Illustrated Living History Series

INDIAN HANDCRAFTS

C. Keith Wilbur

Chelsea House Publishers

Philadelphia

Acknowledgments

The completion of this book demanded many hours of research.
Although much was discovered by poring over dusty tomes, the most
rewarding answers came from talking with the experts. I owe much
to them, and wish to commend the following people in particular:
Joelle Stein, Research Associate, Plimoth Plantation, Plymouth,
MA, for helpful trade shirt suggestions; curators William Henry
Harrison and Richard Reed of the Fruitlands Museum, Harvard, MA,
for their many fruitful conversations; the late Chief
Tantaquidgeon for visits at his Uncasville, CT, museum; the late
Bill Fowler, dean of New England archaeologists, for many
inspiring conversations.

First published in hardback edition in 1997 by Chelsea House Publishers.

Library of Congress Cataloging-in-Publication Data

Wilbur, C. Keith, 1923-
Indian Handcrafts / C. Keith Wilbur.
p.   cm. --(Illustrated living history series)
Originally published: Chester, Conn. : Globe Pequot Press, c 1990.
Summary: Describes and gives instructions for making a variety of traditional Indian tools, implements,
clothing, toys, ornaments, and other items.
Includes bibliographical references (p.) and index.
ISBN 0-7910-4528-5
1. Indians of North America--Industries--Juvenile literature. 2. Indian craft--North America--Juvenile
literature. [1. Indians of North America--Industries. 2. Indian Craft.] I.Title. II.Series: Wilbur, C. Keith,
1923- Illustrated living history series.
[E98.I5W55 1996]
680'.89'97--dc20
                                                                  96-41650
                                                                    CIP
                                                                    AC

CONTENTS

PREFACE

A question-and-answer period followed a talk on the New England Indians down in Connecticut. A young New London girl ~ about seven years old, I'd say ~ stood up and said, "I like the Indian things you've shown ~ where is the nearest Indian store?"

Not an unreasonable question. Her world of today has given scant encouragement to individual creativity and ingenuity. There's more than enough television, prepared craft kits, painting by numbers, plastic models, greeting cards, and so on to blunt the sharpest mind. It is sometimes hard to remember a time when the Algonquian people lived by their wits. From the bounty of nature they were able to shape their needs ~ simple, functional, and attractive objects for the family.

The wilderness materials are still there for the collecting, and this treasure hunt can be an exciting part of any project. Don't hesitate to visit your local Indian museum for inspiration. The following pages describe the ancient method for crafting some of these New England Indian artifacts. Following each such description are a few suggestions for using more modern tools, should one wish. I have made and tested each of these handcrafts, and being a make-do-or-do-without New Englander, it pleases me to say that they needn't cost a penny.

I hope you'll join in spirit with our Indians, past and present, by crafting some of their prized possessions. And if you chance to meet a seven-year-old youngster looking for an Indian store, please show her some of your completed pieces. It may just turn her in a different direction!

ATLATL ~ A THROWING STICK

(Early Archaic, 5,000 ~ 3,000 B.C.)

The ancient Indian hunting spear was a sometimes thing. If the hunter were to have any chance at a meal, he must stalk to within 70 feet of the game. Beyond that, he might as well be on the other side of the Connecticut River, for his weapon lacked two basics ~ distance and accuracy.

Some 7000 years ago, the Early Archaic Indians changed all that. By extending the length of the throwing arm, the spear could now be cast up to 300 feet. This extension was the atlatl ~ little more than a stick with an end hook that propelled the spear by centrifugal force.

This was the same principle as swinging a bucket of water in a circle: The water is forced outward against the bucket bottom, preventing spillage; released, the bucket will fly off with great force, much like a baseball pitch. The spear shaft ~ called the atlatl dart ~ shot off in much the same way.

To date, no atlatls have weathered New England's damp and acidic soil. But there were those throwing sticks that used weights to give extra heft for better control and power. They give some hint about the throwing stick's construction. Made of a relatively soft and workable stone such as chlorite or sedimentary stones such as sandstone, they have survived the ravages of time. In many, a central hole was drilled to taper from $\frac{5}{8}$ inch to $\frac{1}{2}$ inch. This was wedged onto the atlatl shaft from the smaller hook end ~ and probably lashed to prevent it from accidentally flying off. And from this we know that the atlatl hook could be no larger than $\frac{1}{2}$ inch in diameter, while the tapered shaft was $\frac{5}{16}$ inch in diameter somewhere around its center. Likely some sort of hand stop was necessary at the larger end.

CONJECTURAL ATLATL WITH OVAL WEIGHT. THE END HOOK HELD THE DART, WHICH IN TURN RESTED IN THE WEIGHT GROOVE.

A WORD ABOUT THE ATLATL WEIGHT CONSTRUCTION: THE EARLY ARCHAICS USED THE OVAL WEIGHT. BUSINESS-LIKE AND UNADORNED, IT HAD A GROOVE DOWN ITS UPPER SURFACE FOR USE AS A DART REST. WITHOUT SUCH AN ACCOMMODATION, THE DART SHAFT WOULD BE SLANTED TOO HIGH TO BE GRASPED BY THE FINGER AND THUMB. IT IS THE EARLIEST WEIGHT FORM.

THE SHAPE WAS PECKED WITH AN END PICK.

1

A GRITTY STONE ABRADER
OF SCHIST OR SANDSTONE SMOOTHED
OFF THE PECK MARKS.

A GROOVE WAS SCOURED INTO
THE SURFACE AS A REST FOR
THE DART SHAFT.

¼ X (ONE-QUARTER
ACTUAL SIZE)

A CENTER HOLE WAS
DRILLED WITH A PITHY STICK THAT
HELD A FINE WET SAND.

The Late Archaic culture (3000 B.C. to A.D. 300) introduced a new version of the atlatl weight. The oval form was obsolete. Not only functional but handsome, the raw material was selected for varied colors and graining. Very much aware of the spirit world about them, the Late Archaics may have believed that these weights had mystical powers that would guarantee success for the hunter.

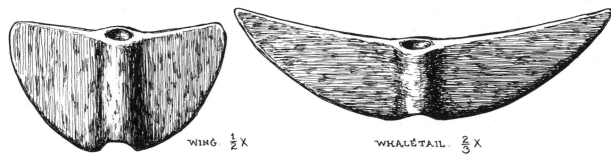

WING. ½ X

WHALETAIL. ⅔ X

The bowtie was the humble cousin to the wing and whaletail weights. Found in either a roughly chipped or polished state, it had no perforation for wedging onto the throwing stick. Instead, the bowtie was lashed in place.

BOWTIE. ⅔ X

ATLATL CONSTRUCTION

Not all atlatls boasted of weights. A simpler style used more wood at the hook end to make a stone weight unnecessary.

(CONJECTURAL)

A LIKELY SAPLING
WAS BENT TO STRETCH
THE WOOD FIBERS, THEN
SAWED THROUGH WITH A
CHIPPED STONE KNIFE.

A STICK, GROOVED AT ONE END
TO HOLD A STONE DRILL,
WAS ROTATED BE-
TWEEN THE
PALMS.

A TWIG WAS INSERTED INTO
THE HANDLE HOLE AS A HAND STOP.

2

ATLATL MAKING TODAY

The throwing stick may be made, of course, from a sapling in the old way. The ancient hunter cut a stick to his liking, with a length somewhere between 18 and 25 inches. By increasing the length of the hook end, more weight could be added to the throw. The pattern is of average size and shape, open to variations.

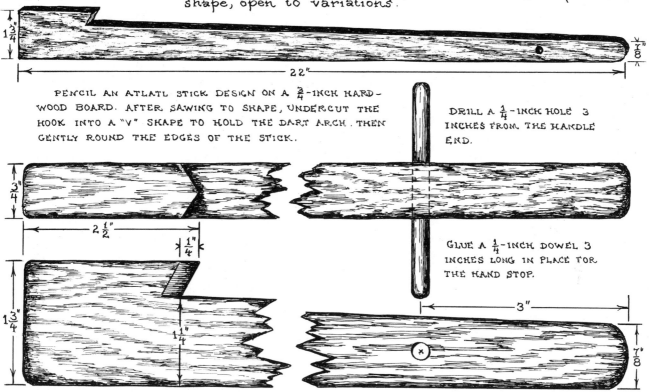

PENCIL AN ATLATL STICK DESIGN ON A $\frac{3}{4}$-INCH HARD-WOOD BOARD. AFTER SAWING TO SHAPE, UNDERCUT THE HOOK INTO A "V" SHAPE TO HOLD THE DART ARCH. THEN GENTLY ROUND THE EDGES OF THE STICK.

DRILL A $\frac{1}{4}$-INCH HOLE 3 INCHES FROM THE HANDLE END.

GLUE A $\frac{1}{4}$-INCH DOWEL 3 INCHES LONG IN PLACE FOR THE HAND STOP.

YOU MAY WISH TO ADD AN ATLATL WEIGHT TO GIVE THE STICK MORE THROWING HEFT.

ATLATL DART

The spear of earlier Paleo-American days (10,000 ~ 7000 B.C.) was altered to accommodate the atlatl throwing stick. The new compound dart was made up of a mainshaft between 4 and 5 feet long. The smaller or notched base end averaged about $\frac{3}{8}$ inch in diameter. The larger or foreshaft end was $\frac{5}{8}$ inch. Western examples were of a long straight branch of a pithy-centered wood such as willow. Into this soft center was inserted a foreshaft of hardwood or bone, tapered to fit snugly. Its opposite end was notched to hold the chipped stone point.

IN 1973, ONE OF NEW ENGLAND'S MOST INTRIGUING INDIAN ARTIFACTS WAS FOUND IN A CHATHAM, MASSACHUSETTS, MARSH. SENT TO DR. MAURICE ROBBINS OF THE BRONSON MUSEUM, THE CORNER~REMOVED FELSITE PROJECTILE POINT PROVED TO BE EARLY ARCHAIC IN ORIGIN. WITH A BIT OF DETECTIVE WORK, DR. ROBBINS

3

FOUND THAT THE POINT WITH ITS WOODEN SHAFT WAS INDEED A FORESHAFT TO A SPEAR—OR AN ATLATL DART. A RARITY INDEED!

HAFTING THE ATLATL FORESHAFT

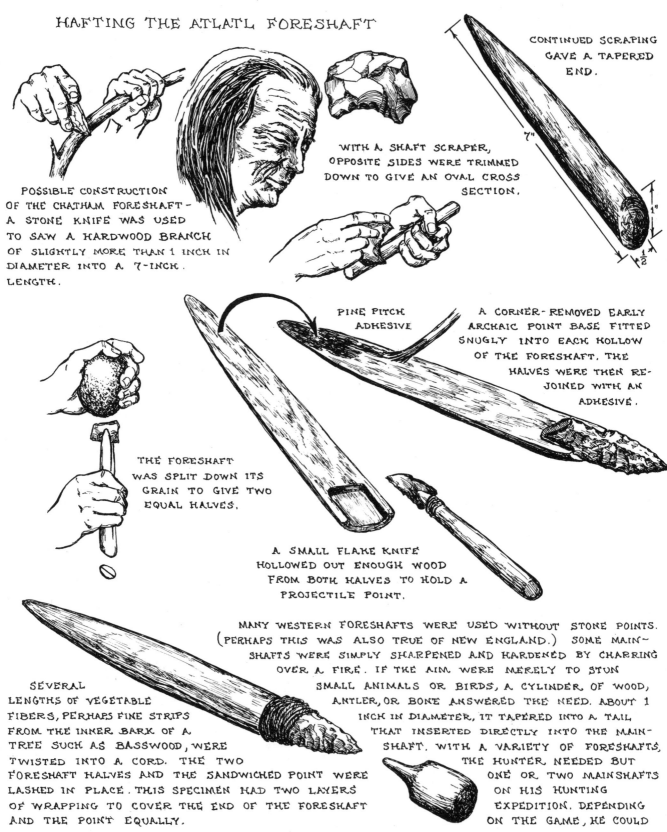

CONTINUED SCRAPING GAVE A TAPERED END.

7"

1"

½"

WITH A SHAFT SCRAPER, OPPOSITE SIDES WERE TRIMMED DOWN TO GIVE AN OVAL CROSS SECTION.

POSSIBLE CONSTRUCTION OF THE CHATHAM FORESHAFT— A STONE KNIFE WAS USED TO SAW A HARDWOOD BRANCH OF SLIGHTLY MORE THAN 1 INCH IN DIAMETER INTO A 7-INCH LENGTH.

PINE PITCH ADHESIVE

A CORNER-REMOVED EARLY ARCHAIC POINT BASE FITTED SNUGLY INTO EACH HOLLOW OF THE FORESHAFT. THE HALVES WERE THEN RE-JOINED WITH AN ADHESIVE.

THE FORESHAFT WAS SPLIT DOWN ITS GRAIN TO GIVE TWO EQUAL HALVES.

A SMALL FLAKE KNIFE HOLLOWED OUT ENOUGH WOOD FROM BOTH HALVES TO HOLD A PROJECTILE POINT.

SEVERAL LENGTHS OF VEGETABLE FIBERS, PERHAPS FINE STRIPS FROM THE INNER BARK OF A TREE SUCH AS BASSWOOD, WERE TWISTED INTO A CORD. THE TWO FORESHAFT HALVES AND THE SANDWICHED POINT WERE LASHED IN PLACE. THIS SPECIMEN HAD TWO LAYERS OF WRAPPING TO COVER THE END OF THE FORESHAFT AND THE POINT EQUALLY.

MANY WESTERN FORESHAFTS WERE USED WITHOUT STONE POINTS. (PERHAPS THIS WAS ALSO TRUE OF NEW ENGLAND.) SOME MAIN-SHAFTS WERE SIMPLY SHARPENED AND HARDENED BY CHARRING OVER A FIRE. IF THE AIM WERE MERELY TO STUN SMALL ANIMALS OR BIRDS, A CYLINDER OF WOOD, ANTLER, OR BONE ANSWERED THE NEED. ABOUT 1 INCH IN DIAMETER, IT TAPERED INTO A TAIL THAT INSERTED DIRECTLY INTO THE MAIN-SHAFT. WITH A VARIETY OF FORESHAFTS, THE HUNTER NEEDED BUT ONE OR TWO MAINSHAFTS ON HIS HUNTING EXPEDITION. DEPENDING ON THE GAME, HE COULD

4

SELECT THE MOST SUITABLE FORESHAFT OR POINT, INSERT IT, AND LET FLY. AND IF A WOUNDED QUARRY MADE OFF WITH THE POINT, THE MAINSHAFT WAS LIKELY TO BE SHAKEN LOOSE AND NOT LOST.

DART MAINSHAFT RECONSTRUCTION

No New England specimens are known. Western examples, however, average 50~75 inches in length. The base or notched end was $\frac{3}{8}$ inch in diameter and the foreshaft end $\frac{5}{8}$ inch. Since really straight saplings are hard to come by, cut a 5~foot length of pine, $\frac{1}{2}$ inch x $\frac{1}{2}$ inch square. With a drawshave or plane, trim off the four edges to give an octagonal cross section. It won't be tapered, as a sapling would be, but it WILL be straight.

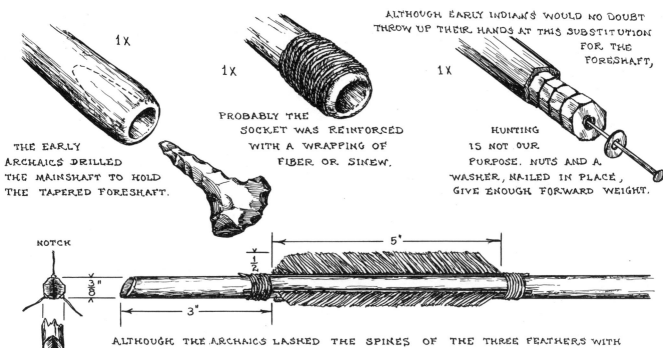

1X

THE EARLY ARCHAICS DRILLED THE MAINSHAFT TO HOLD THE TAPERED FORESHAFT.

1X

PROBABLY THE SOCKET WAS REINFORCED WITH A WRAPPING OF FIBER OR SINEW.

ALTHOUGH EARLY INDIANS WOULD NO DOUBT THROW UP THEIR HANDS AT THIS SUBSTITUTION FOR THE FORESHAFT,

1X

HUNTING IS NOT OUR PURPOSE. NUTS AND A WASHER, NAILED IN PLACE, GIVE ENOUGH FORWARD WEIGHT.

NOTCH

$\frac{3}{8}$"

5'

$\frac{1}{2}$

3"

ALTHOUGH THE ARCHAICS LASHED THE SPINES OF THE THREE FEATHERS WITH TWISTED FIBER OR SINEW (SEE TECHNIQUE UNDER "ARROWS"), TODAY THE FELTCHING MAY BE GLUED AS WELL. LASH THE SPINES OF THE FEATHERS WITH STURDY THREAD, EACH FEATHER WILL BE 120 DEGREES FROM ITS NEIGHBOR FOR EQUAL SPACING. ONE FEATHER SHOULD BE IN LINE WITH THE NOTCH AND WILL BE UPPERMOST WHEN THROWN. WHEN THE FEATHERS ARE IN THE PROPER POSITION, APPLY WHITE GLUE UNDER EACH SPINE WITH A TOOTHPICK. COAT THE LASHINGS AS WELL.

THROWING THE ATLATL DART

With the right hand grasping the throwing-stick handle and resting against the hand stop, hold the dart between the thumb and forefinger. The dart notch rests in the atlatl spur. Place the left foot forward and the right foot at a right angle. With the throwing arm extended behind the shoulder, bring it smartly forward in an overhand sweep. A left-handed throw is, of course, done just the opposite. But remember~this potentially dangerous weapon must be used with responsibility and care.

 # BOWS

The Late Archaics (3000 B.C. ~ A.D. 300), creators of those imaginative atlatl weights, one day learned of a better way to send a projectile to its mark. Introduced by Indian culture from the West, the bow and arrow soon became the ultimate weapon for hunting and warfare. Silent, quick, and far more accurate than the old atlatl dart, it knew no rival for many centuries, until the European matchlock exploded on the scene.

FOR NEW ENGLAND BOWS, HICKORY WAS A FAVORITE, ALTHOUGH ASH, OAK, AND WITCH HAZEL WERE USED WITHOUT APOLOGY.

New England bows were long bows. Therefore a length of 5 to 6 feet, free from branches or knots, furnished the raw material for bows. (The short western bows, of course, had to be bent to a greater arc for shooting. Wrapping and backing of rawhide or sinew were often used to prevent the wood from fracturing.)

6'

A TREE OF 6 TO 8 INCHES IN DIAMETER WAS SELECTED~ JUST SMALL ENOUGH WITH A GROOVED AX OR HATCHET WITHOUT RESORTING TO FIRE. (ANYTHING LARGER REQUIRED THE BLISTER-RAISING CHORE OF CONTROLLED BURNING WHILE GRADUALLY CHIPPING AWAY THE CHAR.)

FULL-GROOVED AX

HATCHET

CELT

POSSIBLY A CELT WAS THEN USED AS A WEDGE TO HALVE THE LOG DOWN THE GRAIN.

FURTHER SPLITTING GAVE A WEDGE OF WOOD. IN THE CASE OF HICKORY THE WHITE OUTER RINGS WERE MORE ELASTIC AND RESILIENT. THE DARK CENTER WAS SPLIT OFF AND DISCARDED.

CONJECTURALLY, A ROUGHING KNIFE MAY HAVE BEEN USED WHILE THE WOOD WAS STILL GREEN.

A SHAFT ABRADER WAS WORKED AS A FILE TO SMOOTH THE ROUGHING-KNIFE SCARS. WHEN THE WOOD HAD DRIED, A SHAFT SCRAPER OF QUARTZ OR QUARTZITE REFINED THE SHAPE.

BY SLASHING ACROSS THE WOOD FIBERS TOWARD THE BODY, THE COURSE STONE ROUGHED OUT THE BOW.

SHAPES ~ The few Algonquian bows preserved to date are largely round, oval, or "D" shaped on cross section.

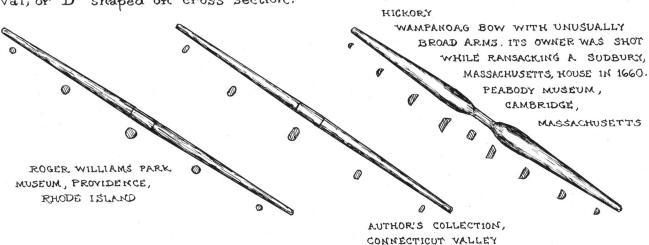

HICKORY
WAMPANOAG BOW WITH UNUSUALLY BROAD ARMS. ITS OWNER WAS SHOT WHILE RANSACKING A SUDBURY, MASSACHUSETTS, HOUSE IN 1660. PEABODY MUSEUM, CAMBRIDGE, MASSACHUSETTS

ROGER WILLIAMS PARK MUSEUM, PROVIDENCE, RHODE ISLAND

AUTHOR'S COLLECTION, CONNECTICUT VALLEY

And so the Late Archaic hunter had his bow ~ rugged and serviceable. The bows shown above were later versions of his craftsmanship. The shooting distance was less than spectacular. A reconstructed 1660 Sudbury bow shot an arrow for a surprising 173 yards, however.

Generally, the accuracy of the Indian bow failed at a distance of more than 30 to 40 feet. This weapon was certainly inferior to the modern bows that bristle with sights, pulleys, and sundry gimcracks. The Algonquian made up for this lack, however, with his hunting prowess. His backyard was the forest, and he knew the habits of the wild creatures. Patience was part of his being, and he knew he could stalk the game to well within range of his weapon.

CRAFTING TODAY'S BOW

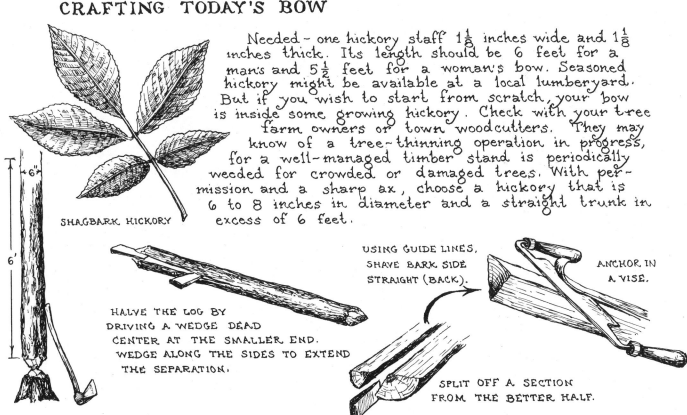

Needed ~ one hickory staff 1⅛ inches wide and 1⅛ inches thick. Its length should be 6 feet for a man's and 5½ feet for a woman's bow. Seasoned hickory might be available at a local lumberyard. But if you wish to start from scratch, your bow is inside some growing hickory. Check with your tree farm owners or town woodcutters. They may know of a tree-thinning operation in progress, for a well-managed timber stand is periodically weeded for crowded or damaged trees. With permission and a sharp ax, choose a hickory that is 6 to 8 inches in diameter and a straight trunk in excess of 6 feet.

SHAGBARK HICKORY

6'

6"

HALVE THE LOG BY DRIVING A WEDGE DEAD CENTER AT THE SMALLER END. WEDGE ALONG THE SIDES TO EXTEND THE SEPARATION.

USING GUIDE LINES, SHAVE BARK SIDE STRAIGHT (BACK).

ANCHOR IN A VISE.

SPLIT OFF A SECTION FROM THE BETTER HALF.

DRAW LINES 1⅛ INCHES APART DOWN THE LENGTH OF THE BACK, WITH A SPOKE SHAVE OR DRAWKNIFE, SQUARE THE SIDES. LASTLY, SQUARE OFF THE REMAINING SIDE ~ THE BOW BELLY.

THE BOW STOCK, BE IT READIED IN INDIAN FASHION FROM LIVE WOOD AND ROUGH-SHAVED OR SEASONED AND CUT TO SIZE AT THE LUMBERYARD, IS READY FOR SHAPING. A VISE IS NECESSARY.

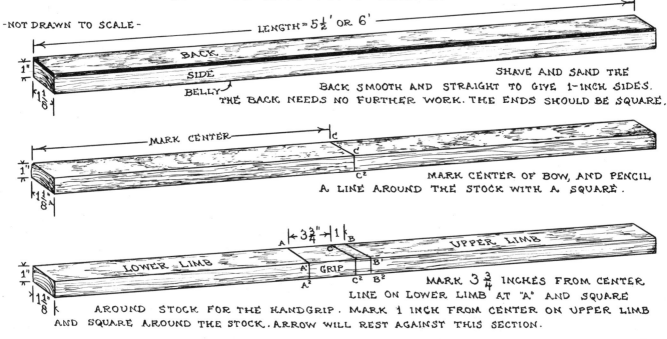

-NOT DRAWN TO SCALE-

LENGTH = 5½' OR 6'

BACK
SIDE
BELLY

SHAVE AND SAND THE BACK SMOOTH AND STRAIGHT TO GIVE 1-INCH SIDES. THE BACK NEEDS NO FURTHER WORK. THE ENDS SHOULD BE SQUARE.

MARK CENTER

MARK CENTER OF BOW, AND PENCIL A LINE AROUND THE STOCK WITH A SQUARE.

LOWER LIMB   GRIP   UPPER LIMB

MARK 3¾ INCHES FROM CENTER LINE ON LOWER LIMB AT "A" AND SQUARE AROUND STOCK FOR THE HANDGRIP. MARK 1 INCH FROM CENTER ON UPPER LIMB AND SQUARE AROUND THE STOCK. ARROW WILL REST AGAINST THIS SECTION.

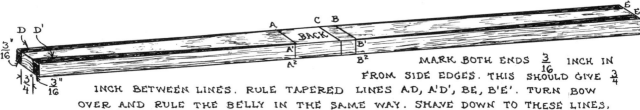

BACK

MARK BOTH ENDS 3/16 INCH IN FROM SIDE EDGES. THIS SHOULD GIVE 3/4 INCH BETWEEN LINES. RULE TAPERED LINES AD, A'D', BE, B'E'. TURN BOW OVER AND RULE THE BELLY IN THE SAME WAY. SHAVE DOWN TO THESE LINES.

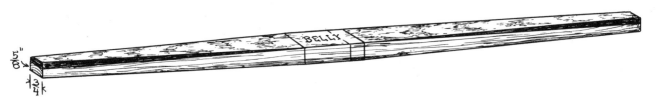

BELLY

TROUBLE SPOTS ~

WITH THE BOW LIMBS TAPERED BUT NOT YET ROUNDED, IT'S TIME TO CHECK THE RUN OF THE GRAIN. IF ANY GRAIN LINE CROSSES FROM SIDE TO SIDE TO MEASURE LESS THAN 15 INCHES, THE BOW MAY WELL FRACTURE AT THIS WEAK POINT. IF SO, YOU'VE MADE YOURSELF SOME FANCY KINDLING.

FURTHER, KNOTS CAN SPELL TROUBLE IF LOCATED IN THE CENTER OF THE BOW. SUCH WEAK POINTS EARN A DISCARD.

15" OR MORE

SMALL KNOTS ALONG THE EDGES RARELY CAUSE PROBLEMS.

MORE ON GRAIN~ ANNULAR RINGS SHOULD, ON CROSS SECTION,
CURVE FROM BACK TO BELLY. ALSO, THE GRAIN SHOULD RUN DOWN
THE SIDES OF THE BOW, NOT DOWN THE BACK OR BELLY.

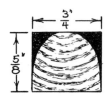

ROUNDING THE BELLY

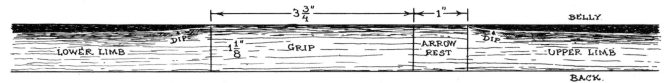

LOWER LIMB   DIP   1⅛"   GRIP   3¾"   ARROW REST   1"   DIP   BELLY   UPPER LIMB   BACK.

BETTER BOWS HAVE A SLIGHT DIP AT THE BELLY, EITHER SIDE OF THE GRIP AND ARROW REST.
ROUND THE BELLY WITH A SPOKESHAVE OR DRAWKNIFE. AND EASY DOES IT~
WOOD CAN'T BE REPLACED.

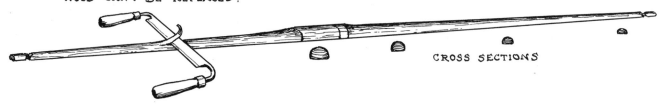

CROSS SECTIONS

NOTCHES -
    WITH A KNIFE OR ROUND
FILE, ROUGH OUT THE NOTCHES.
SAND THESE GROOVES ROUND AND
SMOOTH TO PREVENT CHAFING OF
THE BOWSTRING.

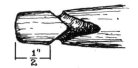

½"   ½"

BOWSTRING —
    BOWSTRINGS ARE INEXPENSIVE AND MADE FOR THE JOB. KEEP YOURS WELL WAXED
    WITH BEESWAX. FIRST, TIE THE BOWSTRING KNOT AT ONE END. THEN SLIP
    THE KNOT OVER AND DOWN THE UPPER LIMB
    TO THE LOWER LIMB NOTCH, AND SECURE THE
    PERMANENT TIMBER HITCH. THIS SHOULD
    LEAVE THE BOWSTRING KNOT ABOUT 4
    INCHES SHORT OF THE UPPER LIMB NOTCH.

BOWSTRING KNOT -
ONE OF THE OLDEST-KNOWN KNOTS

TIMBER HITCH

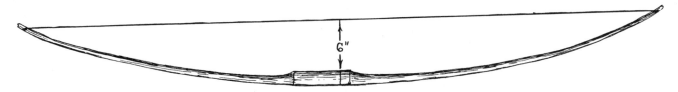

6"

WHEN STRUNG, THE STRING SHOULD BE ABOUT 6 INCHES FROM THE INSIDE
OF THE BOW GRIP. CHANCES ARE, THE BOW WILL BE TOO STIFF TO BEND TO
THE 6-INCH DISTANCE.
    FIRST, REMOVE AN EVEN STRIP OF WOOD
        FROM THE BELLY OF
        BOTH LIMBS.   IF THE BOW STILL RESISTS
                        BENDING, REMOVE A BIT OF
                        WOOD ALONG THE BELLY SIDES.
        STILL TOO STIFF FOR BOWSTRING KNOT TO SEAT
    INTO THE UPPER LIMB NOTCH? REPEAT THE FIRST STEP (1).

9

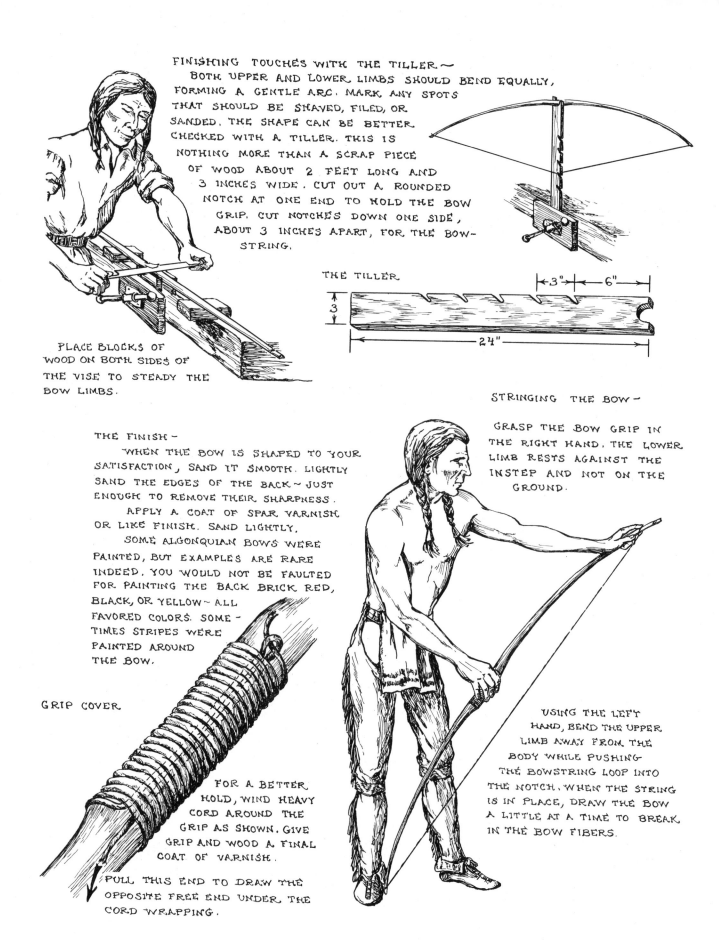

FINISHING TOUCHES WITH THE TILLER ~
BOTH UPPER AND LOWER LIMBS SHOULD BEND EQUALLY,
FORMING A GENTLE ARC. MARK ANY SPOTS
THAT SHOULD BE SHAVED, FILED, OR
SANDED. THE SHAPE CAN BE BETTER
CHECKED WITH A TILLER. THIS IS
NOTHING MORE THAN A SCRAP PIECE
OF WOOD ABOUT 2 FEET LONG AND
3 INCHES WIDE. CUT OUT A ROUNDED
NOTCH AT ONE END TO HOLD THE BOW
GRIP. CUT NOTCHES DOWN ONE SIDE,
ABOUT 3 INCHES APART, FOR THE BOW-
STRING.

THE TILLER

← 3" → ← 6" →
3
← 24" →

PLACE BLOCKS OF
WOOD ON BOTH SIDES OF
THE VISE TO STEADY THE
BOW LIMBS.

STRINGING THE BOW ~

GRASP THE BOW GRIP IN
THE RIGHT HAND. THE LOWER
LIMB RESTS AGAINST THE
INSTEP AND NOT ON THE
GROUND.

THE FINISH ~
WHEN THE BOW IS SHAPED TO YOUR
SATISFACTION, SAND IT SMOOTH. LIGHTLY
SAND THE EDGES OF THE BACK ~ JUST
ENOUGH TO REMOVE THEIR SHARPNESS.
APPLY A COAT OF SPAR VARNISH
OR LIKE FINISH. SAND LIGHTLY.
SOME ALGONQUIAN BOWS WERE
PAINTED, BUT EXAMPLES ARE RARE
INDEED. YOU WOULD NOT BE FAULTED
FOR PAINTING THE BACK BRICK RED,
BLACK, OR YELLOW ~ ALL
FAVORED COLORS. SOME-
TIMES STRIPES WERE
PAINTED AROUND
THE BOW.

GRIP COVER

FOR A BETTER
HOLD, WIND HEAVY
CORD AROUND THE
GRIP AS SHOWN. GIVE
GRIP AND WOOD A FINAL
COAT OF VARNISH.

PULL THIS END TO DRAW THE
OPPOSITE FREE END UNDER THE
CORD WRAPPING.

USING THE LEFT
HAND, BEND THE UPPER
LIMB AWAY FROM THE
BODY WHILE PUSHING
THE BOWSTRING LOOP INTO
THE NOTCH. WHEN THE STRING
IS IN PLACE, DRAW THE BOW
A LITTLE AT A TIME TO BREAK
IN THE BOW FIBERS.

10

ARROWS

By today's standards, the Algonquian arrow was a crude affair. Accuracy and distance were found wanting ~ and little wonder. Nature provided few straight and sturdy branches that could withstand the lengthwise snap of the bowstring. But there were those shrubs and reeds that answered the purpose. Saxton Pope, in his _Bows and Arrows_, was able to identify some of the ancient arrowwood in many museum collections. Most proved to be hazel, dogwood (Cornus nuttallii), arrow-wood (Pluchea sericea), and serviceberry (Amelanchier alnifolia). Rare indeed were a few examples of split hickory. Wedging off strips of this hard, fibrous wood with stone tools must have been a formidable task.

PROBABLE ARROW MAKING OF THE LATE ARCHAIC CULTURE

NOTCHER

SHAFT ABRADER

WOOD FIBERS WERE STRETCHED AND SAWED THROUGH WITH A NOTCHER.

IN SOME SHAFTS, THE ARROW END WAS DRILLED TO ACCOMMODATE THOSE ARROW POINTS WITH THICKER BASES.

THE BARK WAS PEELED, AND ANY KNOTS AND HUMPS WERE SCRAPED SMOOTH WITH A SHAFT ABRADER. FRESH WOOD WAS MOST EASILY WORKED.

THE ARROW LENGTH WAS 29 INCHES OR LESS. A BOW COULD NOT BE DRAWN LONGER THAN THIS, THEREFORE THE AVERAGE ARROW LENGTH WAS 26 INCHES.

THE BEST INDIAN ARROWS WERE $\frac{5}{16}$ INCH OR LESS IN DIAMETER; HOWEVER, SOME HUNTING ARROWS AVERAGED $\frac{1}{2}$ INCH IN DIAMETER.

IN ANY EVENT, A NOTCHER SAWED A SLOT IN THE THINNER END OF THE BRANCH TO HOLD THE BOWSTRING.

IN LINE WITH THE BOWSTRING NOTCH A LARGER AMOUNT OF WOOD WAS REMOVED TO BED THE ARROW POINT BASE.

SOME NEW ENGLAND ARROWS WERE KNOBBED FOR A BETTER FINGER GRIP. FORWARD OF THIS, A GENTLE TAPER WAS PROVIDED FOR ATTACHMENT OF THE SHAFT FEATHERS.

STRAIGHTENING THE SHAFT

BY EXPERIMENTATION, WILLIAM FOWLER FOUND THAT CONTINUED SCRAPING OF THE SHAFT GAVE ENOUGH HEAT TO PRODUCE A DRY CRUST AROUND THE GREEN CENTER. WITH FREQUENT STRAIGHTENING WITH THE HANDS, THE SHAFT DRIED RIGID AND PERMANENTLY STRAIGHT.

A CROOKED BRANCH COULD ALSO BE IMPROVED BY HEATING IT OVER COALS. WITH THE CROOK BENT TO AN OPPOSITE CURVE, THE SHAFT COOLED "STRAIGHT AS AN ARROW."

FLETCHING THE ARROW —
TURKEY WING FEATHERS WERE PREFERRED.

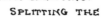

SOME FEATHERS WERE STRIPPED,
BUT THE RIB WAS THIN AND
MORE FRAGILE THAN OCCURRED WITH SPLITTING.

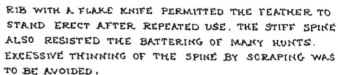

SPLITTING THE
RIB WITH A FLAKE KNIFE PERMITTED THE FEATHER TO
STAND ERECT AFTER REPEATED USE. THE STIFF SPINE
ALSO RESISTED THE BATTERING OF MANY HUNTS.
EXCESSIVE THINNING OF THE SPINE BY SCRAPING WAS
TO BE AVOIDED.

STRIPPED   SPLIT

ALGONQUIAN ARROW,
AUTHOR'S COLLECTION
X1

THE FEATHERS WERE TRIMMED WITH FRONT AND REAR RIB EXTENSIONS. THESE
WERE LASHED TO THE ARROW SHAFT. THE HIGHER THE FEATHERS, THE GREATER
THE AIR DRAG. THEREFORE, TO PREVENT LOSING VELOCITY AND STRIKING FORCE,
EACH FEATHER WAS TRIMMED LONG AND NARROW.

GRAIN

THREE FEATHERS WERE USED FOR EACH FLETCHING — EACH LASHED PARALLEL TO THE SHAFT.

BY AIR FRICTION, THE FEATHERS KEPT THE REAR OF THE SHAFT IN LINE WITH THE
ARROW POINT. THE THREE SHAFT FEATHERS WERE CUT FROM THE SAME FEATHER. LIKE
CONTOURS ACTED AS PLANES THAT REVOLVED EQUALLY TO GIVE AN AXIAL ROTATION.
FINE SINEW BOUND THE FEATHERS BY LASHING; GLUE CONTENT AND SHRINKAGE
ON DRYING HELD THE ENDS FIRMLY. SINCE NO GLUE WAS USED TO SECURE THE
REMAINDER OF EACH RIB, THE ARROW'S FLIGHT HAD A LESS-THAN-PERFECT STABILITY.

SOME SHAFTS WERE TAPERED AT THE
FEATHER END WITH A REAR NOTCHED
KNOB FOR A BETTER FINGER GRIP.

THE THICKER FORWARD END WAS NOTCHED TO HOLD
THE ARROW POINT. LASHING WAS AGAIN DONE WITH
WATER-SOFTENED SINEW (TENDON FIBERS) OR GUT
(ELASTIC TISSUE FROM THE INTESTINE).

REPRODUCING THE ARROW

A walk through the New England woodlands today seems to yield few
specimens suitable for a straight arrow shaft. Now it is against our principles to
use anything but nature's raw materials, but you may find that birch dowels
would be a reasonable substitute. Purchase (also against our principles!) some
straight-grained dowels. These should be free from knots. Dowels $\frac{5}{16}$ inch in
diameter would be best. Trim each to a 28-inch length for men, 25-26 inches
for women.

NOTCHING

Secure the dowel in a vise and cut a notch $\frac{1}{8}$-inch wide and $\frac{3}{8}$-inch
deep. Fold a piece of fine sandpaper and smooth the notch well. Sand the

12

entire shaft and apply a finish similar to that for the bow.

FLETCHING

Turkey wing feathers work as well as they did centuries ago. Check the Yellow Pages in the telephone directory. Turkey farms are not scarce hereabouts. Call early in the fall and ask for a few feathers to be set aside. Thanksgiving flocks should have little use for their plumage.

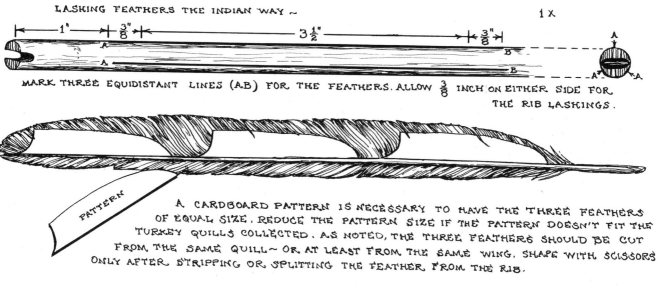

LASHING FEATHERS THE INDIAN WAY ~

1" · 3/8" · 3 1/2" · 3/8"

1 X

MARK THREE EQUIDISTANT LINES (AB) FOR THE FEATHERS. ALLOW 3/8 INCH ON EITHER SIDE FOR THE RIB LASHINGS.

PATTERN

A CARDBOARD PATTERN IS NECESSARY TO HAVE THE THREE FEATHERS OF EQUAL SIZE. REDUCE THE PATTERN SIZE IF THE PATTERN DOESN'T FIT THE TURKEY QUILLS COLLECTED. AS NOTED, THE THREE FEATHERS SHOULD BE CUT FROM THE SAME QUILL ~ OR AT LEAST FROM THE SAME WING. SHAPE WITH SCISSORS ONLY AFTER STRIPPING OR SPLITTING THE FEATHER FROM THE RIB.

GRAIN OF WOOD. 3/8" 1/2" COCK FEATHER 3/8"

1 X

AVOID FEATHERS WITH BROKEN FIBERS. RUFFLED FIBERS MAY BE EASILY STRAIGHTENED AFTER HOLDING THE FEATHER OVER STEAM FROM A KETTLE SPOUT.

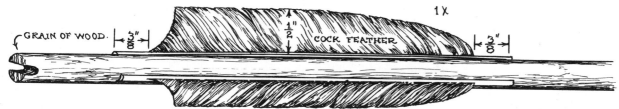

COCK FEATHER

USE A STURDY THREAD TO LASH THE RIB ENDS IN PLACE ON THE THREE MARKS PREVIOUSLY DRAWN ON THE SHAFT. IF YOU WISH, CATCH THE RIB END WITH A FEW TURNS OF SCOTCH TAPE BEFORE LASHING. IT'S A HELP TO SECURE THE SHAFT IN A VISE.

LASHING TECHNIQUE

REMOVE THE TAPE AND COAT THE THREAD WITH WHITE GLUE.

GLUING THE STRIPPED FEATHER ~

① ②

1" COCK FEATHER

TODAY, MOST FEATHERS ARE GLUED DIRECTLY TO THE SHAFT. THE THIN CURVED UNDERSURFACE OF THE STRIPPED RIB WILL HOLD FIRMLY TO GIVE A RUGGED FLETCHING. FIRST GLUE AND PIN ① THE FIRST FEATHER PERPENDICULAR TO THE NOTCH. STRETCH THE RIB ALONG THE PENCIL LINE AND PIN AT ②. REPEAT FOR THE TWO REMAINING FEATHERS. THE COCK FEATHER MAY BE COLORED.

As for decorative arrow bands, there are too few New England arrow examples to indicate their purpose. It has been suggested that painted bands of different colors or number indicated the type of arrow points. If so, the hunter could quickly select from the quiver the arrow that was best suited for the quarry being stalked. Possibly, too, the bands represented arrow ownership.

The arrow decoration is followed with a final varnishing and sanding.

ARCHERY FORM

With your bow-and-arrow efforts largely behind you, a few pointers on the correct shooting form might be helpful. Making the arrow points will follow shortly.

POSITION ~ Stand with the feet comfortably apart and at right angles to the target. The left shoulder and the head face the target.

ARMING THE BOW ~ Hold the bow parallel to the ground with the grip held loosely against the web between the thumb and first finger. Place the arrow notch in the string with the cock feather facing upward and at a right angle to the string. The first finger is above the notch and the middle and index fingers below.

AIMING ~ Draw back the bowstring while straightening the left arm, using the shoulders to do the work. The right finger rests at the corner of the mouth. Estimate the arrow's trajectory to the target. The bow is now at a right angle to the ground.

SHOOTING ~ Release the right finger pads smoothly and equally. Keep your shooting position until the arrow has landed ~ ideally, on target.

SHOOTING SAFETY

You have in your hands a weapon that demands your close attention and care.
1. Never draw on a target you don't intend to shoot.
2. Never shoot into the air. The arrow may seek out the unexpected.
3. The shooting field should be free of paths where people might wander.
4. Consider the possibility of a ricocheting arrow.
5. A densely wooded backdrop may hide approaching people ~ or at best, lose one of those nicely crafted arrows.

14

ARROW POINTS

New England has never wanted for stony soil. But as far as the Indian craftsman was concerned, quantity did not make up for quality. Stones that chipped with a conchoidal fracture made the best raw material, but there was scant little of that. Flint~hard and glasslike~was favored. Chert (hornstone), jasper, and chalcedony fractured in like manner but were scarce. Felsite, quartzite, and quartz, although less easily worked, did yield a reasonable chip to percussion and pressure flaking. The latter were plentiful and could be found in veins of rocks or in random chunks.

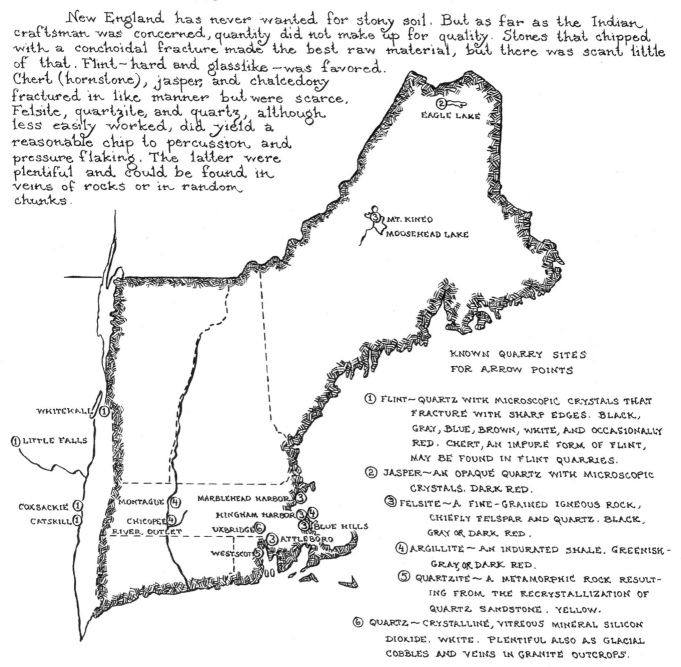

KNOWN QUARRY SITES
FOR ARROW POINTS

① FLINT~QUARTZ WITH MICROSCOPIC CRYSTALS THAT FRACTURE WITH SHARP EDGES. BLACK, GRAY, BLUE, BROWN, WHITE, AND OCCASIONALLY RED. CHERT, AN IMPURE FORM OF FLINT, MAY BE FOUND IN FLINT QUARRIES.

② JASPER~AN OPAQUE QUARTZ WITH MICROSCOPIC CRYSTALS. DARK RED.

③ FELSITE~A FINE-GRAINED IGNEOUS ROCK, CHIEFLY FELSPAR AND QUARTZ. BLACK, GRAY OR DARK RED.

④ ARGILLITE~AN INDURATED SHALE. GREENISH-GRAY, OR DARK RED.

⑤ QUARTZITE~A METAMORPHIC ROCK RESULTING FROM THE RECRYSTALLIZATION OF QUARTZ SANDSTONE. YELLOW.

⑥ QUARTZ~CRYSTALLINE, VITREOUS MINERAL SILICON DIOXIDE. WHITE. PLENTIFUL ALSO AS GLACIAL COBBLES AND VEINS IN GRANITE OUTCROPS.

At the quarry, chunks of stone were split from rock outcroppings. Small surface stones weathered with minute fractures and were therefore bypassed. With an eye toward carrying the raw materials back home, the craftsman percussed rough blanks slightly larger than the future points. At the quarries noted above, masses of chips and spawls gave some indication of the extent of this industry~and it was considerable. Once back in the village, the blanks would be either traded or buried as "cache blades." Underground, the blanks kept fresh for later refining.

Lacking a quarry, glacial cobblestones found along the shores of lakes, rivers, and the ocean made excellent substitutes. Blanks were hammered off the core and roughed out before burying.

ARROW POINT NOMENCLATURE

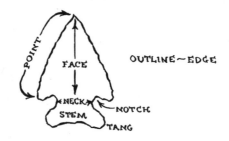

POINT
FACE
OUTLINE~EDGE
NECK
STEM
NOTCH
TANG

PECUSSION CHIPPING~

THE QUARRY STONE OR COBBLE, RANGING BETWEEN A SOFTBALL AND A LARGE BOWLING BALL, RESTED ON AN ANVIL OF STONE OR LOG AND WAS STRUCK WITH A HAMMERSTONE AT SOMEWHAT OF A RIGHT ANGLE. THE FOLLOW~THROUGH BLOW CARRIED THE HAMMERSTONE IN THE SAME PATH AS THE DESIRED FRACTURE.

ANVIL

A SMALLER, MORE OVAL ROCK WAS PERCUSSED TO FIRST GIVE A FLAT SURFACE.

ANVIL

LONG SPAWLS WERE THEN FRACTURED FROM THIS STRIKING PLATFORM.

USING A SMALL HAMMERSTONE, THE SPAWL WAS ROUGH-SHAPED.

THE SPAWL WAS STRUCK SO THAT THE FOLLOW~THROUGH WOULD TAKE THE SAME PATH AS THE CHIP TO BE REMOVED.

WRONG~ PRODUCED A STUBBY CHIP

THE SPAWL RESTED FIRMLY ON THE EDGE OF A WOODEN ANVIL. WHEN PROPERLY PERCUSSED IN THIS WAY, THE HAMMERSTONE DID NOT STRIKE THE ANVIL. THE BEST FLAKE WOULD SEPARATE MORE THAN HALF WAY ACROSS.

RIGHT

THE RESULTING ROUGHED-OUT SHAPE WAS A BLANK. IF THE CHIPS WERE TOO SHORT, A HUMP WAS LEFT IN THE CENTER. THIS RESULT WAS A TURTLEBACK AND JOINED THE DISCARDS AT THE QUARRY HEAP.

PRESSURE CHIPPING~

THE BLANK WAS REFINED BY PRESSURE FLAKING. A PIECE OF BONE OR ANTLER WITH A SMALL ROUNDED END WAS PRESSED AGAINST THE EDGE TO REMOVE A CHIP FROM THE UNDERSURFACE.

WITH THE BLANK RESTING ON THE EDGE OF THE ANVIL, PRESSURE WAS DOWN AND INWARD. SOMETIMES A TWIST OF THE FLAKING TOOL HELPED.

16

ANOTHER METHOD OF PRESSURE FLAKING ~

THE BLANK WAS HELD FIRMLY AGAINST A PALM PROTECTOR ~ A THICK PIECE OF LEATHER. THE FLAKING TOOL ~ SOFT ENOUGH TO GRAB THE EDGE OF THE BLANK ~ PRESSED AGAINST THE BASE OF THE THUMB FOR SUPPORT.

HOW NOT TO FLAKE: HERE, THE BLANK IS UNSUPPORTED BETWEEN THE BASE OF THE THUMB AND THE LITTLE FINGER. WITH ~ OUT SUPPORT, THE BLANK MIGHT BREAK UNDER PRESSURE.

LEATHER PALM PROTECTOR WITH THUMB HOLE ~ A HANDY ADDITION

FLAKING TECHNIQUE ~

AFTER A SUCCESSFUL FLAKE, THE BLANK WAS TURNED OVER AND AN ADJACENT CHIP REMOVED.

AGAIN, THE PRESSURE WAS DOWNWARD AND INWARD, WITH AN OCCASIONAL TWISTING OF THE FLAKING TOOL.

NOTCHING ~

IF THE POINT WAS THIN AND WELL SHAPED, THE INDIAN CRAFTSMAN FINISHED THE POINT BY NOTCHING.

TRIANGULAR

TAPERED-STEM

LEAF

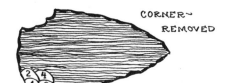

CORNER ~ REMOVED

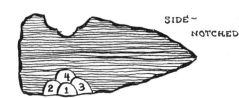

SIDE ~ NOTCHED

THE FLAKING WAS DONE IN THE ORDER SHOWN. THE ARROW POINT WAS TURNED OVER AND THE PROCESS REPEATED UNTIL THE NOTCH WAS DEEP ENOUGH. THE SHARP EDGES OF THE NOTCH WERE DULLED TO PREVENT ANY CUTTING OF THE ARROW SHAFT LASHING.

REPRODUCING THE ARROW POINT

There is no substitute for the time-honored Indian method of making arrow points; however, a few thoughts about flaking today are in order.

1. Wear SAFETY GLASSES. This is a must.

2. Antler-flaking tools are hard to come by. Bone could be the answer, then and now. If you are on friendly terms with a neighborhood dog, see if it can spare a weathered sample from its bone cache. Of course, there's always the butcher, but fresh bones should be well boiled and dried.

CUT TWO PARALLEL SLOTS DOWN THE LENGTH OF THE BONE. ROUND AND TAPER ON A GRINDING WHEEL OR FILE.

$\frac{5}{8}''$

USE A HACKSAW.

17

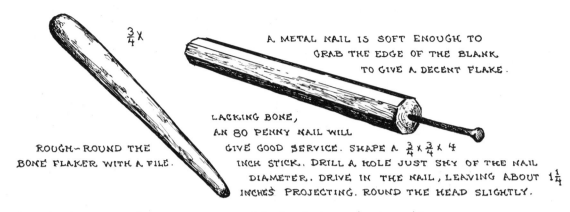

$\frac{3}{4}$ X

ROUGH-ROUND THE
BONE FLAKER WITH A FILE.

A METAL NAIL IS SOFT ENOUGH TO
GRAB THE EDGE OF THE BLANK
TO GIVE A DECENT FLAKE.

LACKING BONE,
AN 80 PENNY NAIL WILL
GIVE GOOD SERVICE. SHAPE A $\frac{3}{4}$ X $\frac{3}{4}$ X 4
INCH STICK. DRILL A HOLE JUST SHY OF THE NAIL
DIAMETER. DRIVE IN THE NAIL, LEAVING ABOUT $1\frac{1}{4}$
INCHES PROJECTING. ROUND THE HEAD SLIGHTLY.

One last suggestion— try an old toothbrush handle.
3. The anvil for percussion flaking works well on any large stone. For pressure flaking, a squared stump 1 foot in diameter and $2\frac{1}{2}$ feet tall provides a comfortable height. Lacking this arrangement, any piece of wood on a bench top will do.

ARROW POINTS OF OTHER MATERIALS

By historic times— certainly by the beginning of the seventeenth century— stone arrow points had been largely displaced by other materials. Willoughby made note of this transition in the 1901 American Anthropologist : "Gosnold in 1602 found the natives supplied with 'copper' points, 'some very red, some a paler color' (brass?): Waymouth three years later saw arrows headed with points made from the long shank-bone of the deer; Champlain at about the same date found them tipped with the tail of the horseshoe crab; Mourt's Relation refers to arrowheads of brass, eagle claws, and hartshorn;* Higgeson, writing in 1629, speaks of bone and brass arrowtips; Wood also mentions brass points, and writes of the feathering of the arrows with the wing and tail feathers of the eagle."

ANTLER POINTS

Little went to waste in the Algonquian camp. Deer horn was no exception.

HORSESHOE CRAB - NOT A CRAB, BUT RELATED
TO SPIDERS DESCENDED FROM A VARIETY 400
MILLION YEARS OLD.

THE POINT WAS THEN DRILLED
AT ITS BASE. THE ARROW
SHAFT WOULD BE WEDGED
INTO THIS HOLE.

A GROOVE WAS
GROUND AROUND
THE ANTLER PRONG,
THEN BROKEN FREE.

$\frac{1}{2}$ X

$\frac{1}{2}$ X

ONE
BARB

TWO
BARBS

SCRAPING AND GRINDING
GAVE A SYMMETRICAL POINT.

FLAT BASE.
THE BASES WERE SHAPED BY
GRINDING, THEN THE POINT WAS
FINISHED BY POLISHING.

*Horn of harts or stags— deer antler.

BONE POINTS

Strong, easily worked cylindrical, of various diameters, and already provided with a centered hole nearly ready for hafting to the arrow shaft ~ it seemed that nature had provided the ideal raw material for arrow points. Bone had all these qualities, and was appreciated by hunters from the latter part of the Late Archaic period onward.

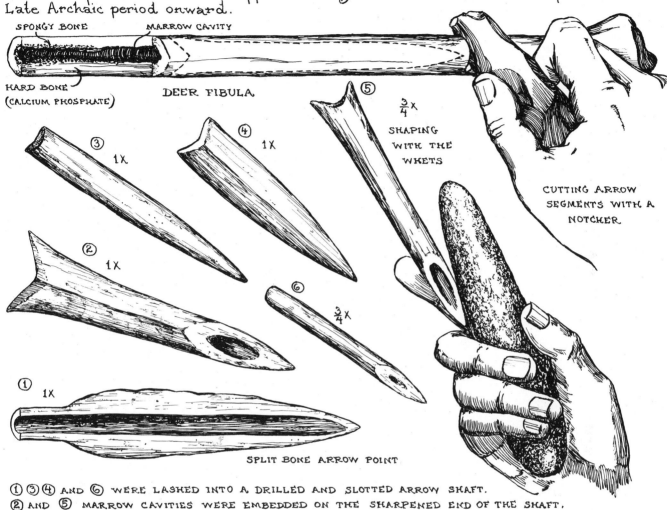

SPONGY BONE

MARROW CAVITY

HARD BONE (CALCIUM PHOSPHATE)

DEER FIBULA

③ 1X

④ 1X

⑤ ¾ X

SHAPING WITH THE WHETS

CUTTING ARROW SEGMENTS WITH A NOTCHER

② 1X

⑥ ¾ X

① 1X

SPLIT BONE ARROW POINT

① ③ ④ AND ⑥ WERE LASHED INTO A DRILLED AND SLOTTED ARROW SHAFT.
② AND ⑤ MARROW CAVITIES WERE EMBEDDED ON THE SHARPENED END OF THE SHAFT.

Reproducing The Bone Point ~

A useful length of the bone arrow point might be between 2 and 2½ inches. Old and weathered bones are ready to work. However, most of the butcher shop discards are considerably larger in diameter than the deer fibula. Therefore the marrow cavity will be too large to be held by the arrow shaft.

CUT THE BONE TO LENGTH WITH A HACKSAW, THEN MAKE A SERIES OF LENGTHWISE CUTS TO GIVE THE BEST WIDTHS. SHAPE WITH A FILE OR GRINDSTONE.

THIN THE STEM TO FIT THE ARROW SHAFT NOTCH

19

METAL ARROW POINTS

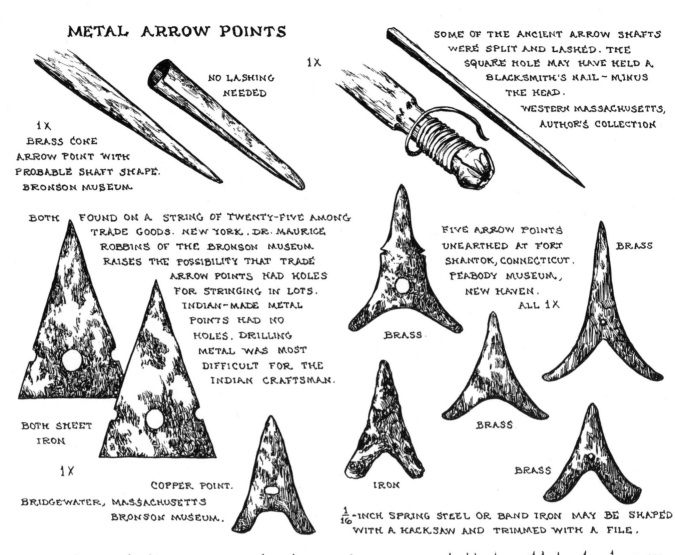

SOME OF THE ANCIENT ARROW SHAFTS WERE SPLIT AND LASHED. THE SQUARE HOLE MAY HAVE HELD A BLACKSMITH'S NAIL ~ MINUS THE HEAD.
WESTERN MASSACHUSETTS, AUTHOR'S COLLECTION

1X

1X
BRASS CONE ARROW POINT WITH PROBABLE SHAFT SHAPE. BRONSON MUSEUM.

NO LASHING NEEDED

BOTH FOUND ON A STRING OF TWENTY-FIVE AMONG TRADE GOODS. NEW YORK. DR. MAURICE ROBBINS OF THE BRONSON MUSEUM RAISES THE POSSIBILITY THAT TRADE ARROW POINTS HAD HOLES FOR STRINGING IN LOTS. INDIAN-MADE METAL POINTS HAD NO HOLES. DRILLING METAL WAS MOST DIFFICULT FOR THE INDIAN CRAFTSMAN.

FIVE ARROW POINTS UNEARTHED AT FORT SHANTOK, CONNECTICUT. PEABODY MUSEUM, NEW HAVEN.
ALL 1X

BRASS

BRASS

BOTH SHEET IRON

1X

COPPER POINT. BRIDGEWATER, MASSACHUSETTS BRONSON MUSEUM.

BRASS

IRON

BRASS

BRASS

$\frac{1}{16}$-INCH SPRING STEEL OR BAND IRON MAY BE SHAPED WITH A HACKSAW AND TRIMMED WITH A FILE.

Although the arrow points shown above were probably brought by traders or made by colonial blacksmiths, the Algonquians were eager to try their hand with the shiny, durable metals. Copper and brass were favorites. In 1640, Captain Underhill wrote of the foresight of the Saybrook, Connecticut, garrison during the Pequot War of 1637. A Dutch trading ship was not allowed to weigh anchor for the Pequot country, "...saying that they would supply the Indians with kettles and other articles of metal, which would immediately be turned into arrow heads." How the sturdy kettles were cut into shape remains a mystery.

More easily worked sheet copper and brass were crafted into many a useful object by the tribesmen. But of these, arrow points were the most numerous. Iron was more difficult to manage, for it was harder than brass and copper and had to be hammered to shape. Therefore iron points were relatively rare.

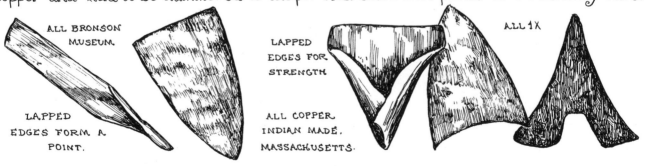

ALL BRONSON MUSEUM

LAPPED EDGES FOR STRENGTH

ALL 1X

LAPPED EDGES FORM A POINT.

ALL COPPER INDIAN MADE. MASSACHUSETTS.

LASHING ARROW POINTS

A fine, strong thread was needed to make a strong and secure lashing without bulk. Several kinds were by-products of a successful hunt.

TENDONS OR SINEWS

Muscles blend into a white fibrous cord~ the tendon~ that is in turn attached to a bone. To move the bone~ and the extremity that encases it~ the muscle contracts to pull the tendon. Motion is the result.

The hind leg of the deer had tendons of considerable length, made up of parallel fibrous strands. These were split into strips and dried. Several of these strips were held in the arrowsmith's mouth until well softened and pliable.

TENDON

TWO OR THREE TWISTED STRANDS GAVE ADDED STRENGTH TO THE LASHING. ONCE SOFTENED, THE STRANDS WERE ROLLED ON THE THIGHS. THE LEFT HAND ROLLED THE STRANDS TOWARD THE BODY WHILE THE RIGHT HAND TWISTED THE FIBERS AWAY. THE ARROW POINT WAS LASHED WHILE THE TWISTED THREAD WAS WET AND PLIABLE. THE FIBERS SHRANK AS THE THREAD DRIED TO GIVE A TIGHT, RUGGED LASHING.

GUT

Each deer carcass contributed many feet of small intestine (each hunter had 20 feet of his own). Each of these digestive tubes had a number of layers, the most important to the arrow maker being the sub~ mucosal layer. It was basically a sheath with a network of strong elastic and fibrous strands~ strong enough to be used today as violin and tennis-racket strings and surgical sutures. (Although known as catgut, the submucosal layer is usually donated by hogs and sheep and not the cat.)

MUCOUS LAYER

SEROUS COAT   MUSCLE LAYERS   SUBMUCOSAL LAYER

The Algonquian method of preparing gut is a matter of speculation, but probably the intestine was first split open. Both sides were scraped to the submucosal layer, then split into ribbons. These were dried, and later moistened and twisted into two-or three-strand threads, much like the tendon preparation. They were kept moistened for pliability in lashing.

SINEWSTONE ~FOR SMOOTHING BOTH TENDON AND GUT STRIPS
$\frac{1}{3}$ X

It's not easy to find a ready supply of small intestines or tendons for lashing arrow points. A willing—and successful—deer hunter might fill your wants, but consider heavy thread or fine string until the real thing comes along.

On cross section~

A thin point might need only a slot in the shaft.

A thicker point would fit only if the end of the shaft were drilled and notched.

Depth of shaft notch~

Expanded stems or side-notched points required only a shallow slot for hafting. Lashing was secured around the notches.

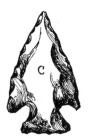

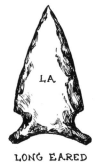

CORNER-NOTCHED

SIDE-NOTCHED

LONG EARED

EA = EARLY ARCHAIC.
     8500~5000 B.C.
LA = LATE ARCHAIC.
     3000 B.C.~ A.D. 300
C = CERAMIC-WOODLAND.
     A.D. 300~1676

Parallel stems, tapered stems, and unstemmed points needed a deeper slot. And without notches in the point, the lashing was more secure when it included the point edge.

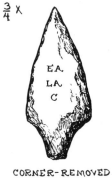
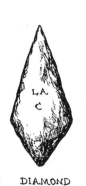

PARALLEL STEM

TRIANGULAR

TAPERED STEM

SMALL STEM

CORNER-REMOVED

DIAMOND

LEAF

Special points~

METAL~

1 X

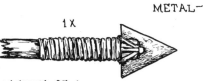

LASHING OF A COPPER-POINTED ARROW FROM THE SOUTHEASTERN INDIANS. (AMERICAN ANTHROPOLOGIST, N.S. 3, 1901)

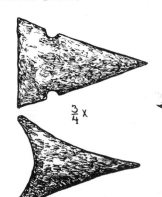

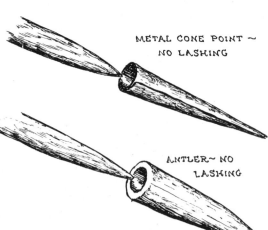

METAL CONE POINT ~ NO LASHING

ANTLER~ NO LASHING

INDIAN-MADE METAL POINTS, WITHOUT THE PERFORATION, HAD SIDE NOTCHING OR EARS FOR HAFTING.

 # DECOYS

The killing of any wild creature was motivated by survival. Necessity alone sent the hunter stalking. Since every bird, beast, and fish was given a spirit by the great god Cautantowit, extinguishing such a gift was not to be taken lightly. The Algonquian's reverence and deep respect for nature may be seen by the following

ABNAKI PRAYER

Our fathers spoke to the animals they had killed thus~

I am sorry that I had to kill you, Little Brother, but I had need of your meat. My Children were hungry and crying for food. Forgive me, Little Brother. I honor your courage, your strength and your beauty. Each time I pass this place I will remember you and do honor to your spirit. Forgive me, Little Brother. See, I smoke in your memory. I burn tobacco.

The arrow and its predecessor, the atlatl dart, had a limited range. High-flying waterfowl would contribute nothing to the cooking pot unless they could be lured to the marsh~ and the hidden hunter. Early Indian decoys were grass-filled bird skins. Later, artificial lures were fashioned from the bulrushes that bristled around the water's edge. A 1687 account by the French explorer Baron Lahontan described the decoys used on Lake Champlain: "For a decoy they have the skins of geese, bustards and ducks, dried and stuffed with hay. The two feet being made fast with two nails to a small piece of light plank which floats around the hut."

In 1924, eleven canvasback ducks and duck heads were unearthed in a Lovelock, Nevada, cave. Crafted of tule~ a lengthy, western variety of the common bulrush~ they were perfectly preserved in a basket some four feet below the cave floor. Some were cloaked in duck skins, others painted to simulate the colors of the canvasback, and still others undecorated.

This remarkable find has not been duplicated in New England, although the art was alive and well with the Algonquians. It is likely that the local decoys were not much different from the Nevada composite drawn here.

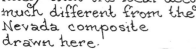

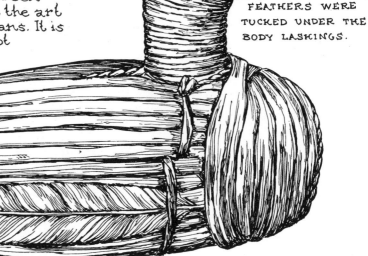

FEATHERS WERE
TUCKED UNDER THE
BODY LASHINGS.

 ABOUT ½ X

The Lovelock decoys are estimated to be between 1,000 and 2,000 years old. Bulrush stems were bent around the duck's neck and lashed together with twists of the same stems. The tail was cut to shape, and white duck feathers were tucked under the front and back lashings to give a realistic appearance. The painted colors gave the finishing touch~ hard for a south~ bound canvasback to resist.

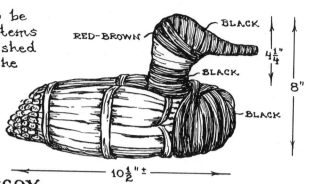

RED-BROWN
BLACK
BLACK
BLACK
4¼"
8"
10½" ±

REPRODUCING THE DUCK DECOY

For a close-up of these lures, see the display at the Museum of the American Indian in New York City. Our New England efforts will follow the same general construction with cat-o-nine-tails. Harvest in the fall and dry them for two or three days. The leaf should shrink about a third its width.

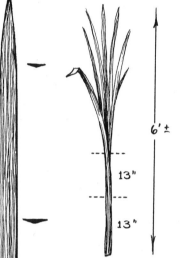

6' ±

13"

13"

CUT TWO LENGTHS OF 13 INCHES EACH FROM LOWER PORTION OF THE LEAF BUNCH. DON'T SEPARATE.

1X

CATTAIL LEAF

9"

CRISSCROSS THE TWINE TO BRING THE HEAD DOWN. THIN SISAL TWINE OR NATURAL RAFFIA GIVES AN AUTHENTIC LOOK TO YOUR LASHING.

BUNDLE A NUMBER OF THE 13~INCH LENGTHS AND TIE WITH STRING. USE FRESH AND PLIABLE LEAVES. AFTER BINDING THE BUNDLE TO THE GENERAL SHAPE, DRY, AND REMOVE THE TEMPORARY LASHINGS. BIND AND COVER WITH MOIST LEAVES.

BECAUSE I LIKED THE GREENS AND WHITES OF THE CATTAIL LEAVES, I BOUND THE HEAD AND NECK TO USE THESE NATURAL COLORS (BUT IT MIGHT NOT FOOL A REAL DUCK!).

BEND BACK SOME OF THE LEAVES AGAINST THE TWINE TO FILL OUT THE HEAD.

TIES

CUT THE SHAPE OF THE BILL.

SPLIT THE LEAF DOWN THE MIDDLE AND BIND WITH THE FLAT OF THE LEAF NEXT TO THE HEAD AND NECK.

DAMPEN THE SPLIT LEAF BEFORE BINDING. USE THE BRIGHT GREEN END TO COVER THE BILL AND HEAD.

START BY COVERING END OF THE BILL. THEN BIND UP TOWARD THE HEAD.

GO AS FAR AS THE LENGTH OF THE LEAF WILL PERMIT. SECURE END UNDER THE BINDING.

TWIST THE LEAF WHEN CROSSING UNDER THE NECK.

CONTINUE WINDING THE SPLIT GREEN LEAF, CROSSING UNDER THE CHIN. BARE AREAS ON THE HEAD AND NECK ARE NOW COVERED.

BODY~

CUT 16 OR MORE CATTAIL STALKS, EACH ABOUT 28 INCHES IN LENGTH. A CATTAIL STALK WILL PROVIDE TWO LENGTHS. THE DIAMETERS WILL RANGE BETWEEN $\frac{5}{8}$ AND $\frac{3}{4}$ INCH.

GREEN.

WHITE.

├─ 5" ─┤

TO BEND THE STALKS AROUND THE NECK, A PART MAY BE CUT OUT FOR A ROUNDED CURVE OR THE STALK FIBERS MAY BE CRUSHED AT THE CENTER. DAMPENING IS OPTIONAL.

BEND EACH STALK AROUND THE NECK, HOLDING THE ENDS TOGETHER BETWEEN THE KNEES. WHEN THE BODY IS FULL ENOUGH, TIE THE BUNDLE BEHIND THE NECK WHILE THE ENDS ARE STILL IN THE LEG VISE.

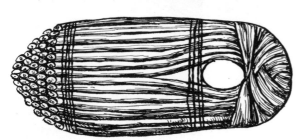

28"

28"

NEXT, TIE THE REAR LASHING. THE TAIL IS TRIMMED ~ THE SOFT STALKS ARE EASILY CUT WITH THE JACKKNIFE. IF YOU WISH, BIND THE BREAST WITH A CRISSCROSSED GREEN LEAF ~ MUCH LIKE A TURBAN. OF COURSE, YOU MAY PAINT THE DECOY AS THE INDIANS DID.

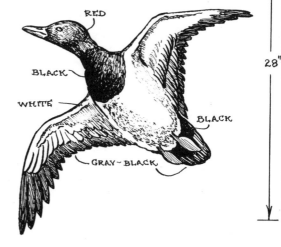

RED

BLACK

WHITE

BLACK

GRAY-BLACK

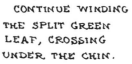

GOOSE DECOY

The decoy craft is still flourishing among such tribes as the Crees of the northern Great Lakes. Several of their tamarack twig examples are exhibited at the American Indian Archaeological Institute of Washington, Connecticut. Since there are no known New England specimens of this practical artistry, improvisation from our native materials would seem in order.

In nature's vast supermarket grow many possibilities. Whatever is chosen — fresh-cut branches, grasses, reeds, leaves, or vines — all must be well dried to reach a final shrinkage. To restore pliability, the stalks should receive a soaking and then be kept moist while being worked.

BRANCHES ~ CHOOSE THIN, STRAIGHT SHOOTS FROM THE WHITE BIRCH, COTTONWOOD, HAZELNUT, MULBERRY, POPLAR, SERVICEBERRY, WILLOW, WEEPING WILLOW, AND A HOST OF OTHERS. SUN-DRY AND SOAK FOR SEVERAL DAYS. IF BENDING IS DIFFICULT, ESPECIALLY WHEN WORKING THE DECOY HEAD, THE FIBERS MAY BE CRUSHED WITH PLIERS (JAW-WRAPPED WITH PLASTIC ELECTRICAL TAPE TO PREVENT MARRING THE BARK).

GRASSES ~ BEACH GRASS, BROOMCORN, REDTOP, REED GRASS, SEDGE, AND CANADIAN BLUE-GRASS. TO PRESERVE THE COLOR, CUT FOR DEEP GREEN IN JUNE. FOR LIGHTER GREEN, AMBER, AND REDS, COLLECT IN JULY. TIE IN BUNDLES AND HANG WITH THE POINTS DOWNWARD IN OUTDOOR SHADE. FOR BLEACHED HAY AND SHADES OF BROWN, DRY IN THE SUN. HALF AN HOUR BEFORE USING IT, SOAK THE DRIED GRASS IN COLD WATER (HOT WATER WILL BLEACH THE COLORS).

LEAVES ~ CATTAIL, HOLY GRASS, AND IRIS COME TO MIND. HARVEST IN THE SUMMER OR FALL AND DRY IN THE SHADE FOR SOFT GREEN COLORS.

VINES ~ BOSTON AND ENGLISH IVY, CLEMATIS, HONEYSUCKLE, WISTERIA, AND SUCH CULTIVATED VARIETIES THAT NEED PRUNING AROUND THE YARD. SELECT THE LONG AND FLEXIBLE ONE-YEAR SHOOTS IN THE FALL OR WINTER. REMOVE THE LEAVES, SHAVE THE KNOBS FLUSH, AND DRY. SOAK UNTIL MANAGEABLE.

THIN SISAL TWINE OR NATURAL RAFFIA BLENDS WELL WITH THE NATURAL COLORS. TRY QUICK AND TEMPORARY LASHINGS. LET DRY. WITH THE BRANCHES DRIED TO SHAPE, REPLACE LASHING IN A MORE ARTISTIC WAY.

SIZES MAY VARY FROM 5 INCHES UP TO 20 INCHES, DEPENDING ON THE RAW MATERIALS.

CATTAIL LEAVES MAY BE SPLIT INTO LENGTHS FOR SMALLER DECOYS.

CRUSH INDIVIDUAL BRANCHES IF BENDING MAY CAUSE BREAKAGE.

LASH THE SMALLER ENDS OF SIXTEEN OR SO STRAIGHT LENGTHS. THEN SEPARATE THE BUNDLE INTO TWO EQUAL SECTIONS.

BEND THE UPPER HALF TO FORM THE HEAD, AND LASH TO FORM THE CURVE.

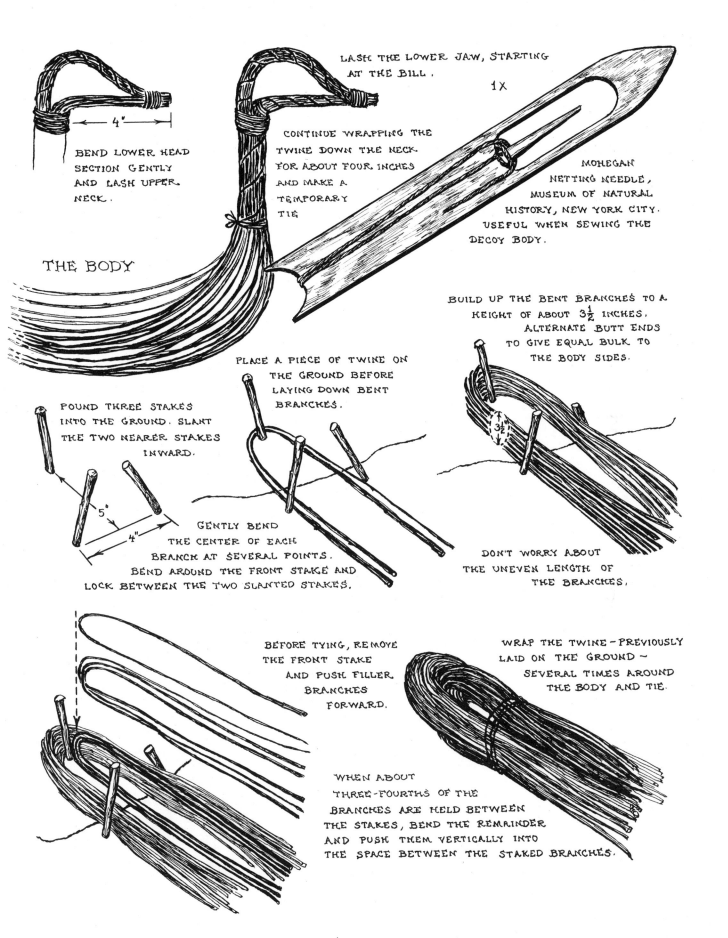

BEND LOWER HEAD SECTION GENTLY AND LASH UPPER NECK.

4"

LASH THE LOWER JAW, STARTING AT THE BILL.

1X

CONTINUE WRAPPING THE TWINE DOWN THE NECK FOR ABOUT FOUR INCHES AND MAKE A TEMPORARY TIE

MOHEGAN NETTING NEEDLE, MUSEUM OF NATURAL HISTORY, NEW YORK CITY. USEFUL WHEN SEWING THE DECOY BODY.

THE BODY

BUILD UP THE BENT BRANCHES TO A HEIGHT OF ABOUT 3½ INCHES. ALTERNATE BUTT ENDS TO GIVE EQUAL BULK TO THE BODY SIDES.

PLACE A PIECE OF TWINE ON THE GROUND BEFORE LAYING DOWN BENT BRANCHES.

POUND THREE STAKES INTO THE GROUND. SLANT THE TWO NEARER STAKES INWARD.

3½

5"

4"

GENTLY BEND THE CENTER OF EACH BRANCH AT SEVERAL POINTS. BEND AROUND THE FRONT STAKE AND LOCK BETWEEN THE TWO SLANTED STAKES.

DON'T WORRY ABOUT THE UNEVEN LENGTH OF THE BRANCHES.

BEFORE TYING, REMOVE THE FRONT STAKE AND PUSH FILLER BRANCHES FORWARD.

WRAP THE TWINE — PREVIOUSLY LAID ON THE GROUND — SEVERAL TIMES AROUND THE BODY AND TIE.

WHEN ABOUT THREE-FOURTHS OF THE BRANCHES ARE HELD BETWEEN THE STAKES, BEND THE REMAINDER AND PUSH THEM VERTICALLY INTO THE SPACE BETWEEN THE STAKED BRANCHES.

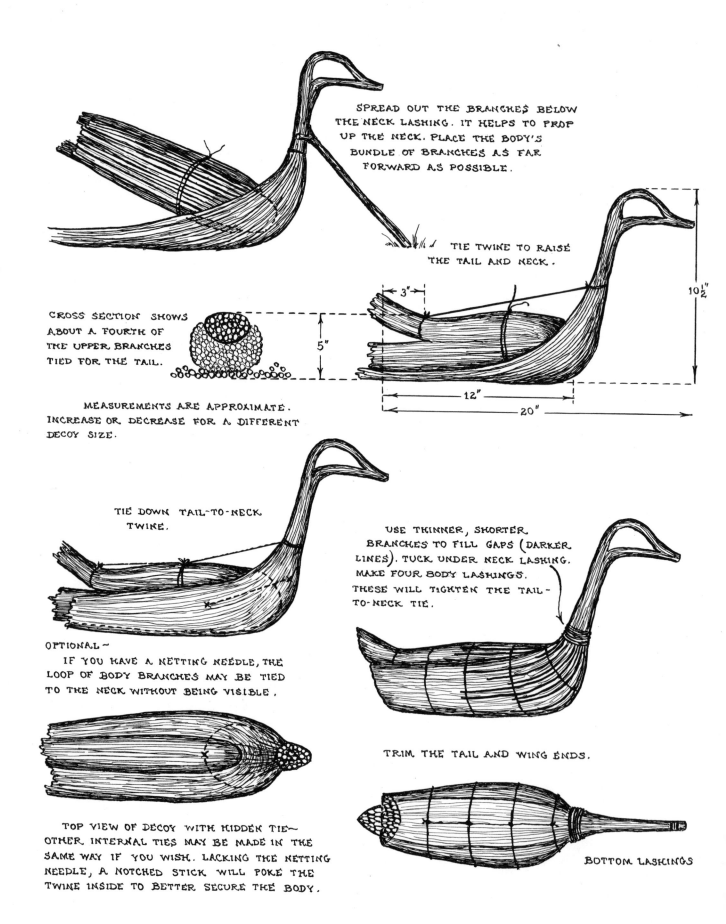

SPREAD OUT THE BRANCHES BELOW
THE NECK LASHING. IT HELPS TO PROP
UP THE NECK. PLACE THE BODY'S
BUNDLE OF BRANCHES AS FAR
FORWARD AS POSSIBLE.

TIE TWINE TO RAISE
THE TAIL AND NECK.

3"

10½"

CROSS SECTION SHOWS
ABOUT A FOURTH OF
THE UPPER BRANCHES
TIED FOR THE TAIL.

5"

12"

20"

MEASUREMENTS ARE APPROXIMATE.
INCREASE OR DECREASE FOR A DIFFERENT
DECOY SIZE.

TIE DOWN TAIL-TO-NECK
TWINE.

USE THINNER, SHORTER
BRANCHES TO FILL GAPS (DARKER
LINES). TUCK UNDER NECK LASHING.
MAKE FOUR BODY LASHINGS.
THESE WILL TIGHTEN THE TAIL-
TO-NECK TIE.

OPTIONAL ~
IF YOU HAVE A NETTING NEEDLE, THE
LOOP OF BODY BRANCHES MAY BE TIED
TO THE NECK WITHOUT BEING VISIBLE.

TRIM THE TAIL AND WING ENDS.

TOP VIEW OF DECOY WITH HIDDEN TIE~
OTHER INTERNAL TIES MAY BE MADE IN THE
SAME WAY IF YOU WISH. LACKING THE NETTING
NEEDLE, A NOTCHED STICK WILL POKE THE
TWINE INSIDE TO BETTER SECURE THE BODY.

BOTTOM LASHINGS

✝ SNARE

The Pilgrims learned about Indian snares first hand. Shortly after the Plymouth landing, several members of the party suddenly found their feet heading skyward~neatly entrapped in a noose of twine. Tied in turn to a bent sapling, the trap worked as well for man as for beast. The Wampanoags must have had many a chuckle over their campfires.

A large noose, baited with acorns or such, was pegged to

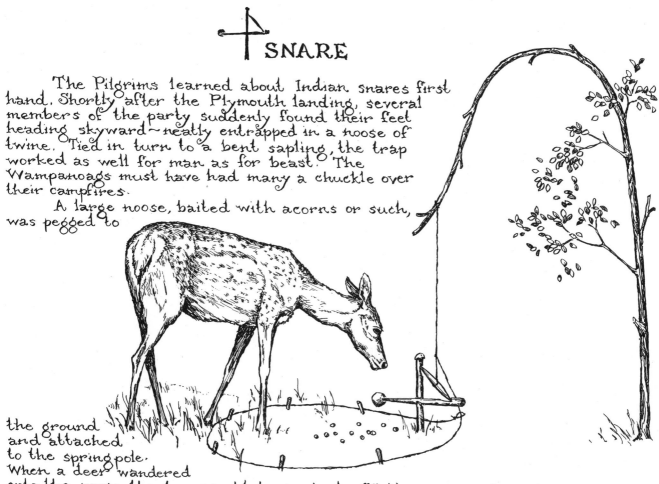

the ground and attached to the springpole. When a deer wandered onto the noose, the loop would be pushed off the pegs and quickly tightened around the antlers, neck, or legs. The purpose was not to actually lift the animal off the ground but rather to maintain enough tension on the loop to keep it from being shaken off. The bent sapling also helped to counterbalance the weight of the animal. As Roger Williams made note in his <u>A Key into The Language of America</u>, the snares had to be checked daily or the wolf would leave little but the bones for the stew pot.

In historic times, the Algonquian hunter added a trigger mechanism to his snare rig. An invention brought by the Yankee settlers, the "figure 4" could be whittled out on the spot. Simple and sure~fire, it soon was preferred for most Indian snares, deadfalls, and cage traps throughout New England.

REPRODUCING THE "FIGURE 4"

SAW A LENGTH OF PINE $\frac{3}{8}$ INCH SQUARE AND A MINIMUM LENGTH OF 40 INCHES. WHITTLE NOTCHES TO A DEPTH OF $\frac{1}{4}$ INCH. BRANCHES OF $\frac{1}{2}$~$\frac{5}{8}$ INCH IN DIAMETER MAY BE USED INSTEAD.

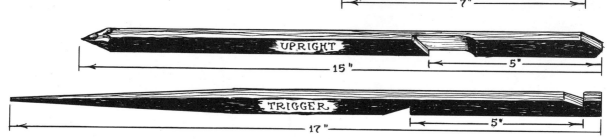

CATCHSTICK — 7"

UPRIGHT — 15" — 5"

TRIGGER — 17" — 5"

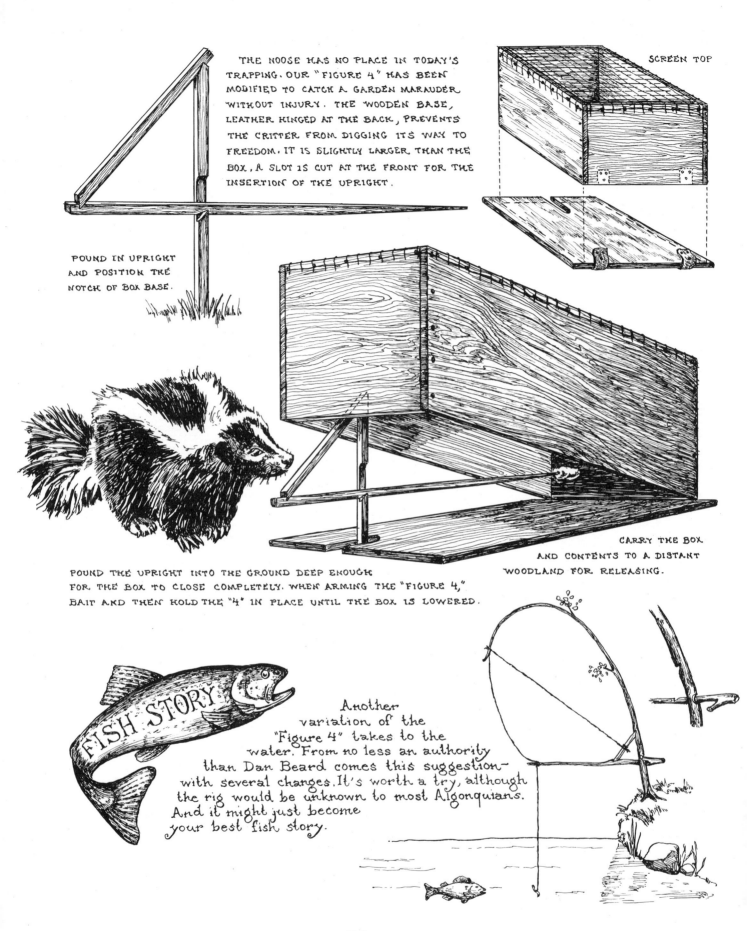

THE NOOSE HAS NO PLACE IN TODAY'S TRAPPING. OUR "FIGURE 4" HAS BEEN MODIFIED TO CATCH A GARDEN MARAUDER WITHOUT INJURY. THE WOODEN BASE, LEATHER HINGED AT THE BACK, PREVENTS THE CRITTER FROM DIGGING ITS WAY TO FREEDOM. IT IS SLIGHTLY LARGER THAN THE BOX, A SLOT IS CUT AT THE FRONT FOR THE INSERTION OF THE UPRIGHT.

SCREEN TOP

POUND IN UPRIGHT AND POSITION THE NOTCH OF BOX BASE.

CARRY THE BOX AND CONTENTS TO A DISTANT WOODLAND FOR RELEASING.

POUND THE UPRIGHT INTO THE GROUND DEEP ENOUGH FOR THE BOX TO CLOSE COMPLETELY. WHEN ARMING THE "FIGURE 4," BAIT AND THEN HOLD THE "4" IN PLACE UNTIL THE BOX IS LOWERED.

FISH STORY

Another variation of the "Figure 4" takes to the water. From no less an authority than Dan Beard comes this suggestion— with several changes. It's worth a try, although the rig would be unknown to most Algonquians. And it might just become your best fish story.

30

FISH SPEARS

Not all seafood needed a fishline and hook, for all the eastern Indian tribes had their expert spearmen. Before European trade goods were available, the fish spear points were crafted of bone and antler. The bone was prepared by scoring, separated into lengths, and shaped as in the "Bone Points" section (p.19).

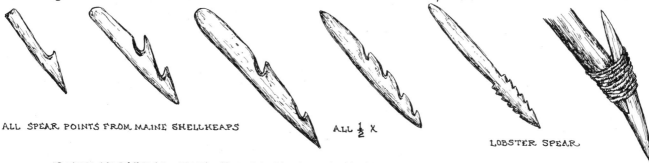

ALL SPEAR POINTS FROM MAINE SHELLHEAPS   ALL ½ X

LOBSTER SPEAR

REPRODUCING THE BONE FISH SPEAR

WITH A SHARP, COLD CHISEL, SCORE AND SEPARATE THREE SHAFTS OF BONE.

SHAPE AN EQUAL CURVE ON BOTH SIDES WITH A FILE, SANDER, OR GRINDER.

USE A RAT-TAIL FILE FOR THE CURVES.

GRIND INNER CURVE OF BONE FLAT. SKETCH THE POINT OUTLINE ON FACE.

USE A HACKSAW TO PRODUCE THE ROUGH DESIGN.

IRON FISH SPEARS

Gladys Tantaquidgeon noted the use of these iron heads by the Gay Head Indians of Martha's Vineyard.

Smaller fish, eels, and frogs are better caught with a two-pronged spear.

MODERN IRON SPEARHEAD FOR SPEARING SKATE ⅓ X±

OLD STYLE ~   THE LOOP PREVENTED THE SPEAR~ HEAD FROM BEING FORCED INTO THE SHAFT.

IRON.

AFTER CUTTING BARBS WITH A SHARP, COLD CHISEL, BEND THE OTHER END IN A VISE. PLACE IN THE GROOVE AND POUND TO SECURE.

USE ⅜ INCH RODS OF IRON OR ALUMINUM.

THE POLE IS 7~8 FEET LONG AND 1~1¼ INCHES IN DIAMETER AT THE BUTT END. GROOVES ARE CUT INTO BOTH SIDES. IF WOOD PRONGS ARE USED, TRY A FIBROUS WOOD SUCH AS HICKORY OR ASH~ OR EVEN BAMBOO. PLACE IN GROOVES AND LASH WITH WIRE. CHECK YOUR LOCAL FISHING LAWS~ 400 YEARS MAY HAVE SEEN CHANGES.

WOOD

PURSE NET

When spring came to New England, the return of the alewives was not far behind. Otherwise known as herring, they stormed up the freshwater streams that emptied into the ocean. The Algonquians were ready for this annual herring "run" with nets, scooping quantities ashore for eating and fertilizing the gardens.

John Josselyn, in his <u>Two Voyages to New England</u>, described these fish catchers as "nets like a purse put upon a round hooped stick with a handle." Roger Williams further noted that netting was made of hemp (Indian hemp or Apocyanum cannabinum). The inner bark of basswood and other vegetable fibers were probably also used.

REPRODUCING THE PURSE NET

Consider not only the Indian hemp but also leatherwood, swamp milkweed, or nettle. And aside from basswood, there are slippery elm, white oak, hickory, white and red cedar. (Details are under "Lacings" p.63 and "Thread and Cordage" p.66.) On the other hand, there's work enough ahead. You may wish to use fish line or string as a reasonable netting substitute. While you are mulling this over, the netting frame should be under way.

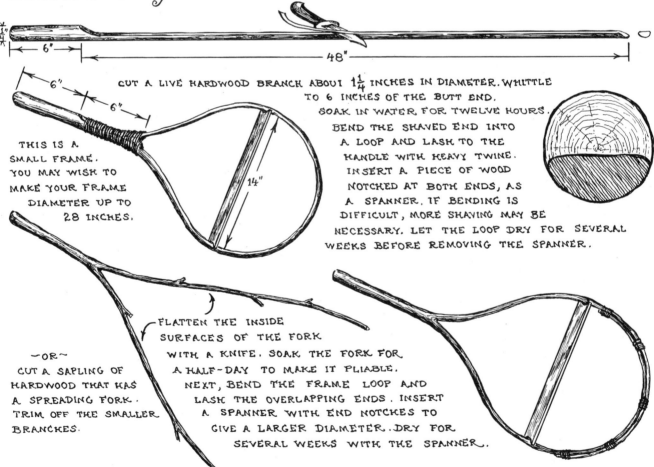

1¼"

6"

48"

6"

6"

THIS IS A SMALL FRAME. YOU MAY WISH TO MAKE YOUR FRAME DIAMETER UP TO 28 INCHES.

14"

CUT A LIVE HARDWOOD BRANCH ABOUT 1¼ INCHES IN DIAMETER. WHITTLE TO 6 INCHES OF THE BUTT END. SOAK IN WATER FOR TWELVE HOURS. BEND THE SHAVED END INTO A LOOP AND LASH TO THE HANDLE WITH HEAVY TWINE. INSERT A PIECE OF WOOD NOTCHED AT BOTH ENDS, AS A SPANNER. IF BENDING IS DIFFICULT, MORE SHAVING MAY BE NECESSARY. LET THE LOOP DRY FOR SEVERAL WEEKS BEFORE REMOVING THE SPANNER.

~OR~ CUT A SAPLING OF HARDWOOD THAT HAS A SPREADING FORK. TRIM OFF THE SMALLER BRANCHES.

FLATTEN THE INSIDE SURFACES OF THE FORK WITH A KNIFE. SOAK THE FORK FOR A HALF-DAY TO MAKE IT PLIABLE. NEXT, BEND THE FRAME LOOP AND LASH THE OVERLAPPING ENDS. INSERT A SPANNER WITH END NOTCHES TO GIVE A LARGER DIAMETER. DRY FOR SEVERAL WEEKS WITH THE SPANNER.

LASH THE NET FRAME HANDLE,
OR, IF THE FORKED BRANCH IS USED, SECURE THE OVERLAPPING ENDS WITH FIVE LIKE LASHINGS.

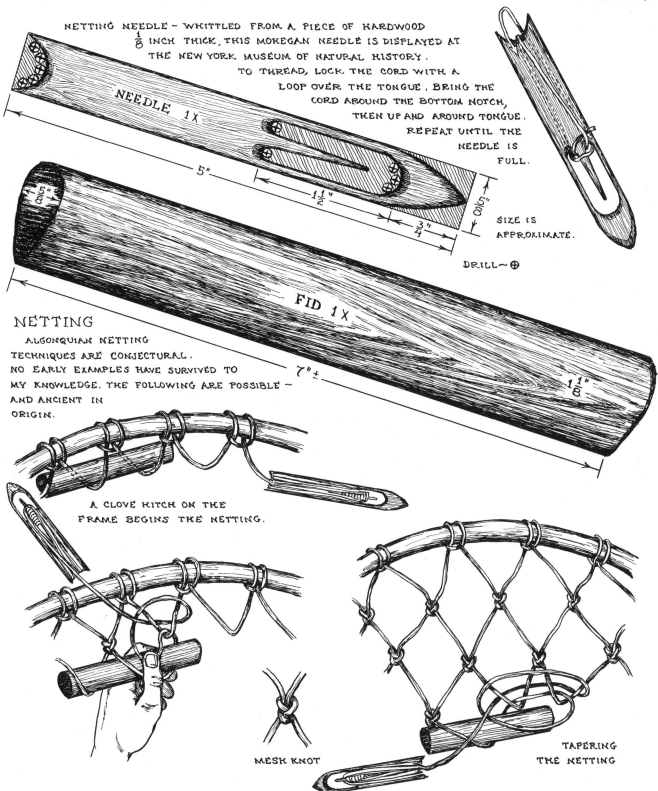

NETTING NEEDLE ~ WHITTLED FROM A PIECE OF HARDWOOD $\frac{1}{8}$ INCH THICK, THIS MOHEGAN NEEDLE IS DISPLAYED AT THE NEW YORK MUSEUM OF NATURAL HISTORY.
TO THREAD, LOCK THE CORD WITH A LOOP OVER THE TONGUE, BRING THE CORD AROUND THE BOTTOM NOTCH, THEN UP AND AROUND TONGUE. REPEAT UNTIL THE NEEDLE IS FULL.

NEEDLE 1X

5"

1$\frac{1}{2}$"

$\frac{3}{4}$"

SIZE IS APPROXIMATE.

DRILL ~ ⊕

FID 1X

7"±

1$\frac{1}{8}$"

NETTING

ALGONQUIAN NETTING TECHNIQUES ARE CONJECTURAL. NO EARLY EXAMPLES HAVE SURVIVED TO MY KNOWLEDGE. THE FOLLOWING ARE POSSIBLE ~ AND ANCIENT IN ORIGIN.

A CLOVE HITCH ON THE FRAME BEGINS THE NETTING.

MESH KNOT

TAPERING THE NETTING

The preceding netting method works handily for larger fish. But for collecting minnows or other bait, frogs, crayfish, or the like, here is another~ and easier~ way to make your netting. No netting needle or fid is necessary.

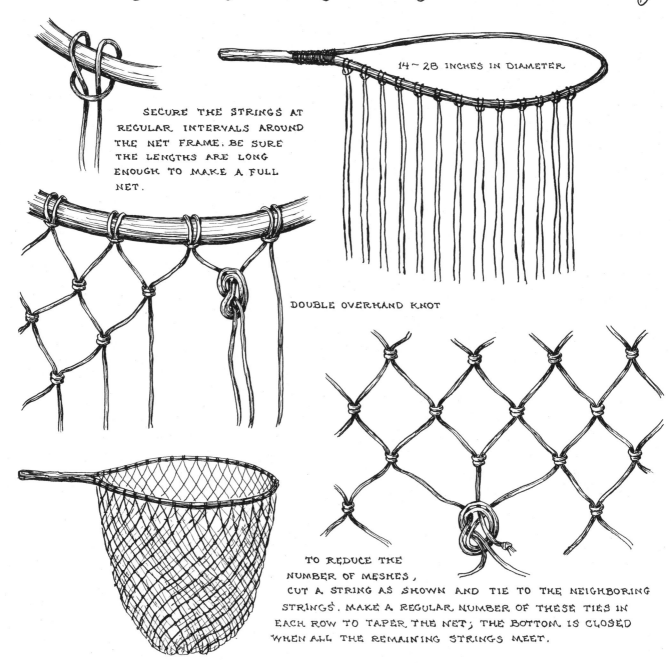

SECURE THE STRINGS AT REGULAR INTERVALS AROUND THE NET FRAME. BE SURE THE LENGTHS ARE LONG ENOUGH TO MAKE A FULL NET.

14 ~ 28 INCHES IN DIAMETER

DOUBLE OVERHAND KNOT

TO REDUCE THE NUMBER OF MESHES, CUT A STRING AS SHOWN AND TIE TO THE NEIGHBORING STRINGS. MAKE A REGULAR NUMBER OF THESE TIES IN EACH ROW TO TAPER THE NET; THE BOTTOM IS CLOSED WHEN ALL THE REMAINING STRINGS MEET.

If the mesh on your net is small enough, try catching some minnows for bait. Locate a school of fish and sprinkle bread crumbs on the water. Place a stone inside the net to prevent the string from floating. Hold the handle with both hands and rest the net on the river bottom under the crumbs. When the minnows are lunching, bring the net up with a sudden sweep.

A crayfish, while not exactly a lobster, makes a tasty meal none-the-less. Since the crustacean swims backward~tail first~ approach it slowly while placing the net to its rear. With luck, the crayfish will net itself.

THE WIGWAM

Morton, in his New English Canaan, described it this way: "They gather Poles in the woodes and put the great end of them in the ground, placing them in forme of a circle or circumference and, bending the topps of them in form of an Arch they bind them together with the Barke of Walnut trees which is wondrous tuffe so that they make the same round on the Topp."

This was the round house ~ as snug and warm as the best houses of the colonists. Its curved surface could baffle the worst of New England's storms. Its larger relative, the long house, was reborn centuries later ~ 1941, to be exact ~ at Quonset Point, Rhode Island. The Quonset hut served our troops throughout World War II and continues as efficient barns, restaurants, and dwellings.

THE ROUND HOUSE

FRAMING THE WIGWAM WAS MAN'S WORK. GREEN SAPLINGS OF ANY WOOD, 10-12 FEET IN LENGTH, WERE CUT WITH A NOTCHER. BENDING HELPED BY STRETCHING THE WOOD FIBERS. THE BUTTS WERE AT LEAST AN INCH IN DIAMETER.

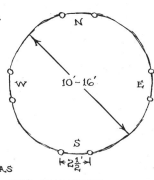

A CIRCLE OR AN OVAL WAS SCRATCHED INTO THE EARTH. THE DIAMETER RANGED BETWEEN 10 AND 16 FEET. SINCE DOORWAYS WOULD BE ON THE NORTH AND SOUTH SIDES, A PAIR OF SAPLINGS WERE EMBEDDED AT THESE POINTS ABOUT 2½ FEET APART. TWO LIKE PAIRS WERE ALSO SECURED AT THE EAST AND WEST SIDES.

EACH SAPLING WAS ANCHORED AT LEAST 1 FOOT IN THE GROUND.

EACH SAPLING WAS BENT AND LASHED TO ITS OPPOSITE. THE HEIGHT WAS 6-7 FEET.

THE OVERLAP OF THE OPPOSITE SAPLINGS WAS AT LEAST 1 FOOT. IT WAS THEN LASHED IN PLACE WITH THE INNER BARK STRIPS OF BASSWOOD, HICKORY, SLIPPERY ELM, OR WALNUT.

THE CIRCUMFERENCE ARCS BETWEEN THE PAIRS OF LASHED SAPLINGS WERE MARKED FOR HOLES (HERE MARKED "X"). THE DISTANCE BETWEEN HOLES WAS EQUAL ~ AND AS CLOSE TO 2 FEET AS POSSIBLE.

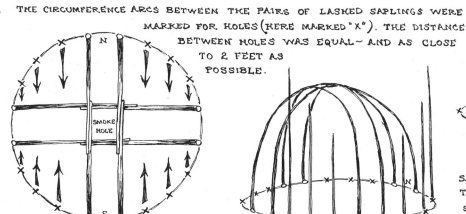

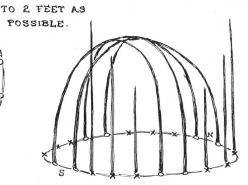

THINNER AND SHORTER SAPLINGS WERE USED AS THE LASHED ARCHES BECAME SMALLER.

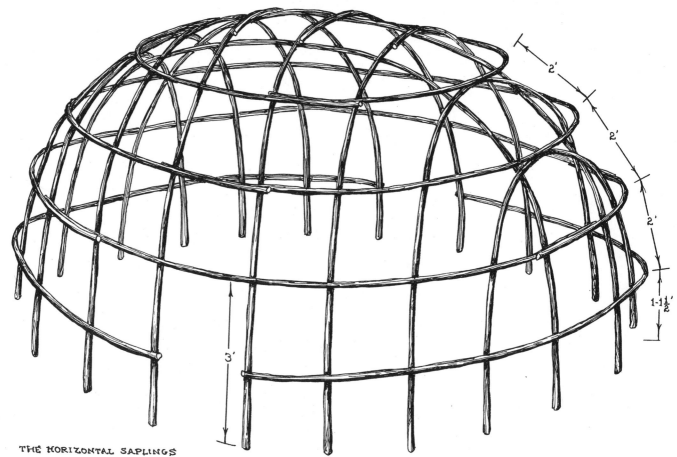

THE HORIZONTAL SAPLINGS
WERE THINNER THAN THE STURDIER
UPRIGHT ARCH SUPPORTS. THE LOWEST RING WAS LASHED 1~1½ FEET ABOVE THE GROUND. OPENINGS
WERE LEFT FOR THE NORTH AND SOUTH ENTRANCES. THE SECOND ROW WAS LASHED 2 FEET ABOVE
THE FIRST. IT COMPLETELY ENCIRCLED THE WIGWAM TO GIVE A 3~FOOT HEIGHT TO BOTH ENTRANCES.
ADDITIONAL HORIZONTAL RINGS WERE 2 FEET APART.

LASHING

BAST WAS THE CORD MADE FROM
THE FRESH INNER BARK OF BASSWOOD,
HICKORY, SLIPPERY ELM, AND WALNUT.
AN INCH-WIDE LENGTH OF BARK WAS
STRIPPED TOWARD THE TOP OF THE
TREE~THE LONGER THE BETTER.

THE OUTER BARK WAS PEELED
OFF AND DISCARDED.

SQUARE KNOT
FINISHES
LASHING.

ONE OF MANY LASHINGS~BUT THE CROSSED
SAPLINGS MAY BE POSITIONED AND
THE TWINE TIGHTENED WITH-
OUT HELP.

THE INNER BARK
WAS CUT INTO THIN
STRIPS. THEY COULD BE USED
IMMEDIATELY OR COILED AND
STORED. THE STRIPS WOULD THEN BE
SOAKED FOR SEVERAL HOURS BEFORE USING.

THE LONG HOUSE

These larger dwellings were favored in the wintry months - especially in northern New England. The long house was a sort of one-story apartment house, with a number of tribespeople sharing the warmth. A four-family 'long house would have several fireplaces. Six or more families would require three or more fires with as many smoke holes in the roof. Forty souls would need a long house of some 50 feet in length. But by all standards, the ceremonial long house was mammoth. Some were as long as 200 feet, with a width of up to 30 feet.

The long house was basically a stretched-out round wigwam. Construction began with two parallel rows of freshly cut poles. Again, opposites were bent over and lashed to their opposites, giving a long row of equal arches. Closing the ends was accomplished in two ways: Semicircles of poles were bent over to join the main arch framework, or the end poles were placed in a perpendicular position to give flat ends. Two or more entrances were part of the structure, depending on its size.

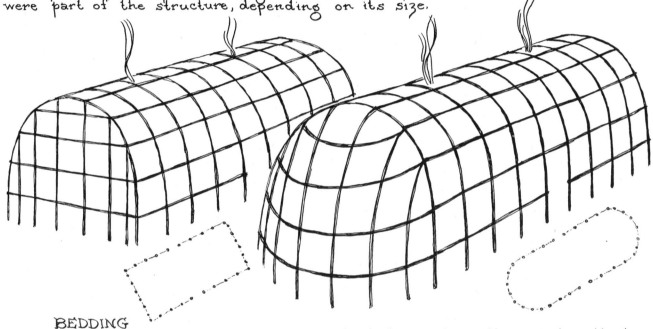

BEDDING

Bed frames were made before either the round or the long house was sheathed. Forked sticks were embedded an equal distance from the wigwam wall. They supported outer side rails 12-18 inches above the ground. A second bed rail was lashed to the wig-wam framework. Small branches, between $\frac{1}{2}$ -1 inch in diameter, were lashed to the rails. Mats and furs were laid over the surface for comfortable sitting or sleeping

Beds often ran along both sides of the long house - with gaps left for the entrances, of course. And they were sizable - 6 to 8 feet in width. Sleepers could lie three or four deep, snug and warm.

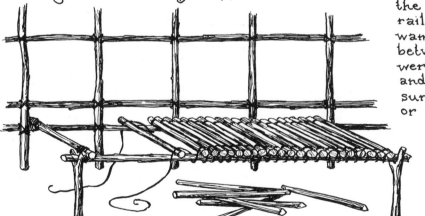

FIREPLACES

Fireplaces were usually lined with small fieldstones. Smoke holes were provided directly over the hearth. As a rule, one fireplace would serve two families. The average round house sheltering one or two families would therefore have a single central hearth. Long houses with four families required two fires, while six, eight, or more such groups would have three, four, or more fires.

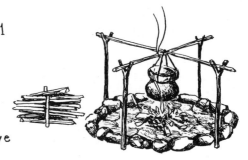

RECONSTRUCTING THE WIGWAM FRAME

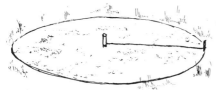

OUTLINE THE WIGWAM WITH A STRING OF THE DESIRED RADIUS. LOOP ONE END AROUND A STAKE. THE OTHER END, TIED TO A STICK, MARKS THE DIAMETER.

HORIZONTAL SAPLINGS ARE 1 INCH OR LESS IN DIAMETER, FOR EASIER BENDING.
LASH WITH TWINE SUCH AS IS USED ON PACKAGES.

MAKE 1-FOOT HOLES FOR ANCHORING THE SAPLINGS. USE A STAKE OR A CROWBAR.

SAPLINGS ~ THINNING OUT SUCH WEED TREES AS THE BLIGHT-RIDDEN CHESTNUT OR RED MAPLE IS GOOD FOREST MANAGEMENT. THEY YIELD POOR TIMBER BUT FINE FRAME POLES.

BUT ANY STRAIGHT HARDWOOD SAPLING THAT IS STRAIGHT AND CROWDING OTHER TREES WILL DO NICELY.

LEAVE A LOWER BRANCH PROJECTION TO POUND THE POLE INTO THE HOLES.

BUTT ENDS

COVERING THE FRAME

There was no want of sheathing for the wigwam frame. Bark did a decent job of covering tree trunks ~ and was no less efficient for keeping out the elements and holding in the fireplace heat. The pliable white birch bark of northern New England was an ideal covering, but the more southerly regions found basswood, walnut, elm, ash, chestnut, fir, cedar, and spruce perfectly satisfactory.

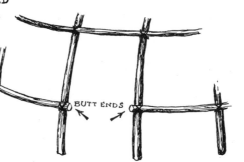

6-9'

TWO ENCIRCLING CUTS WERE MADE, ONE AT THE BASE AND THE SECOND CUT 6-7 FEET ABOVE THE FIRST. A PERPENDICULAR CUT CONNECTED BOTH.

A SPUD WAS USED TO PRY THE BARK LOOSE. MOST PIECES WOULD BE 3-4 FEET WIDE, DEPENDING ON THE TREE DIAMETER.

SPUDS ~ ONE A WOODEN WEDGE-SHAPED POLE AND TWO OF STONE, MASSACHUSETTS

2'

ALL ⅙ X

DESCRIBED BY WILLIAM FOWLER IN THE MASSACHUSETTS ARCHAEOLOGICAL BULLETIN," VOL. 37, 1976

BARK WIGWAMS WERE SHINGLED, STARTING AT THE DOORWAY WITH THE LOWEST ROW.

BARK WAS DRIED FLAT UNDER THE WEIGHT OF STONES BEFORE USING.

THE SMOOTH SIDE OF THIS BARK FACED THE INTERIOR OF THE WIGWAM.

SOME WIGWAMS, AS ON THE LEFT, WERE SHINGLED WITH THE LENGTH OF THE BARK LAID PARALLEL TO THE GROUND. THE NEARER ONE HAD ITS BARK STRIPS RUNNING VERTICALLY. TOUGH AND SUPPLE BRANCHES, OR WITHES, HELD THE COVERING IN PLACE. THE 18-INCH SMOKE HOLE AT THE TOP WAS SCREENED AGAINST THE WIND WITH A MAT. THIS COULD BE PIVOTED BY AN ATTACHED SAPLING.

Today, there can be no compromise when it comes to collecting bark. A stripped tree will become a rotting skeleton within a year ~ a monument to a vandal's thoughtlessness. Removing smaller pieces of this protective layer will just as surely doom the tree ~ it just takes a bit longer to die. But for Indian-lore enthusiasts, the answer may be found at any lumbering operation. Timber that is to be felled for lumber has no use for its skin. Talk to your local forester, tree-farm grower or logger. Generally, trees are marked by the forester for cutting. Ask for permission to harvest all the bark needed to cover your wigwam.

CATTAIL MATS

Cattail mats rivaled the bark strips for wigwam coverings ~ and for a number of reasons. Consider that each cattail stalk matured in a single season and that each was identical to its neighbor. The stalks could be harvested without fear of depleting the supply, for the vast meshwork of roots, or more properly rhizomes, guaranteed an even larger crop the following year. They were easily gathered (if wet feet were no problem) and were light to carry when sewn into mats. Further, these same mats provided excellent insulation against the extremes of New England weather. The Pilgrims were quick to learn such advantages and early on thatched their roofs with these stalks.

CATTAILS WERE COLLECTED IN THE LATE SUMMER. EACH STALK WAS STRIPPED OF ITS LOOSE OUTER LAYERS AND DRIED IN THE SUN.

CATTAIL (TYPHA LATIFOLIA L.)

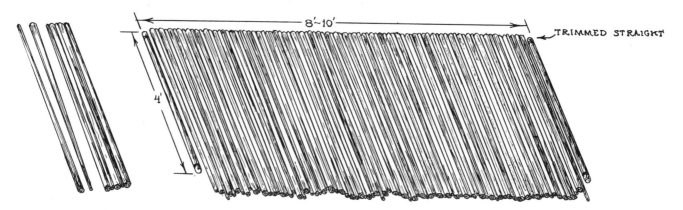

8'~10'

4'

TRIMMED STRAIGHT

THE CATTAIL STALKS WERE LAID PARALLEL ON A FLAT PIECE OF GROUND. BECAUSE EACH STALK TAPERED, THE BUTTS AND SMALL ENDS ALTERNATED IN THE ROW.

ON ONE SIDE, THE ENDS OF THE STALKS WERE TRIMMED EVENLY. STRAIGHT PEELED STICKS WERE NOTCHED AT BOTH ENDS AND WERE HELD PARALLEL TO THE STALKS. PEGS, DRIVEN INTO THE GROUND, HELD THE STICKS IN PLACE.

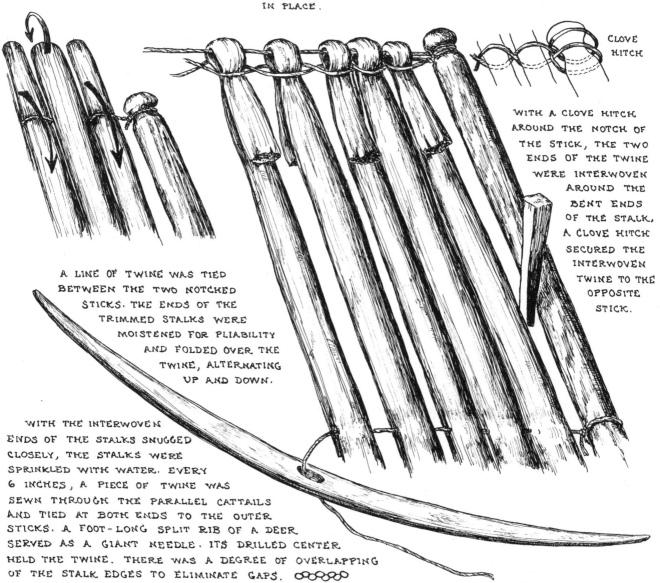

CLOVE HITCH

A LINE OF TWINE WAS TIED BETWEEN THE TWO NOTCHED STICKS. THE ENDS OF THE TRIMMED STALKS WERE MOISTENED FOR PLIABILITY AND FOLDED OVER THE TWINE, ALTERNATING UP AND DOWN.

WITH A CLOVE HITCH AROUND THE NOTCH OF THE STICK, THE TWO ENDS OF THE TWINE WERE INTERWOVEN AROUND THE BENT ENDS OF THE STALK. A CLOVE HITCH SECURED THE INTERWOVEN TWINE TO THE OPPOSITE STICK.

WITH THE INTERWOVEN ENDS OF THE STALKS SNUGGED CLOSELY, THE STALKS WERE SPRINKLED WITH WATER. EVERY 6 INCHES, A PIECE OF TWINE WAS SEWN THROUGH THE PARALLEL CATTAILS AND TIED AT BOTH ENDS TO THE OUTER STICKS. A FOOT-LONG SPLIT RIB OF A DEER SERVED AS A GIANT NEEDLE. ITS DRILLED CENTER HELD THE TWINE. THERE WAS A DEGREE OF OVERLAPPING OF THE STALK EDGES TO ELIMINATE GAPS.

40

THE MATMAKER SAT ON THE CATTAILS DURING THE SEWING PROCESS. WITH ONE HAND SHE RAISED AND STEADIED THREE OR FOUR STALKS AND, WITH THE OTHER, PUSHED THROUGH THE NEEDLE.

WHEN THE PARALLEL ROWS OF STITCHES WERE FINISHED, THERE REMAINED ONLY THE TRIMMING AND TWINE INTERWEAVING OF THE UNFINISHED EDGE.

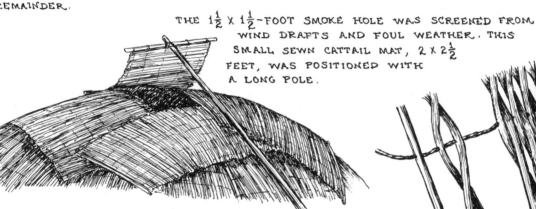

ONE THING FURTHER: DOUBLE CORDS~ EACH A FOOT LONG ~ WERE TIED TO THE NOTCHED ENDS OF THE STICKS. THESE WERE SECURED TO THE WIGWAM FRAMEWORK. NOTE THAT THE SECOND ROW OF HORIZONTAL FRAME SAPLINGS WAS AS HIGH AS THE MATS WERE WIDE. OTHER MATS - OR OCCASIONALLY BARK SLABS - COVERED THE REMAINDER.

THE $1\frac{1}{2}$ X $1\frac{1}{2}$-FOOT SMOKE HOLE WAS SCREENED FROM WIND DRAFTS AND FOUL WEATHER. THIS SMALL SEWN CATTAIL MAT, 2 X $2\frac{1}{2}$ FEET, WAS POSITIONED WITH A LONG POLE.

INTERIOR MATS

There were other mats to be crafted— handsome coverings for the interior of the wigwam.
Bulrushes were the preferred raw material, found by the same swamps that yielded the cattails. The stalks were harvested in July, then dried and bleached in the summer sun. Some lengths were dyed to give the mats color and design.

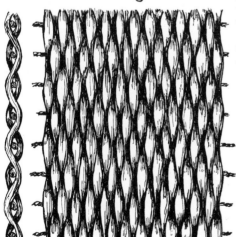

ABOVE IS SHOWN A DIFFERENT TWIST. MOST INTERIOR MATS WERE WOVEN, BUT OCCASIONALLY THEY WERE TWISTED, THEN SEWN MUCH LIKE THE CATTAIL OUTSIDE MATS.

TYPICAL WOVEN RUSH MAT WITH BASSWOOD BARK TWINE

41

SOFT-STEM, OR GREAT, BULRUSH (SCIRPUS VALIDUS VAHL) OFTEN GREW TO A 6-FOOT HEIGHT, WITH A ROUND STEM, UPWARD TO 1 INCH IN DIAMETER.

THE ENDS OF THE RUSHES WERE BRAIDED, THEN SUSPENDED FROM A CROSSBAR. THE MAT MAKER WOVE A BASSWOOD TWINE (THE WEFT) IN AND OUT OF THE SUSPENDED STALKS. BEGINNING AT THE TOP, THE TWINE WAS WOVEN FROM LEFT TO RIGHT, THE ROWS OF TWINE WERE ABOUT ½ INCH APART. WHEN THE BOTTOM WAS REACHED, THE ENDS WERE BRAIDED IN THE SAME MANNER AS THE UPPER EDGE.

THE BURDEN STRAP WAS USED TO CARRY THE MATS TO THE CAMPSITE.

THESE INTERIOR MATS NOT ONLY DECORATED THE WALLS OF THE WIGWAM BUT ALSO GAVE EXCELLENT INSULATION WITH THE DEAD AIR SPACE BETWEEN IT AND THE OUTSIDE MATS. THEY ALSO COVERED THE BEDS AND OCCASIONALLY WERE USED FOR SITTING ON, FOR SERVING MEALS, DRYING CORN AND BERRIES, AND EVEN FOR WRAPPING THE DEAD AT BURIAL.

MAT LOOMS

Willoughby, in his _Antiquities of the New England Indians_, wrote that "the poorer wigwams were sometimes covered with a thatch of reeds, grass or corn-husk, or with the boughs of trees." Since the method of weaving these varied materials is uncertain, you might wish to try a modern-day mat loom. Now if you'd rather not risk being the owner of a "poorer" wigwam, there's always the ancient way to sew cattails or weave rushes!

SCRATCH A RECTANGLE ON FLAT GROUND 6 FEET LONG AND 44 INCHES WIDE. POUND STURDY STICKS AT EACH END AS SHOWN. TIE THE PERMANENT AND MOVABLE WARP STRINGS 6 INCHES APART.

PROCEDURE~ RAISE THE MOVABLE WARP BAR ABOVE YOUR HEAD. HAVE A HELPER LAY WELL-DRIED CATTAILS OR REEDS OR SMALL BUNCHES OF CORNHUSKS OR HAY ON THE PERMANENT WARP STRINGS. BRING THE MOVABLE BAR DOWN TO THE GROUND. THEN PLACE ANOTHER BUNDLE OF MATTING AT THE ANGLE BETWEEN THE MOVABLE WARP AND THE PERMAN-ENT WARP. UP GOES THE MOVABLE BAR, AND ANOTHER ROW OF MATTING IS DONE.

TRIM EDGES

TIE

10'

MOVABLE WARP

3'

6'

--- ~SCRATCHED OUTLINE

PERMANENT WARP

6'

3'

4" 6" 6" 6" 6" 6" 4"

TIE WARP STRINGS AT BOTH ENDS.

DUGOUT CANOES

The native Americans were astounded at the size of the early European sailing ships. Where, indeed, did trees grow to such a gargantuan size— large enough to hollow a vessel of such proportions?

William Wood, in his 1634 New England's Prospect, described the dugout as made of pine "burned hollow, [then] scraping them smooth with clam shells and oyster shells, cutting their outsides with stone hatchets. These boats be not above a foot and a half or two feet wide and twenty foot long."

It is difficult to imagine these white-pine giants being felled, trimmed, and hollowed by burning ~ and the char being chipped away with primitive tools. Yet experienced craftsmen could trim the sides to within $\frac{3}{4}$ inch and could completely shape and finish an average canoe in just three weeks.

BLUE-GREEN NEEDLES IN BUNCHES OF FIVE, WITH LONG TAPERED PINE-CONES.

A FOREST ARISTOCRAT ~ THE GIANT WHITE PINE

CONTROLLED BURNING AND AXING AWAY THE CHAR ULTIMATELY LEVELED THE PINE. THE TOP AND BRANCHES WERE REMOVED IN LIKE MANNER TO GIVE A TRUNK OF THE DESIRED LENGTH. SUPPORTS RAISED THE PIECE TO A WORK-ABLE HEIGHT.

AFTER THE BARK WAS STRIPPED FREE, A FIRE BURNED THE TOP DOWN TO THE GUNWALES.

CHIPPING AND SCRAPING THE CHAR CONTINUED UNTIL THE INSIDE WAS HOLLOWED. THE JUDICIOUS USE OF WATER SNUFFED OUT ANY FLAMES THAT MIGHT EAT INTO THE DUGOUT'S SIDES AND BOTTOM.

HATCHET ~ WILLIAM WOOD NOTED IN 1634 THAT THE INDIANS FINISHED THEIR DUGOUTS BY "CUTTING THEIR OUT-SIDES WITH STONE HATCHETS." LATE ARCHAIC~CERAMIC.

GROOVED AX ~ A HEFTY PIECE OF STONE THAT COULD FELL A TREE WITH THE HELP OF FIRE. LATE ARCHAIC.

CELT~ USEFUL FOR CHIP-PING OUT CHAR. SOME WERE USED WITHOUT HANDLES, AS WEDGES. LATE ARCHAIC ~ CERAMIC.

GOUGE ~ THE GROOVED CUTTING EDGE SCOOPED OUT CHUNKS OF THE BURNED WOOD. LATE ARCHAIC.

QUAHOG SHELL ~ THE OCEAN'S READY-MADE SCRAPER ~ AND CHIPPED STONE SCRAPERS GAVE A SMOOTH FINISH BY REMOVING RESIDUAL CHAR FROM THE INSIDE OF THE CANOE.

43

Ancient descriptions cannot compare with actually SEEING a 500-year-old dugout. In 1965, a severe drought had reduced much of the Great Pond reservoir to muck at Weymouth, Massachusetts. The discovery of the decade began when a group of boys chanced upon a protruding chunk of water-soaked wood. Armed with shovels, they gradually exposed an extremely rare Algonquian dugout canoe, preserved in the mud bottom since A.D. 1450.

Now safely displayed in the Tufts Library at Weymouth, the canoe stands as a monument to the ancient art of burning and scraping a seaworthy craft from a log.

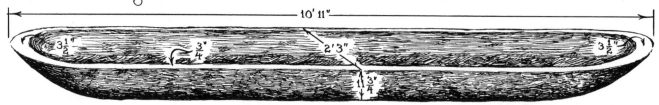

APPROXIMATE MEASUREMENTS OF WEYMOUTH DUGOUT - "MASSACHUSETTS ARCHAEOLOGICAL BULLETIN"
OCTOBER 1968

REPRODUCING THE DUGOUT

Ever since the Weymouth discovery, I hankered to see if a dugout afloat handled more like a log than a canoe. A twentieth-century copy was the answer. It happened that a nearby white pine - just the dimensions of the drawing above - had been struck by lightning. A logger friend dropped the trunk off at my back yard. I attacked the giant with some typical colonial tools. You may wish to burn and scrape in the old way - or even to be ultramodern with a chain saw - your choice.

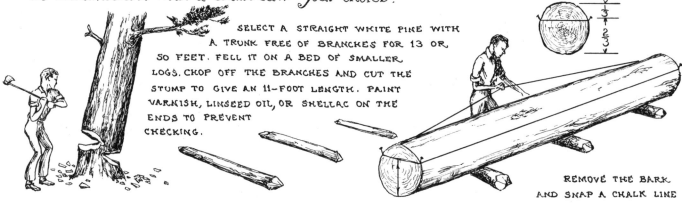

SELECT A STRAIGHT WHITE PINE WITH A TRUNK FREE OF BRANCHES FOR 13 OR SO FEET. FELL IT ON A BED OF SMALLER LOGS. CHOP OFF THE BRANCHES AND CUT THE STUMP TO GIVE AN 11-FOOT LENGTH. PAINT VARNISH, LINSEED OIL, OR SHELLAC ON THE ENDS TO PREVENT CHECKING.

REMOVE THE BARK AND SNAP A CHALK LINE TWO-THIRDS OF THE WAY FROM THE LOG BOTTOM. USE WET CHARCOAL DUST ON THE CHALK LINE IF THE CHALK IS DIFFICULT TO SEE.

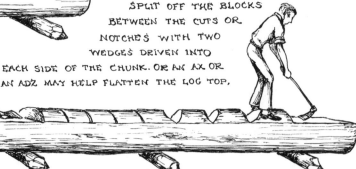

CUT DOWN TO THE CHALK LINES WITH A SAW. SPACE CUTS ABOUT 8 OR 9 INCHES APART, OR CUT NOTCHES DOWN TO THE CHALK LINES. MAKE NOTCHES ABOUT 12 INCHES APART.

SPLIT OFF THE BLOCKS BETWEEN THE CUTS OR NOTCHES WITH TWO WEDGES DRIVEN INTO EACH SIDE OF THE CHUNK. OR AN AX OR AN ADZ MAY HELP FLATTEN THE LOG TOP.

44

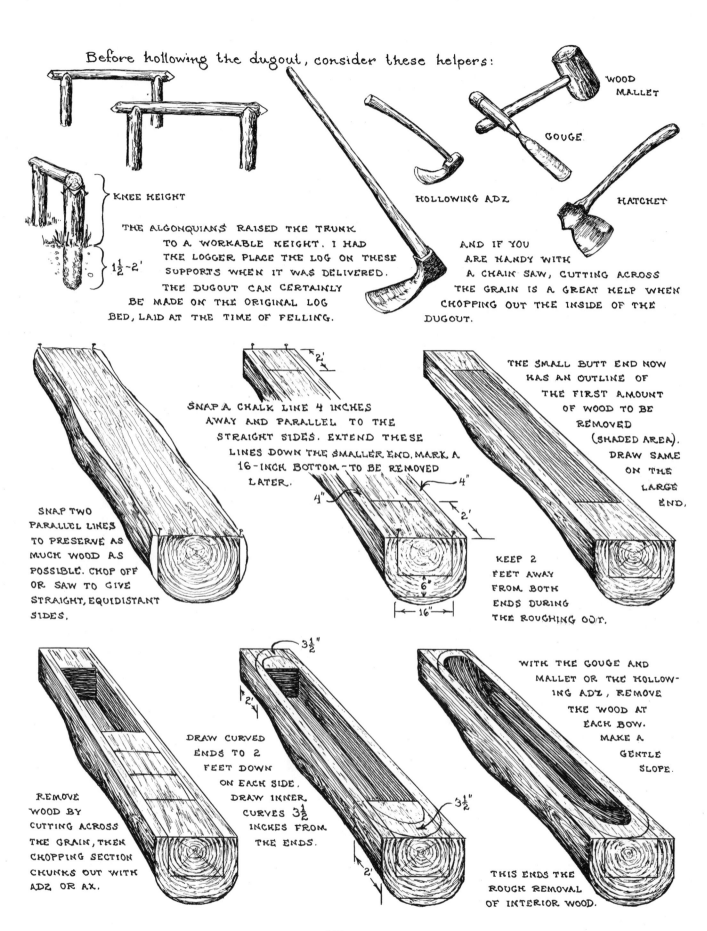

Before hollowing the dugout, consider these helpers:

WOOD MALLET

GOUGE

HOLLOWING ADZ

HATCHET

KNEE HEIGHT

1½ - 2'

THE ALGONQUIANS RAISED THE TRUNK TO A WORKABLE HEIGHT. I HAD THE LOGGER PLACE THE LOG ON THESE SUPPORTS WHEN IT WAS DELIVERED. THE DUGOUT CAN CERTAINLY BE MADE ON THE ORIGINAL LOG BED, LAID AT THE TIME OF FELLING.

AND IF YOU ARE HANDY WITH A CHAIN SAW, CUTTING ACROSS THE GRAIN IS A GREAT HELP WHEN CHOPPING OUT THE INSIDE OF THE DUGOUT.

SNAP A CHALK LINE 4 INCHES AWAY AND PARALLEL TO THE STRAIGHT SIDES. EXTEND THESE LINES DOWN THE SMALLER END. MARK A 16-INCH BOTTOM — TO BE REMOVED LATER.

2'

4"

4"

2'

6"

16"

SNAP TWO PARALLEL LINES TO PRESERVE AS MUCH WOOD AS POSSIBLE. CHOP OFF OR SAW TO GIVE STRAIGHT, EQUIDISTANT SIDES.

THE SMALL BUTT END NOW HAS AN OUTLINE OF THE FIRST AMOUNT OF WOOD TO BE REMOVED (SHADED AREA). DRAW SAME ON THE LARGE END.

KEEP 2 FEET AWAY FROM BOTH ENDS DURING THE ROUGHING OUT.

3½"

2'

3½"

2'

REMOVE WOOD BY CUTTING ACROSS THE GRAIN, THEN CHOPPING SECTION CHUNKS OUT WITH ADZ OR AX.

DRAW CURVED ENDS TO 2 FEET DOWN ON EACH SIDE. DRAW INNER CURVES 3½ INCHES FROM THE ENDS.

WITH THE GOUGE AND MALLET OR THE HOLLOWING ADZ, REMOVE THE WOOD AT EACH BOW. MAKE A GENTLE SLOPE.

THIS ENDS THE ROUGH REMOVAL OF INTERIOR WOOD.

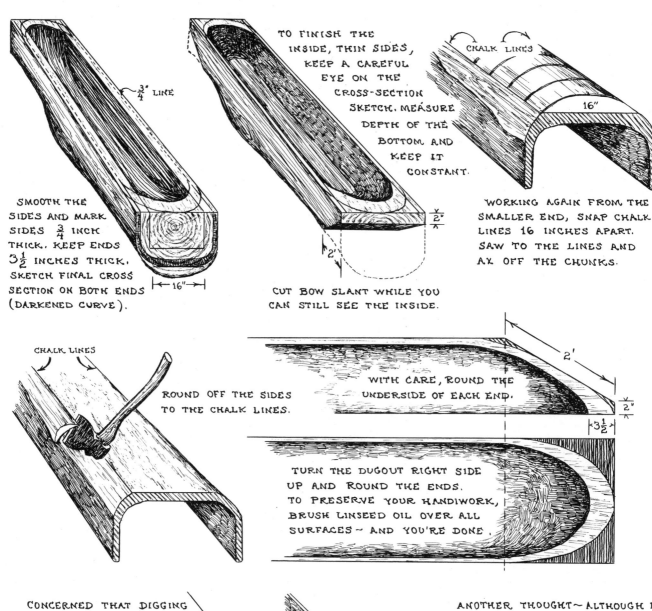

SMOOTH THE SIDES AND MARK SIDES $\frac{3}{4}$ INCH THICK. KEEP ENDS $3\frac{1}{2}$ INCHES THICK. SKETCH FINAL CROSS SECTION ON BOTH ENDS (DARKENED CURVE).

$\frac{3}{4}$" LINE

16"

TO FINISH THE INSIDE, THIN SIDES, KEEP A CAREFUL EYE ON THE CROSS-SECTION SKETCH. MEASURE DEPTH OF THE BOTTOM AND KEEP IT CONSTANT.

CUT BOW SLANT WHILE YOU CAN STILL SEE THE INSIDE.

$\frac{1}{2}$"

2'

CHALK LINES

16"

WORKING AGAIN FROM THE SMALLER END, SNAP CHALK LINES 16 INCHES APART. SAW TO THE LINES AND AX OFF THE CHUNKS.

CHALK LINES

ROUND OFF THE SIDES TO THE CHALK LINES.

WITH CARE, ROUND THE UNDERSIDE OF EACH END.

2'

$\frac{1}{2}$"

$3\frac{1}{2}$

TURN THE DUGOUT RIGHT SIDE UP AND ROUND THE ENDS. TO PRESERVE YOUR HANDIWORK, BRUSH LINSEED OIL OVER ALL SURFACES ~ AND YOU'RE DONE.

CONCERNED THAT DIGGING OUT THE DUGOUT MIGHT CHOP HOLES THROUGH THE SIDES OR BOTTOM? YOU MIGHT TRY THESE TWO IDEAS TO AVOID MAKING A LEAKY WOODEN BATHTUB.

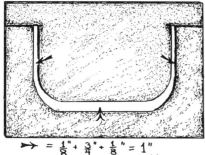

$\rightarrow = \frac{1}{8}" + \frac{3}{4}" + \frac{1}{8}" = 1"$

$\rightarrow = \frac{1}{8}" + 1" + \frac{1}{8}" = 1\frac{1}{4}"$

CUT OUT A CARDBOARD PATTERN TO FIT YOUR PARTICULAR LOG. CUT OFF $\frac{1}{8}$ INCH EXTRA ON INSIDE AND OUTSIDE PATTERNS FOR EASIER INSERTION IN THE DUGOUT.

ANOTHER THOUGHT ~ ALTHOUGH I FOUND IT UNNECESSARY. DIP HARDWOOD SLIVERS INTO INK TO A POINT SLIGHTLY GREATER THAN THE WIDTH OF THE SIDE. MAKE A HOLE WITH AN AWL, NAIL, OR DRILL AND DRIVE IN THE SLIVER. REMOVE INSIDE WOOD UNTIL THE COLOR SHOWS.

PADDLES

No dugout should be up a creek without a paddle – or probably several paddles. With all of the dugout making through the centuries, it would seem that a number of preserved specimens would be available for study. Not so. William Fowler described a single discovery in 1880 at Canoe Place, Long Island. From the approximate measurements of this rarity, several efficient paddles can be crafted with little difficulty.

But using the dugout-canoe tools of stone and fire was anything but easy for the Algonquians. Just how these stubby paddles were fashioned is speculative. No early writer made mention of the techniques involved.

HARDWOODS WERE APPARENTLY USED. THE LONG ISLAND EXAMPLE WAS OAK. MAPLE WAS MENTIONED IN A 1735 ACCOUNT. CELTS MAY HAVE BEEN USED AS WEDGES TO SPLIT THE LOG. A "V" SHAPED SLAB COULD THEN BE SPLIT FREE. TO FREE A PADDLE FROM THIS WOODEN CHUNK COULD BE DONE ONLY BY WEARISOME BURNING AND SCRAPING.

The Weymouth dugout or my reproduction will carry several passengers with comfort – If they sit on the bottom to keep the center of gravity as low as possible.

2½"

20½" — 1⅛"

SAWING AND SHAPING THE PADDLE FROM A PINE PLANK IS EASIEST.

7½"

14"

But paddling in this position makes it difficult to take a decent scoop of water with the blade. To move the canoe with any sort of muscle, kneeling – if the knees are well cushioned – will propel the dugout with surprising speed.

Make no mistake – the dugout is no floating log. The bottom edges act as a keel to keep the canoe on a straight course. The low free-board keeps the vessel manageable when the wind is broadside. And the flat bottom allows for a rapid change in direction with a few outward sweeps of the paddle. Further, portaging this dry pine vessel can be handled easily by two adults. The dugout experience, after many forgotten decades, can also be yours.

TRADE SHIRT

Probably no single article of clothing has so much history sewn into it as the trade shirt. Yet not a one has been preserved through the centuries. Its humble origin was European, and it was worn as underwear to protect the outerwear from grease and perspiration. It was roomy enough to use as a nightgown.

When the trade shirt crossed the Atlantic, it soon became high on the New England Indian want list. No need to work skins into a shoulder mantle when a few of these same furs could be traded for a colorful cloth shirt.

Linen was the usual material ~ perhaps dyed to pleasure the Indian trade tastes. Calicoes may also have been used. Imported from and named for Calicut, India, the East India Company shipped back the cotton goods in quantity, and by the third quarter of the seventeenth century, demand had increased "to a passion." Some calico was woven with colorful stripes or checks, and some boasted of painted designs. Later, the Americans imitated these goods by printing designs with carved wooden blocks.

WARRIOR'S TRADE SHIRT, WOMAN'S SHIRT AND A RIFLE OR HUNTING SHIRT WIDELY WORN IN THE COLONIES

No doubt about it ~ the trade shirt had become an all~American favorite. Both Indians and colonists appreciated its practicability during the French and Indian War years. And early in the Revolution, Washington issued the shirt to his threadbare troops. In his General Orders of 1776, he wrote that "no dress can be cheaper, nor more convenient, as the wearer may be cool in warm weather and warm in cool weather by putting on undercloaths which will not change the outward dress, Winter or Summer ~ Besides which it is a dress justly supposed to carry no small terror to the enemy, who think every such person is a complete marksman."

The trade shirt (or hunting or rifle shirt ~ depending on the wearer) was well established among the western tribes. Frontier settlers, hunters, and trappers

COLLAR

18½"

FOLD

COLLAR GUSSET

3½"

FOLD ALL DOTTED LINES UNDER ¼ INCH TO FINISH ROUGH EDGES

8"

SHIRT BACK

30¼"

2½"

3½"

22"

SLEEVE

WRIST SLIT GUSSET

8½"

17½"

FOLD

11"

FOLD

FOLD

CUFF

5¼"

4"

CUT SLITS

9½"

SLEEVE SLIT

8"

UNDERARM GUSSET

8"

SHIRT FRONT

30¼"

2½"

SIDE-SLIT GUSSET

8"

LENGTH ABOUT HIP LEVEL

29"

48

recognized the counterparts that covered each back. The traditional covering continues to be worn by western tribespeople. And here in New England, your bit of fancy stitching can keep the original trade shirt alive and well.

STITCHING ~ EARLY SEWING WAS FINE AND INVISIBLE; THAT IS, VERY LITTLE OF THE STITCHING SHOWS ON THE OUTSIDE. THE ENCIRCLED NUMBERS SHOW THE KIND OF STITCH USED FOR EACH SEAM. PIN IN PLACE BEFORE YOUR THREAD MAKES IT FINAL.

A SEWING MACHINE MAKES ② EASIER.

Now the professional dressmaker or tailor may well snicker in their thimbles at the following how-to description. But if the only use you've made of a needle was to dig out a splinter, perhaps the drawings will be helpful.

This trade shirt will fit an average man. But for women and children AND to be certain, use the pattern measurements to make a crude shirt from an old sheet or whatever. Take it in or let it out, according to your size. The shirt should extend to the midthigh.

SHIRT BODY

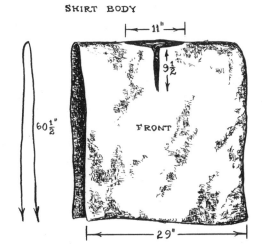

VERTICAL NECK SLIT

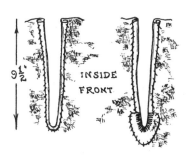

FRONT INSIDE ~ FOLD SIDES OF SLIT BACK ⅛ INCH AND SEW. REINFORCE WITH A HEART-SHAPED SCRAP.

A BUTTONHOLE STITCH GIVES ADDED REINFORCEMENT.

FOLD THE OBLONG OF CLOTH IN HALF. TO MAKE THE NECK OPENING, CENTER AN 11-INCH CUT ON THE FOLD. MAKE A 9½-INCH VERTICAL SLIT FOR THE NECK OPENING.

TAKE SMALL GATHERS ABOUT ⅛ INCH FROM THE NECK EDGE, FOUR OR FIVE PUCKERS FOR EACH INCH.

NECK OPENING

2 NECK GUSSETS

TURN UNDER THE GUSSET EDGES AND SEW TO BOTH CORNERS OF THE NECK SLIT. ALSO STITCH THE FOLD TO HOLD THE SHAPE.

49

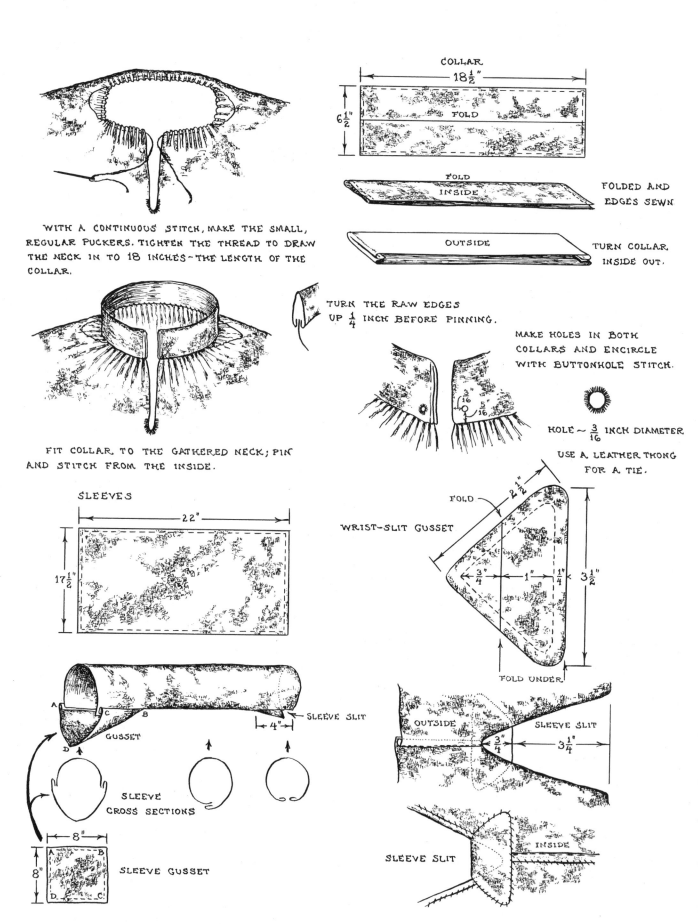

WITH A CONTINUOUS STITCH, MAKE THE SMALL, REGULAR PUCKERS. TIGHTEN THE THREAD TO DRAW THE NECK IN TO 18 INCHES ─ THE LENGTH OF THE COLLAR.

COLLAR
18½"
6½"
FOLD

FOLD
INSIDE
FOLDED AND EDGES SEWN

OUTSIDE
TURN COLLAR INSIDE OUT.

FIT COLLAR TO THE GATHERED NECK; PIN AND STITCH FROM THE INSIDE.

TURN THE RAW EDGES UP ¼ INCH BEFORE PINNING.

MAKE HOLES IN BOTH COLLARS AND ENCIRCLE WITH BUTTONHOLE STITCH.

3/16   5/16

HOLE ~ 3/16 INCH DIAMETER

USE A LEATHER THONG FOR A TIE.

SLEEVES
22"
17½"

WRIST-SLIT GUSSET
FOLD
2½"
¾"   1"   1¼"   3½"
FOLD UNDER

A C B
GUSSET
D
4" ← SLEEVE SLIT

SLEEVE CROSS SECTIONS

OUTSIDE
SLEEVE SLIT
¾"   3¼"
INSIDE

8"
A   B
8"
D   C
SLEEVE GUSSET

SLEEVE SLIT

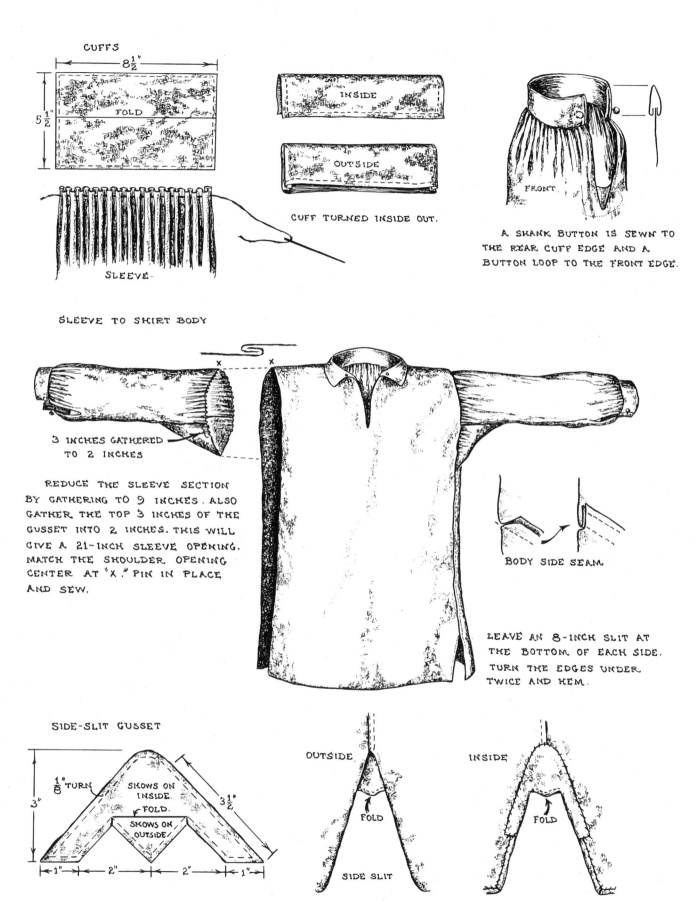

CUFFS

8½"

5½"

FOLD

SLEEVE

INSIDE

OUTSIDE

CUFF TURNED INSIDE OUT.

FRONT.

A SHANK BUTTON IS SEWN TO
THE REAR CUFF EDGE AND A
BUTTON LOOP TO THE FRONT EDGE.

SLEEVE TO SHIRT BODY

x   x

3 INCHES GATHERED
TO 2 INCHES

REDUCE THE SLEEVE SECTION
BY GATHERING TO 9 INCHES. ALSO
GATHER THE TOP 3 INCHES OF THE
GUSSET INTO 2 INCHES. THIS WILL
GIVE A 21-INCH SLEEVE OPENING.
MATCH THE SHOULDER OPENING
CENTER AT "X." PIN IN PLACE
AND SEW.

BODY SIDE SEAM

LEAVE AN 8-INCH SLIT AT
THE BOTTOM OF EACH SIDE.
TURN THE EDGES UNDER
TWICE AND HEM.

SIDE-SLIT GUSSET

⅛" TURN

SHOWS ON
INSIDE.

FOLD.

SHOWS ON
OUTSIDE

3"

3½"

1"   2"   2"   1"

OUTSIDE

FOLD

SIDE SLIT

INSIDE

FOLD

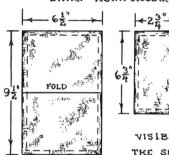

├─ 6½" ─┤   ├─ 2¾" ─┤

FOLD

9½"   6¾"

CUT OUT TWO OF EACH
REINFORCEMENT PATTERNS.
MATCH THE FOLD OF THE LARGER
PIECE TO THE NECK GUSSET
AND THE SLEEVE FOLD. FOLD
UNDER RAW EDGES ¼ INCH AS
USUAL; PIN AND STITCH IN-
VISIBLY TO THE SHIRT BODY. SEW
THE SMALLER PIECE AS SHOWN.

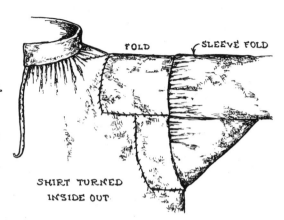

FOLD   SLEEVE FOLD

SHIRT TURNED
INSIDE OUT

FINGER~WOVEN BELT

DIAGONAL

CHEVRON

The trade shirt has want of a belt. Early accounts shed little light on these "girdles" or "sashes." But certainly they added a dash of color ~ and often wealth ~ to the Algonquian dress. Witness Drake's description of King Philip's finery. One of the Wampanoag chieftain's belts was of "black and white wampum in various figures and pictures of many birds and beasts." It was a massive work ~ 9 inches wide and reportedly reaching clear to Captain Church's ankles when draped over his shoulders. Its whereabouts is unknown.

Other lesser Algonquian belts were of buckskin, some decorated with intricate quillwork. There were belts of snakeskin. But a favorite was the belt that was finger woven into chevron or diagonal stripes. Dyed herb fibers* from swamp milkweed and Indian hemp, inner bark strands* from such trees as the bass~ wood and slippery elm, and strips of buckskin were all worked into belts.

In historic times, twisted linen from flax and wool strands were traded as yarn from the colonists. Striking belts were also woven from this source.

These were sturdy and flexible belts, meant to be tied in a soft knot with no need for a buckle. From these belts could be suspended a dressed skin pouch containing fire-making tools or a pipe and tobacco.

REPRODUCING THE WOVEN BELT

LEATHER THONGS

It's an old New England tradition ~ saving odds and ends that might come in handy someday. "Waste not, want not" sound familiar? Then dig out any retired wallets, handbags, or cast-off suede jackets or skirts ~ anything leather. If your scrap stock is scant, try rummage and

PHILIP. *KING* of Mount Hope.

* SEE THE SECTION ON "THREAD AND CORDAGE" ON PG. 66.

52

garage sales or secondhand clothing stores for articles of thin leather. The earth colors of dyed hides make a pleasing blend, from shades of brown down to buff and white.

The literature cites any number of ways to cut leather thongs. Most such instructions use a perfectly round disk of leather, the edge of which is drawn between a sharp blade and a fixed projection. Thick, dampened rawhide (untanned hide) may work with such techniques, but thin and pliable leather such as is used for braiding is better cut by eye with a pair of scissors. Further, an exact circle is wasteful. Any odd piece of leather may be rounded at the corners and a continuous $\frac{1}{8}$-inch strip cut from it. By the way, this is a job for an evening by the fireplace or for a lazy summer day. There's a lot of cutting to make all those belt thongs.

PLANT FIBERS~No need to skin a tree for the inner bark strands or to twist your threads from local herbs if you've a mind for an easier way. String from sisal (a Mexican plant yielding fibers from the leaf), raffia (twine from the Madagascar palm leaf), and jute (cordage from several Asian plants) are all belt-weaving possibilities. Don't forget the ordinary wrapping twine of doubtful heritage. It may be dyed or woven in its natural browns and white. Christmas package string is multicolored and worth considering. And, of course, a sturdy, heavy cotton yarn will duplicate the old Indian belts quite nicely. Check out the rug-yarn counter.

Whatever the material, use no more than two or three colors or the belt will look like three kinds of measles. Better to use two shades of a color along with a contrasting color.

FIGURING THE LENGTH OF STRANDS OR THONGS NEEDED~ Measure the waist and add the length needed to tie a square knot. Also add the length of fringe desired for both belt ends. Double these measurements, since the weaving uses twice the length of each strand or thong to complete the belt.

BELT WIDTH~Plan to line up the strands or thongs to a width that is a third larger than the finished belt, since the weaving will reduce width as well as length.

FOR EXAMPLE ~ TO MAKE A 2-INCH WIDE BELT OF $\frac{1}{8}$-INCH THONGS:

WAIST SIZE 32 X 2 = 68"
10" FOR SQUARE KNOT X 2 = 20"
6" FRINGE ONE END X 2 = 12"
6" FRINGE OTHER END X 2 = 12"
EACH THONG LENGTH = 112"

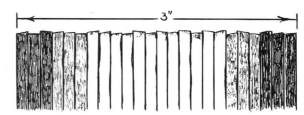

ABOUT TWENTY-FOUR THONGS ARE NEEDED. THERE MUST BE AN EVEN NUMBER OF THONGS TO BRAID THREE OR FOUR STRANDS EACH FOR THE END FRINGES.

CUT

56"

WIND THE THONGS AROUND A PIECE OF CARDBOARD HALF THE LENGTH OF EACH THONG ~ 56 INCHES, IN THIS EXAMPLE. CUT THE THONGS ALONG ONE EDGE OF THE CARD-BOARD TO GIVE EACH THONG A 112-INCH LENGTH.

BRAIDING PATTERNS

Two simple stripe patterns are especially worth trying~ the diagonal and the chevron braid.

DIAGONAL BRAID

SPACE THE COLORS TO YOUR LIKING. EACH COLOR WILL BECOME A STRIPE. THE STRANDS DRAWN HERE ARE SEPARATED FOR CLARITY. ACTUALLY, THE STRANDS ARE SNUG TO ONE ANOTHER FOR WEAVING.

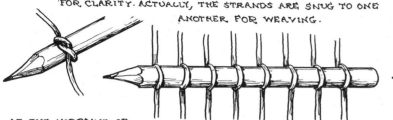

TIE UPPER HALF OF THE STRANDS TO A CHAIR BACK AFTER SECURING WITH AN OVERHAND KNOT.

AT THE MIDPOINT OF EACH STRAND, TIE AN OVERHAND KNOT AROUND A PENCIL OR DOWEL. EQUAL LENGTHS ARE THEREFORE ABOVE AND BELOW THE PENCIL.

SECURE THE FREE LOWER HALF OF THE STRANDS WITH A SHORT STRING JUST BELOW THE PENCIL.

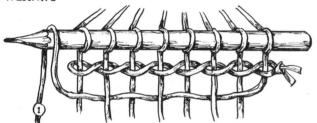

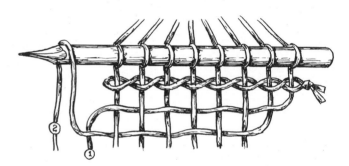

RIGHT-HANDERS WEAVE FROM THE RIGHT AS SHOWN; LEFT-HANDERS FROM THE LEFT. WEAVE THE OUTER STRAND ACROSS AND HANG IT OVER THE PENCIL ①.

WEAVE ② ACROSS, DROP ①, AND HANG ②. THE WEAVE BECOMES DIAGONAL.

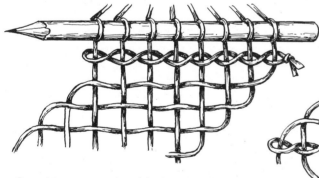

FRINGE~ LESS IS NEEDED IF THE BELT IS FINISHED WITH SEVERAL ROWS OF TWINING AS DRAWN BELOW. NO FRINGE BRAIDING IS NECESSARY.

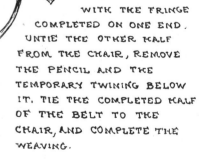

WITH THE FRINGE COMPLETED ON ONE END, UNTIE THE OTHER HALF FROM THE CHAIR, REMOVE THE PENCIL AND THE TEMPORARY TWINING BELOW IT. TIE THE COMPLETED HALF OF THE BELT TO THE CHAIR, AND COMPLETE THE WEAVING.

OR~

THE FRINGE MAY BE BRAIDED IN 3- OR 4-INCH STRANDS, WHICHEVER DIVIDES THE TOTAL NUMBER OF BELT STRANDS EVENLY. FINISH BY TYING THE TWO CENTER STRANDS, (MARKED ➤) WITH A SQUARE KNOT.

54

CHEVRON BRAID

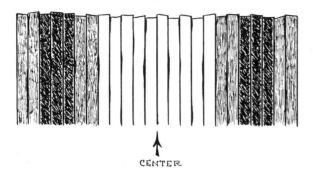

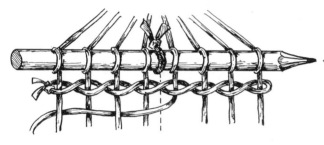

CENTER

AN EVEN NUMBER OF STRANDS OR THONGS MUST BE USED. BE SURE TO ARRANGE THE COLORS FROM THE CENTER SO THAT ONE SIDE IS THE MIRROR IMAGE OF THE OTHER.

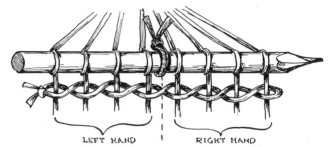

LEFT HAND   RIGHT HAND

TIE THE STRANDS AT THEIR MIDPOINT WITH THE COLORS IN THE PROPER ORDER. ALSO TIE A PIECE OF BRIGHT YARN AROUND THE PENCIL OR DOWEL TO GIVE AN EQUAL NUMBER OF STRANDS ON EITHER SIDE. HOLD EACH GROUP FIRMLY IN EACH HAND.

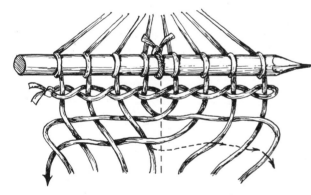

RIGHT-HANDERS FIND WEAVING TO THE RIGHT EASIER, AS SHOWN. LEFT-HANDERS WORK IN REVERSE.

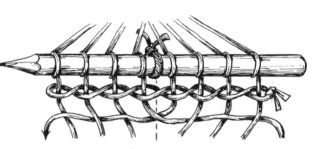

TWIST THE PENCIL IN THE OPPOSITE DIRECTION AND WEAVE AGAIN TO THE RIGHT. THE IDEA IS TO ALTERNATELY CROSS THE TWO STRANDS NEAREST THE CENTER (HERE MARKED WITH THE COLORED YARN ON THE PENCIL AND THE IMAGINARY DOTTED LINE).

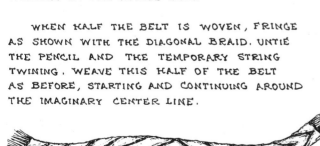

AT THIS POINT, TURN THE PENCIL AND CONTINUE WEAVING ON THE DOTTED LINE.

WHEN HALF THE BELT IS WOVEN, FRINGE AS SHOWN WITH THE DIAGONAL BRAID. UNTIE THE PENCIL AND THE TEMPORARY STRING TWINING. WEAVE THIS HALF OF THE BELT AS BEFORE, STARTING AND CONTINUING AROUND THE IMAGINARY CENTER LINE.

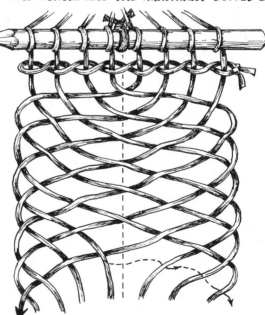

TURN THE PENCIL AND CONTINUE AS SHOWN WITH THE DOTTED LINE. BE SURE TO KEEP THE CENTER DIVISION IN MIND.

55

∫ SNAKESKIN BELT

Colonial writers mention snakeskin belts only in passing. There are no descriptions ~ and no authentic relics ~ for today's craft person to follow. Considering Algonquian handwork in general, however, the following should give a reasonable result.

Since a snakeskin belt makes a poor appearance without a snakeskin, I mentioned my wants to a local reptile fancier.(By the way ~ he gives some excellent live programs on understanding reptiles.)When one of his preformers ~ a yard-long water snake ~ gave up the ghost, its mortal remains went through the following steps:

CUT DOWN THE CENTER OF THE ABDOMEN BUT AVOID SLICING INTO THE INNARDS. CUT JUST SKIN-DEEP AROUND THE HEAD AND AROUND THE ANUS.

 USING THE THUMB, THE LOWER THIRD OF SKIN ON EACH SIDE IS EASILY STRIPPED FREE.

PEEL THE UPPER THIRD OF THE SKIN BACK FROM THE CIRCULAR HEAD CUT. PEEL DOWN TO THE REAR CIRCULAR CUT. THE SKIN SHOULD SEPARATE FREE OF SUBCUTANEOUS TISSUE. THE LENGTH OF TIME FROM THE YEARLY SHEDDING DETERMINES THE SKIN THICKNESS.

OXALIC ACID TAN LIQUOR

WATER	1 GALLON
SALT	1 PINT
OXALIC ACID CRYSTALS	2 OUNCES

REDUCE THE PROPORTIONS TO YOUR NEEDS. A SNAKESKIN NEEDS ABOUT A COFFEE-MUG-SIZED CONTAINER. USE EARTHEN OR GLASS ~ NEVER A METAL CONTAINER. THE MIXTURE NEED ONLY BE APPROXIMATE. SOAK THE SKIN FOR SIX TO TWENTY-FOUR HOURS, AND RINSE IT THOROUGHLY IN WATER. SCRUB THE SKIN BETWEEN THE HANDS TO REMOVE SCALES AND ANY EXCESS TISSUE.

BLOT THE SKIN DRY. STRETCH IT ON A LONG PIECE OF CORRUGATED CARDBOARD, AND TACK WITH FINE BRADS OR COMMON PINS. AFTER IT HAS DRIED FOR SEVERAL DAYS, REMOVE THE SKIN AND TRIM OFF THE PUCKERS WITH SCISSORS.

CARDBOARD STRETCHER.

MAKE THE SKIN PLIABLE WITH A LEATHER SOFTENER.

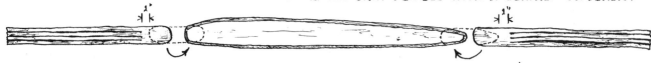

BACK THE SKIN WITH A PIECE OF BUCKSKIN (OR A SUBSTITUTE), CUTTING IT $\frac{1}{4}$ INCH LESS THAN THE SKIN EDGES. USE RUBBER CEMENT TO GLUE THE SKIN TO THIS LEATHER BACKING AND LET IT DRY UNDER THE WEIGHT OF SOME LARGE BOOKS. THEN GLUE THE SKIN EDGES OVER THE BACKING ~ AND IT'S UNDER THE WEIGHTS AGAIN. GLUE TWO STRIPS OF BUCKSKIN TO BOTH ENDS. THE TOTAL BELT LENGTH SHOULD ALLOW FOR SOME SHORTENING FROM BRAIDING AND FOR A SOFT SQUARE KNOT.

PUNCH HOLES AROUND SKIN $\frac{3}{8}$ INCH APART AND $\frac{3}{16}$ INCH FROM EDGE. USE A COTTON RUG YARN OF A BLENDING COLOR TO ANCHOR SKIN EDGE.

END BRAID WITH TWO SQUARE KNOTS.

⬩ ALGONQUIAN FOOTWEAR

The New England Indians preferred a one-piece moccasin without added sole. The centered front seam was characteristic and gave a rather pointed toe. Sinew was stronger than thread and cinched up tightly on drying. Few Indians today, however, opt for the sinew.

By all odds, moosehide was best for durable service, but buckskin was a tolerable substitute. The moccasins were sometimes tied with a thong of the same hide, and in foul weather the flaps could be folded up for protection.

USE HEAVY ALUMINUM FOIL TO SHAPE THE MOCCASIN TO THE FOOT.

EDGE TO JUST BELOW ANKLE.
TRIM OFF EXCESS FOIL.

FLAP ADDED HERE ON CLOTH PATTERN.

FOLD IN HALF—MUST BE SYMMETRICAL.

FLATTEN ROUGH FOIL PATTERN AND TRACE ON A HEAVY PIECE OF CLOTH, ADDING $\frac{1}{8}$ INCH TO FRONT FOR STITCHING. TAKE A FEW STITCHES TO BRING FRONT SEAM (AB) TOGETHER.

SUEDE HAS GIVE, AND THE SYMMETRICAL PATTERN WILL MOLD TO YOUR ASYMMETRICAL FOOT. TEMPORARILY TACK THE BACK OF THE MOCCASIN PATTERN TO CONFORM TO THE HEEL.

FLAP IS $1\frac{1}{2}$ INCHES FROM FLOOR.

Use suede with the roughened surface on both sides. If one side is smooth, scrape it with a hacksaw blade to match the surfaces. Suede is the closest to Indian tanned buckskin. A weight of three or four ounces per square foot of leather will give a strong moccasin. If you've a mind for economy, the flaps may be made of scraps and sewn on separately. Transfer the pattern to the leather with chalk or awl marks. The back of the moccasin is left unmarked and uncut. The cloth pattern will give a rough idea of how long a piece of leather is needed.

USE A WHIPSTITCH TO CLOSE THE CENTER SEAM~ BUT THERE ARE TWO POINTS TO REMEMBER.

$\frac{1}{4}$-INCH WELT INSERTED BEFORE SEWING.

INSIDE SURFACE.

① TURN THE SUEDE INSIDE OUT, FOR THE SEWING IS DONE FROM THE INSIDE FOR THE FRONT SEAM.
② USE A $\frac{1}{4}$-INCH WELT OF THE SAME SUEDE TO SEW BETWEEN THE CENTER SEAM FOR MORE STRENGTH AND BETTER APPEARANCE.

KEEP WHIP-STITCHES EVEN—ABOUT $\frac{1}{8}$ INCH APART AND $\frac{1}{16}$ INCH FROM THE EDGE.

STITCH WITH HEAVY LINEN THREAD OF THE SAME COLOR AS THE LEATHER. START AT THE FLAP AND WORK DOWN TOWARD THE TOE. USE A STURDY NEEDLE, AN AWL TO PUNCH THE HOLES, AND A PAIR OF PLIERS TO COAX THE NEEDLE THROUGH. WAXING THE THREAD WITH AN OLD CANDLE IS A HELP. THE WELT MAY BE TRIMMED AFTER THE MOCCASIN IS TURNED RIGHT SIDE OUT. KNOTS ARE TIED OUTSIDE TO PREVENT CHAFING OF THE SKIN.

PLUS $\frac{1}{8}$"

OUTSIDE.

WITH THE FOOT SNUGGLY IN THE MOCCASIN, MAKE PINCH MARKS ALONG THE BACK OF THE FOOT.

OUTSIDE.

WITH THE MOCCASIN FLATTENED RIGHT SIDE OUT, WHIPSTITCH DOWN TO ABOUT 1 INCH FROM THE BOTTOM.

OUTSIDE.

CUT OUT THE HEEL FLAP.

~OR~

HEEL FLAP FOLDS UP.

WHIPSTITCH THE FLAP RIGHT SIDE OUT

A THONG TIE MAY BE ADDED JUST BELOW THE FLAP FOLD~DOWN.

THE HEEL MIGHT BE PARTIALLY STITCHED AND THE BACK CLOSED WITH TWO THONGS TIED THROUGH TWO REAR HOLES.

MOCCASIN DECORATION

You now have a serviceable pair of moccasins for everyday use. But if the result pleasures you, consider the addition of quillwork, cloth appliqué, beads, or paint for more formal ceremonial footwear. Here follows a brief glimpse of the decorative possibilities that were used by our New England Indians. Your local museum should be a primary source for more specific ideas.

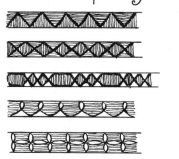

LINEAR-GEOMETRIC

DOUBLE CURVE

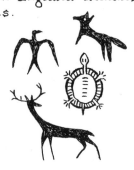

NATURALISTIC FIGURES

FLORAL FIGURES - INFLUENCED BY EARLY FRENCH AND DUTCH SETTLERS

QUILLWORK

Needed: a harvest of porcupine quills collected from roadside casualties or by throwing a blanket over the critter and plucking the harvest from the fabric. Each porky bristles with 30,000 to 40,000 quills. These range up to 5 inches in length, and are white with dark brown tips. They are hollow.

Dyeing was ~ and still can be~ done with local woodland flowers, leaves, roots, and bark (see "Natural Dyes" p.61). Later Algonquians were happy enough with many of the prepared dyes available to the colonists. With this thought in mind, one might consider modern cloth dyes such as Rit. Choose the Indian favorites of black, yellow, red, and blue. Several colors may be preferred to the many ~ and save some white quills for contrast.

Add a package of powdered dye to a quart of water. This concentrated solution will yield more vivid colors. Simmer~ don't boil~ the quills for about half an hour, with frequent stirring. Rinse, then dry on newspaper.

DECORATION~ Use a leather strip of about 1 inch in width to cover the central seam puckers. On this, heavy thread of the same color as the leather is stitched along the outline of the design. Anchor the thread at intervals of ½ inch or less.

The quills are then soaked in warm water for about ten minutes for flexibility. Each quill is flattened with the bowl of a spoon on a hard surface, then wrapped about the thread base in a variety of ways.

EIGHTEENTH CENTURY

NORTHAMPTON HISTORICAL SOCIETY, NORTHAMPTON, MASSACHUSETTS

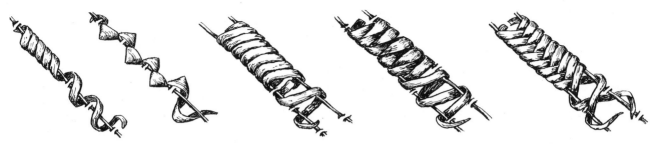

| WRAPPING– SINGLE THREAD | FOLDING– SINGLE THREAD | WRAPPING– DOUBLE THREAD | ONE QUILL~ZIGZAG– DOUBLE THREAD | 2 QUILLS INTERLACED– DOUBLE THREAD |

An Indian woman would soften the quill in her mouth, then flatten it by pulling it between the teeth (with commercial dyes, this is not recommended). Unless stitching a design on birch bark, she would bite or cut off the dark tip. The end tab was bent under the wrapping.

The flaps were also decorated, often with cloth designs or borders tacked halfway through the leather. When the moccasins had outlived their usefulness, the flaps and toe-strip quillwork could be transferred to a new pair.

PAINTED DESIGNS

Buckskin and moosehide clothing was frequently painted~ but sparingly and with an eye to the artistic. Morton described a white moose-skin mantle with a painted border "in form like lace set on by a tailor, and some they stripe in size with works of several fashions very curious according to the several fantasies of the workmen wherein they strive to excel one another." ("Size" is a gluelike substance used to fill pores and give adhesiveness to the paint.) Indians north of the St. Lawrence River still apply colors with a size made from fish roe, using a pointed bone rather than a brush.

MOHEGAN DOT DESIGN PAINTED ON BARK BASKET

Moccasins? Although I have seen no surviving examples, it seems likely that moccasin trims were sometimes painted. You'll not be faulted for using acrylics, tube oil paints, or airplane dope colors. Try some dots ~ used especially in southern New England~ to make an interesting contrast with linear/geometric borders. Try some examples on a scrap of your moccasin leather. If you like it, you're in business.

BEADWORK

We've said little about this subject, for the common glass seed beads were not introduced into New England until 1675~ the beginning of King Philip's War. Following that conflict, there were few Algonquian tribespeople remaining to be concerned about the new decorative possibilities. Still, most later generations of these survivors preferred working their designs rather than continuing the old quillwork artistry. Therefore these tiny trade beads should be considered when dressing up your moccasins. Both embroidery and loom work are old and honored techniques.

Beadwork Embroidery~Probably the earliest beadwork was sewn directly on buckskin clothing as embroidery. It made possible flowing curves and colors unknown with quillwork, and our woodland Indians were quick to bead realistic impressions of the leaves and flowers that they knew so well. These naturalistic designs set off the moccasin flaps nicely. Sinew was used before thread became plentiful.

BEADED FLAP DESIGNS WITH RIBBON APPLIQUÉ BORDER

OUTLINES ARE PENCILED ON BUCKSKIN OR SUEDE.

59

Two threaded needles are needed - one to string a length of beads and another sturdier needle with a heavy thread to secure the string of beads to the design. Both threads are waxed.

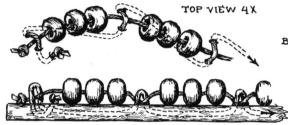

TOP VIEW 4X

SIDE VIEW 4X

USE A SPIRAL ("SPOT" OR "OVERLAY") STITCH OVER THE BEAD THREAD EVERY TWO OR THREE BEADS. SINCE FLAPS ARE WORN UP IN FOUL WEATHER, THE STITCHING DOES NOT GO CLEAR THROUGH THE LEATHER. RATHER, THE BUCKSKIN IS BENT INTO A SMALL HUMP; THEN THE STURDY NEEDLE IS PASSED JUST BELOW THE SURFACE.

ALTHOUGH BEADS ARE SHOWN SEPARATED, THE STITCHED BEADS ARE SNUGGED CLOSELY TO ONE ANOTHER. THE SPIRAL THREAD SHOULD BE HARD TO SEE.

SIDE VIEW 4X

FINISH THE BEAD LENGTH BY HUMPING THE BUCKSKIN. THE HEAVY NEEDLE SECURES THE STITCHING THREAD WHEN ANCHORED IN THE SKIN AND TIED WITH AN OVERHAND KNOT. USING THE SAME NEEDLE, SECURE THE BEAD THREAD IN THE SAME MANNER.

TOP VIEW 1X

FLOWER AND LEAF DESIGNS ARE FIRST OUTLINED WITH BEADS. VARIED COLORS MAY THEN BE USED TO FILL IN THE DESIGN, FOLLOWING THE SAME CURVES AS THE BEADED OUTLINE.

Loom Beadwork ~ The earliest type was the bow loom, with a frame of nothing more than a curved stick. (A fresh branch was bent to shape by tying a cord to both ends and letting it dry for several days.) Near each end was a doubled birch-bark heddle, perforated at short intervals to keep the parallel warp threads in place.

Later, a lashed rectangular frame gave service, with the warp threads strung between the shorter ends.

THE BOW LOOM WAS HELD BETWEEN THE LEGS.

Tied at one end, the spool of thread was brought to the opposite side and wrapped several times. This gave the bead width. It was then returned to the starting end, wrapped again, and returned.

WIDTH OF BEAD

Today's loom may be made in short order from 3/4-inch scrap pine.

BEVEL THE ENDS AND CUT THREAD SLOTS $\frac{1}{8}$ INCH APART AND $\frac{1}{16}$ INCH DEEP WITH A KNIFE BLADE. A NAIL IS DRIVEN INTO EACH END; THE WARP THREADS ARE CAUGHT IN THE SLOTS, LOOPED AROUND THE NAIL, AND RETURNED. USE AN EQUAL NUMBER OF WAXED THREADS TO GIVE AN ODD NUMBER OF BEADS FOR EACH ROW. DRAW YOUR PATTERN WITH THIS IN MIND. USE COLORED PENCILS FOR SHARPER DETAILS ON THE ACCOMPANYING BEAD GRAFT. FOR MORE STRENGTH, ADD AN EXTRA THREAD TO THE TWO OUTSIDE WARP THREADS. OUR EXAMPLE DEALS WITH THE NARROW STRIP THAT COVERS THE FRONT MOCCASIN PUCKERS.

$2\frac{1}{2}$"

THE LENGTH = THE LENGTH OF THE FINISHED BEADED PIECE PLUS 6 INCHES.

60

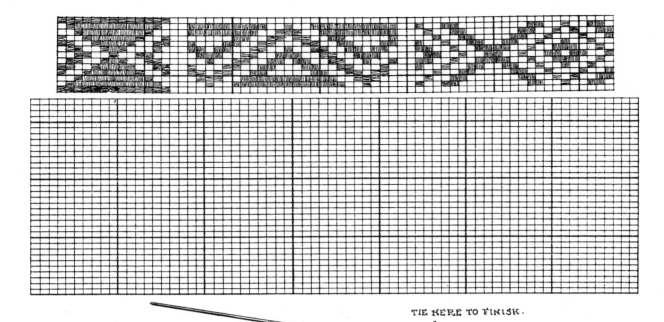

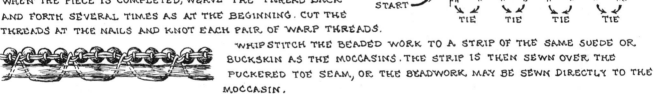

Weaving Procedure ~

TIE THE WEAVING (WEFT) THREAD ONTO THE LEFT DOUBLE
EDGE 3 INCHES FROM THE LOOM END (LEFTIES WILL TIE ONTO THE
RIGHT DOUBLE EDGE). PICK UP THE FIRST ROW OF BEADS ON THE NEEDLE
AND RUN THEM DOWN TO THE KNOT, WITH THE BEADS **UNDER** THE WARP
THREADS, PUSH THEM UP AND INTO PLACE WITH THE INDEX FINGER. KEEP
THE PRESSURE UPWARD AND PASS THE NEEDLE **OVER** THE WARP THREADS.
IF ANY BEADS SAG, YOUR WEAVING THREAD ISN'T ON THE UP AND
UP.

CONTINUE THE PATTERN, REPEATING THE GEOMETRICAL DESIGN.
WHEN THE PIECE IS COMPLETED, WEAVE THE THREAD BACK
AND FORTH SEVERAL TIMES AS AT THE BEGINNING. CUT THE
THREADS AT THE NAILS AND KNOT EACH PAIR OF WARP THREADS.

TIE HERE TO FINISH.

START →

TIE   TIE   TIE   TIE

WHIP STITCH THE BEADED WORK TO A STRIP OF THE SAME SUEDE OR
BUCKSKIN AS THE MOCCASINS. THE STRIP IS THEN SEWN OVER THE
PUCKERED TOE SEAM, OR THE BEADWORK MAY BE SEWN DIRECTLY TO THE
MOCCASIN.

NATURAL DYES ~ If you've ever splashed a piece of blueberry pie down your front, you've already been introduced to this subject.

Quill dyeing can be an exercise in frustration ~ or an exciting adventure into the Indians'
world of color. Here follow a few simplified guidelines that really do work. And try throwing
some other materials into the brew besides quills ~ a piece of string, a length of hemp, a
square of cotton, and a few twists of wool. You may find that the results are pleasing
enough to dye the materials for such as the woven belt, basket lacings, or the trade
shirt. As a bonus, you'll appreciate the possibilities of many common plants and the soft
warm colors that they yield. If you find yourself fired up on the subject, do check the
Bibliography for more specific books about natural dyes.

Equipment ~

    Enamel, steel, or aluminum pan
    Debarked stick for stirring
    Slotted spoon for removing quills
    Soft water from rain or lake. (Hard water contains lime compounds and
        will scum the work)
    Newspaper for drying quills

TASTE TESTS ARE
DEFINITELY NOT
RECOMMENDED.

USE ROOTS.   RED
BEDSTRAW (GALIUM SPECIES)

USE BERRIES.

LEMON-YELLOW
TO TAN-YELLOW

GOLDENROD (SOLIDAGO CANADENSIS)

ROSE-TAN

USE BARK.

BLACK WILLOW (SALIX NIGRA)

USE BERRIES. ROSE
BLACKBERRIES (RUBUS SPECIES)

Raw materials ~
  Flowers ~ gather fresh and use plenty.
  Berries ~ collect slightly overripe and mash.
  Nut hulls and barks ~ use the fresh inner
    bark from a severed branch. Cut into
    pieces or crush and soak overnight in
    the dyeing pan.
  Leaves ~ pick mature fresh leaves; chop if
    large, and soak overnight in dyeing pan.

BROWN

USE HULLS.
BLACK WALNUT
(JUGLANS NIGRA)

Mordants are metallic salts that combine with
  both fibers and dyes to penetrate, brighten,
  and make colors fast. (Iron pots act as a
  mordant but dull or "sadden" color. Brass,
  tin, or copper may brighten.) A time-honored
  weak solution of lye, made by pouring hot
  water over hardwood ashes, was used for
  fabrics by the Indians but will turn
  quills to mush. Clay, rusty water, and oak
  galls (the brown ball on leaves from
  insect activity supplied the mordant tannin)
  were also used. We will try the white alum
  crystals (potassium aluminum sulfate), $\frac{3}{4}$ tablespoon to $\frac{1}{2}$ gallon of soft water. Optional is the
  addition of $\frac{3}{4}$ teaspoon of cream of tartar
  to brighten the color. Proportions may be
  changed, depending on the amount to be dyed.

USE ROOTS.
INDIANS DYED   RED-
QUILLS RED   ORANGE
WITH THEM.
BLOODROOT (SANGUINARIA
CANADENSIS)

BROWN

USE BERRIES.

STAGHORN SUMAC (RUBUS SPECIES)

USE
SKINS.
YELLOW-ORANGE
ONION
(ALLIUM CEPA)

USE BERRIES. PINK-
PURPLE

BLUEBERRIES (VACCINIUM SPECIES)

Procedure: Add quills, raw materials,
  and mordant. Bring to a simmer ~
  just short of boiling ~ about
  180 degrees Fahrenheit or 82
  degrees Celsius. Stir frequently.
  Because quills take longer than
  fabrics* or fibers, simmer quills several
  hours; then rinse and dry on the
  newspaper.

YELLOW WITH ALUM.
BUFF-BROWN
WITHOUT MORDANT.

WHITE OAK

RED OAK

USE INNER BARK AND OAK GALLS.
OAK (QUERCUS SPECIES)

PURPLE

USE BERRIES.
WILD GRAPE (VITIS SPECIES)

USE
LEAVES. GOLD-YELLOW
LILY OF THE VALLEY
(CONVALLARIA MAJALIS)

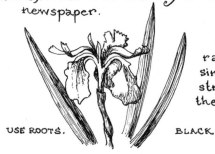

USE ROOTS.   BLACK

YELLOW FLAG IRIS
(IRIS PSEUDACORUS)

*For fabrics, the
raw materials are
simmered, then
strained out of
the dye water.

PURPLE
USE BERRIES.

HUCKLEBERRY
(GAYLUSSACIA BACCATA)

62

LACINGS

 BASSWOOD
 SLIPPERY ELM
 WHITE OAK
 **HICKORY**
 **WHITE CEDAR**   **RED CEDAR**

Just under the outer skin of the growing tree is stored a wondrous supply of lacing, string and rope. This is the cambium layer – the transportation system that carries nutrition from the leaves to the rest of the tree. The wealth of vertical fibers gives the strength needed for the inner bark lacing and the cordage – if one barks up the right tree.

At the top of the preferred list is basswood. Since this tree often grows in clumps, several of the less desirable basswoods may be stripped. The remainder will be freed for better growth. Next, the Algonquians favored the slippery elm, followed by the very serviceable elm, white oak, hickory, and the white and red cedar.

Bark is easily separated in the spring when the sap is running. Crowded trees of 3 to 6 inches in diameter are preferred. A 2-to-4 inch cut was made at the base of the tree. Now stripping the bark is something to experience. The bark is loosened above the cut and strips upward as easily as peeling off one's socks. The strip, gradually tapering, will usually pull free near the top.

SEPARATING THE OUTER BARK FROM THE INNER BARK

TAKE CARE TO PEEL ONLY THE BARK AND NOT YOUR FINGERS.

The fresh strip may be used on the spot for coarse lashings for such as tying wigwam saplings. Bend the supple belt of bark away from the outer layer. The hard, rough surface will snap and be easily peeled back from the white, slippery inner fibers. Narrow strips of between $\frac{1}{8}$ and $\frac{3}{16}$ inch in width may be split off by jabbing a hunting knife in a log, then separating the inner fibers by pulling against the knife blade.

LACING PROCESS

Bark dishes and baskets had need of a thin and narrow strip of inner bark. The broad strips were rolled and tied (with another basswood lacing, of course.), then weighted down in water for seven to ten days. The Indians preferred running water for the soaking process. Following this, the bark strip was bent back and forth to remove the outer bark and to separate the inner layers. The back of a knife may have helped to work the broad sheets free. Thicknesses of between $\frac{1}{16}$ and $\frac{1}{8}$ inch were stripped off with the thumbnail. The lacings could be used while damp or could be hung to dry. An hour or so of soaking made them pliable once again for sewing.

Black willow lacings are not as strong but are quite usable. A collection of thin inner bark is easily stripped in the spring ~ just make a lengthwise slit on either side of the branch. Scrape off the green outer layer and cut ⅛-inch strips with scissors. Avoid the tiny sprout holes that will weaken the lacing. The strips are ready to sew but, as with all lacings, must be moistened if they are dried and stored.

LACINGS FROM PLANTS

Closer to the ground were other lacing producers:

Indian hemp (Apocynum cannabinum), also known as dogbane, supplied a fine, soft fiber that was one of the Algonquian favorites. There is, however, another Indian hemp (Apocynum sativa), an Asiatic cousin that came to the Americas at an unknown date. Its bark gave a coarse and very satisfactory fiber, but its leaves made it an outlaw. Better known as marijuana, it is mentioned only to prevent confusion and then to be forgotten.

Leatherwood (Dirca palustris) was also called moose-wood or wicopy. It thrives in rich moist woodlands. In the 1856 entry in the Journal of Henry D. Thoreau, the bush was noted as growing in

DOGBANE, OR
INDIAN HEMP ~
SMOOTH BARK; MILKY, JUICED
STEM; 2~4 FEET HIGH. GREENISH
WHITE BELL-SHAPED FLOWERS
RESEMBLING LILY OF THE VALLEY,
IN TERMINAL CLUSTERS. PRODUCE
SLENDER, 4-INCH SEED PODS.

SWAMP
MILKWEED

SMOOTH STEM, 2~4
FEET HIGH. LEAVES
LANCE SHAPED. PINK TO
RED FLOWERS.

NETTLE ~
THE FIBROUS STEM GROWS UP TO 6 FEET IN
HEIGHT. STINGING HAIRS MAY BRISTLE FROM THIS
AND THE TOOTH-EDGED LEAVES. OPPOSITE LEAVES.
TINY FLOWERS IN CLUSTERS FROM THE BASES
OF THE UPPER LEAVES.

LEATHERWOOD ~ TOUGH,
PLIABLE BARK 2-6 FEET
HIGH. JOINTED TWIGS.
HAIRY BUD-SCALES IN
EARLY SPRING BEFORE OVAL
LEAVES APPEAR. SMALL
PALE YELLOW FLOWERS.

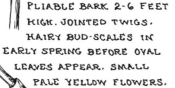

64

plenty near Brattleboro, Vermont: "In its form it is somewhat like a quince bush, though less spreading, its leaves like entire sassafras leaves; ··· It has a remarkably strong thick bark and soft white wood which bends like lead, the different layers separating at the end."

Swamp milkweed (Asclepias incarnata) is found, not surprisingly, in New England's swamps.

Nettle (Urtica dioica), a European native, is found in New England as a weed in waste ground. Its toothed leaves are covered with hairs that secrete a fluid that irritates the skin on contact. All in all, an unlikable plant. A more friendly variety, Urtica procera, has few stinging hairs and is said to be found from Maine to Newfoundland and Labrador. It was processed in the fall when dry, and made excellent fishnets for the Indians.

Generally, the Algonquian people collected these plants in the fall and then soaked the stems until the bark could be peeled without difficulty. A knife slit down the length of the stem made this easier. The outer bark was removed by scrubbing or scraping. The remaining fibrous inner bark layer was of the proper thickness and ready to be split into lacing with the thumbnail. As with the inner bark from the trees, the lacing could be used immediately or dried and stored. Soaking again made it pliable for sewing.

ROOT LACINGS

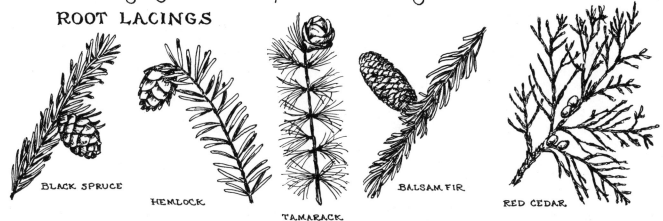

BLACK SPRUCE

HEMLOCK

TAMARACK

BALSAM FIR

RED CEDAR

The roots from these trees are strong and elastic, but the tapered width does give a less uniform lacing and sews with more difficulty. Compared with basswood and other inner bark lacings, they come off second best.

Black spruce and hemlock were preferred, but all the trees shown above have workable roots. The smallest roots near the surface of the soil were teased free. Roots of an average diameter of $\frac{1}{8}$ inch could be laced in the round. Those of a larger diameter were split down the middle – or in quarters, for those expert enough to do it. Starting at the larger end with a knife slit, the two halves were separated by pulling them apart with equal pressure.

When a halved root was laced, the curved surface faced outward. As with all lacing, it was necessary to soak the root for an hour or so until it was elastic enough for sewing.

The thin roots were used for bark vessels. Larger split roots provided a strong sewing material for birch-bark canoes.

AFTER BEING SOAKED IN HOT WATER, THE ROOT WAS DRAWN THROUGH A SPLIT STICK TO REMOVE THE BARK.

65

OUTER BARK   INNER BARK   LACING

THICK LAYERS MAY BE SPLIT   CORDAGE FIBERS

THREAD AND CORDAGE

The same strong inner bark fibers that make efficient lacings need only be freed and twisted into fine string and cordage. And, as with lacings, the bark is stripped free and the outer bark removed and discarded. At this point, the processing of the thread and cordage takes a different trail.

Now if you have plenty of time on your hands, the whole bark can be soaked in water for a month or so. The outer bark will skin off nicely and the woody cement between the fibers will have rotted free.

But if waiting is not to your liking, the retting process may be speeded with several handfuls of hardwood ashes in a pot of boiling water. After ten minutes, you'll have made a batch of lye, Indian fashion. The long strips of inner bark — with the outer bark peeled off — may be coiled and boiled to give a pleasing darker brown. Or, for lighter-colored fibers, the liquid may be poured off the ash sediment and into another pot. (Be careful — caustics are unkind to the skin.) In either case, the inner bark should be boiled on and off for twenty-four hours. The Indian women let it all simmer by the cooking fire for the day. It is said that the boiling gives the fibers added toughness. Rinse the strip well to be rid of the lye.

After the long soak or the short lye boil, the fibers are ready to be separated. If the strips are thin or the layers separated, try rubbing the lengths between the palms. Gently work the fibers free. They will look a bit fuzzy and not like household thread. Or, if the inner bark is thick, work the wet strip back and forth over a smooth barkless pole until the fibers loosen. These plant and tree fibers are known as bast — sometimes called bass — and are now ready to be twisted into thread (two or more fibers) or cord (two or more twisted threads — also called twine or string).

The time-honored technique calls for rolling several of the moist fibers together down the length of the right thigh with the right palm. The fibers will twist together. Now roll the thread back toward the body to tighten the twined thread. Angle the return roll toward the outer thigh while feeding more untwisted fibers to the thigh with the left hand. In an almost continuous motion, twist these fibers down with another push of the palm.

Add another fiber when one length is depleted. If both fibers end near one another, cut off the lesser length to make it 6 inches shorter than the other. Then lay new fiber in place and continue the twisting. The finished thread — or cord, if more fibers are used — will prove to be strong, easily worked and pliable when dry, and as soft as cotton. It may now be woven into a variety of nets, mats, bags, robes, mantles, and belts.

66

BARK CONTAINERS

Consider the white birch~ as handsome a tree as has graced any forest, and it's wrapped in a covering that is waterproof and bugproof, resists decay, and is flexible, light, and easily decorated. Among its many uses by the northern New England tribes was to make such containers as baskets, dishes, bowls, kettles, and spoons.

WHITE BIRCH

(BETULA PAPYRIFERA)

The bark was collected by the men in the spring and into June, when the slit bark practically peeled itself. (In later months, it resisted any efforts to unwind it and would separate into layers in the process). Black spots from knots, however, were apt to anchor the bark locally. To prevent the sheet from tearing, a few blows with a stick would loosen it from the trunk. By the way, very small knot scars were to be found on the best of bark containers.

While finger pressure was enough to ease the bark strip free, the Algonquians used spuds to harvest large amounts. Examples of both stone and wooden spuds are sketched under "Covering the Frame" (p.38) of the wigwam. The bark parted from the trunk with the brown inner layer curling outward. This rugged inner surface became the outside of the bark container. It had many decorative possibilities.

When fresh, the white birch bark sheets were worked much like leather. For storage, they could be flattened by weights. The sheets were never rolled with the white surface outward, for they would set permanently as a cylinder and be useless. To recondition the flattened bark, it needed only to be moistened to make it pliable. It was never soaked for an extended period or placed in hot water, for the sheet would curl so tightly that flattening would be impossible.

A word, again, on collecting bark today: Defacing or killing a white birch is a sorry exchange for any sort of bark container. Vandalism had no part in the Indians' way of life ~ and certainly no place in reproducing their handicrafts. Check out woodlands to be lumbered or trees felled by storms. Even if the wood of a fallen birch has started rotting, the bark will often have enough resin to preserve it for use.

And what of the more plentiful gray birch? Although its bark may be used as a substitute, it is thin; less attractive; has large, unusable black knots; is more rigid; and works like cardboard. It is a poor second best.

GRAY BIRCH (BETULA POPULIFOLIA MARSH)

NOTES ON CRAFTING WHITE BIRCH CONTAINERS

WORK ON THE BARK AS SOON AS POSSIBLE AFTER COLLECTING.
KEEP THE BARK SLIGHTLY DAMP WHILE CUTTING, BENDING, OR LACING IF NOT FRESH.
MAKE A PATTERN OF THE CONTAINER FROM A GROCERY BROWN BAG. VARY THE SIZE
        TO FIT THE SHEET OF BARK. IF THE PAPER MODEL IS TO YOUR LIKING, TRACE
        THE PATTERN ON THE BARK. CHECK THE FOLLOWING DRAWINGS TO BE SURE
        THE FINE BARK STRIATIONS RUN IN THE RIGHT DIRECTION. FOLDING WILL BE
        EASIER AND LACINGS WILL BE LESS LIKELY TO SPLIT THE EDGES.
IF THE CONTAINER IS SMALL, UP TO HALF THE LAYERS OF BARK MAY BE PEELED FROM
        THE WHITE SURFACE FOR EASIER FOLDING. FOR LARGER CONTAINERS, REMOVE SOME

THIN LAYERS OR SHREDS FROM THE WHITE SURFACE TO GIVE AN EVEN APPEARANCE
CUT THE BARK ALONG THE PATTERN OUTLINE WITH SCISSORS. REALLY THICK BARK MAY
HAVE NEED OF TIN SNIPS.

FOLD LINES WILL BE DRAWN DOTTED. SCORE THESE LINES
ALONG A RULER WITH AN AWL. USE PRESSURE
WITHOUT CUTTING THE BARK FIBERS. IF THE
BARK IS NOT FRESH, DAMPEN BEFORE FOLDING
TO PREVENT CRACKING.

PUNCH AWL HOLES FOR LACINGS, KEEPING $\frac{1}{4}$ INCH
FROM THE EDGE OF THE CONTAINER. AFTER
PUNCTURING BOTH SHEETS OF BARK, INSERT
TEMPORARY WOODEN PEGS TO HOLD THE BARK IN PLACE.
(HOLES THROUGH A SINGLE LAYER NEED NOT BE
PEGGED.) THE PEGS ARE REMOVED AS THE
LACING PROGRESSES. A CLOTHESPIN
WILL KEEP THE RIM IN PLACE.

X $\frac{1}{3}$

BONE AWL
SPLINTERED
FROM DEER
AND TURKEY LEG
BONES

TAPERED WOODEN PIN   1 X

LACING THE CONTAINER

CHOOSE THE LACING FROM THE VARIOUS TREE AND PLANT
SOURCES. BASSWOOD IS PREFERRED. NOW YOU MAY WISH TO COLOR
THE LACINGS WITH WOODLAND DYES (CHECK THE LIST IN THE "NATURAL DYES"
SECTION, p.61) OR USE A COMMERCIAL FABRIC DYE ACCORDING TO THE PACKAGE
INSTRUCTIONS. BLUE, DARK GREEN, OR RED COLORS WERE INDIAN FAVORITES; HOWEVER,
THE NATURAL LACING COLOR WILL GIVE A PLEASING CONTRAST TO THE WHITE
BIRCH THAT'S HARD TO BEAT.

THE LACING MUST BE SOAKED FOR AN HOUR OR SO UNTIL PLIABLE. THE LACING FIBERS
TIGHTEN AS THEY DRY. AWL HOLES IN FRESH BARK ALSO TIGHTEN AROUND THE LACING
TO GIVE A MOST DURABLE STITCH.

NO KNOTS ARE USED. THE FREE END IS BENT UNDER THE NEXT STITCH TO SECURE IT.
A VARIETY OF STITCHES MAY BE USED TO HOLD TWO PIECES OF BARK TOGETHER:

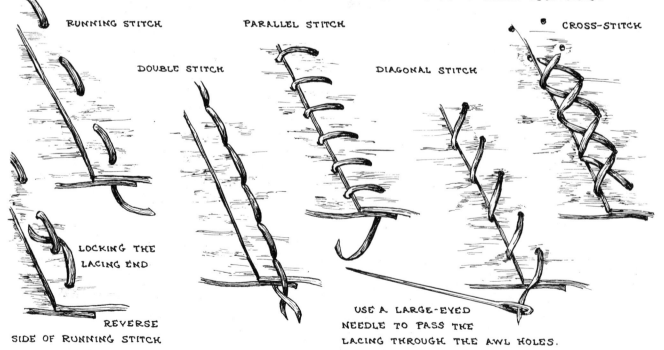

RUNNING STITCH   PARALLEL STITCH   CROSS-STITCH

DOUBLE STITCH   DIAGONAL STITCH

LOCKING THE
LACING END

REVERSE   USE A LARGE-EYED
SIDE OF RUNNING STITCH   NEEDLE TO PASS THE
                           LACING THROUGH THE AWL HOLES.

LACING THE HOOP RIM OF THE CONTAINER PROVIDES BOTH STRENGTH AND DECORATIVE POSSIBILITIES:

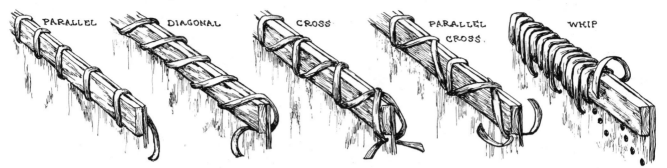

PARALLEL   DIAGONAL   CROSS   PARALLEL CROSS   WHIP

 THE RIM MAY BE A THIN STRIP OF DAMPENED WHITE CEDAR ABOUT $\frac{1}{8}$ INCH THICK AND $\frac{1}{4}$ INCH WIDE (WIDE ENOUGH TO PREVENT THE AWL HOLES FROM SPLITTING THE BARK EDGE). A LIVE MAPLE OR ASH SHOOT, $\frac{1}{4} \pm$ INCH IN DIAMETER, MAY BE SPLIT, ITS BARK SKINNED, AND USED AS A RIM INSTEAD. OR, IF THE GREEN SHOOT IS STIFF, THE ROUNDED SURFACE MAY BE FLATTENED WITH A KNIFE. IF STILL NOT PLIABLE ENOUGH, SOAK IT FOR A FEW HOURS. CONSIDER THE VERY FLEXIBLE WILLOW SHOOTS FOR THE RIM ~ OR EVEN A THICK STRIP OF THE INNER TREE BARK.

WITH THE CONTAINER ENDS LACED, TRY THE RIM STRIP FOR SIZE. ALLOW AN EXTRA 2 INCHES FOR THE RIM OVERLAP.

BEVEL BOTH ENDS OF THE RIM FOR THE OVERLAP. HOLD THE RIM TO THE TOP EDGE OF THE CONTAINER WITH SPRING CLOTHESPINS. WHEN PIECED TOGETHER, THE THICKNESS SHOULD BE THE SAME AS THE REST OF THE RIM. IN PLACE, THE RIM WILL BE ROUND OR OVAL. THIS GIVES AN INTERESTING CONTRAST TO THE SQUARE BASES OF BOXES AND BASKETS.

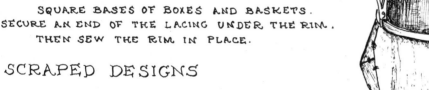

SECURE AN END OF THE LACING UNDER THE RIM. THEN SEW THE RIM IN PLACE.

SCRAPED DESIGNS

WINTER BARK, HARVESTED IN THE SPRING, WAS PRIZED FOR THE DARK BROWN INNER LAYER THAT BECAME THE OUTER SURFACE OF THE CONTAINER. WHEN SCRAPED TO SHOW THE LIGHTER BROWN LAYER UNDERNEATH, STYLIZED NATIVE WOODLAND PLANT DESIGNS COULD ADD TO AN ALREADY HANDSOME BARK. THE SINGLE- AND DOUBLE-CURVED DESIGNS WERE THE BASIC FORMS USED, AND THE ARTISTRY OF THE

SINGLE-CURVE   DOUBLE-CURVE DESIGN

ALGONQUIAN WOMEN WORKED THEM INTO COUNTLESS VARIATIONS. SCRAPINGS WERE EITHER POSITIVE OR NEGATIVE. IF ONLY THE BACKGROUND WERE SCRAPED, THE REMAINING DARK FIGURE WAS POSITIVE. THIS WAS CHARACTERISTIC OF THE COUNTRY NORTH OF THE ST. LAWRENCE RIVER. SCRAPING THE FIGURE ITSELF TO THE LIGHTER LAYER GAVE A NEGATIVE RESULT. THIS WAS THE TECHNIQUE SOUTH OF THE ST. LAWRENCE AND THEREFORE THAT OF THE NEW ENGLAND CONTAINERS.

IN EARLIER DAYS, THE DESIGN WAS TRACED AROUND BIRCH-BARK CUTOUTS WITH AN AWL. NOW A CARDBOARD PATTERN AND PENCIL WILL DO NICELY. WITH A SHARP KNIFE, APPLY JUST ENOUGH PRESSURE TO THE PENCIL OUTLINE TO PENETRATE THE FIRST THIN LAYER OR TWO. THE

POSITIVE   NEGATIVE

DARK SURFACE CAN BE PEELED FREE BETWEEN THE CUT LINES. MOISTENING MAY HELP THE SEPARATION. SCRAPING WITH THE EDGE OF THE BLADE ALSO FREES THE DARK INNER BARK

AN EXAMPLE OF A NEW
ENGLAND WHITE BIRCH
BASKET WITH NEGATIVE
SCRAPED DESIGN ON
LID AND SIDES.

MAKING AND DECORATING
BARK CONTAINERS WAS
USUALLY WOMEN'S
WORK.

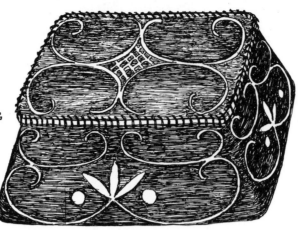

PEABODY MUSEUM,
CAMBRIDGE, MASSACHUSETTS

$\frac{1}{2}$ X

CONTAINER PATTERNS ~ with the foregoing notes in mind

BARK SPOON

FOLD = — — — —   CUT = — · — · — · —

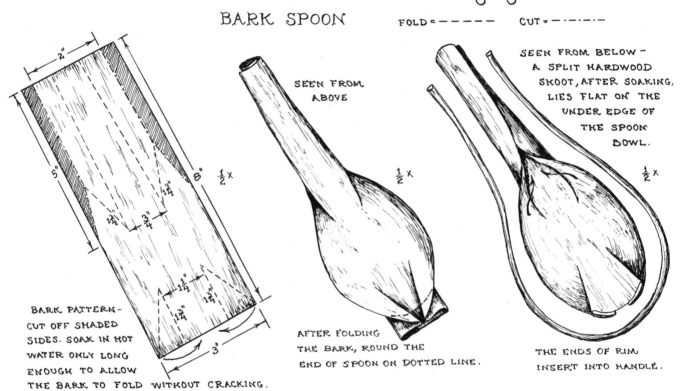

2"

5"   8" $\frac{1}{2}$ X

$1\frac{3}{4}$"
$1\frac{3}{4}$"
$1\frac{1}{4}$" $\frac{3}{4}$"

$1\frac{1}{4}$"
$1\frac{3}{4}$"
$1\frac{1}{4}$"

3"

BARK PATTERN-
CUT OFF SHADED
SIDES. SOAK IN HOT
WATER ONLY LONG
ENOUGH TO ALLOW
THE BARK TO FOLD WITHOUT CRACKING.

SEEN FROM
ABOVE

$\frac{1}{2}$ X

AFTER FOLDING
THE BARK, ROUND THE
END OF SPOON ON DOTTED LINE.

SEEN FROM BELOW -
A SPLIT HARDWOOD
SHOOT, AFTER SOAKING,
LIES FLAT ON THE
UNDER EDGE OF
THE SPOON
BOWL.

$\frac{1}{2}$ X

THE ENDS OF RIM
INSERT INTO HANDLE.

THIS EXAMPLE, ON DISPLAY
AT THE PEABODY MUSEUM IN
CAMBRIDGE, MASSACUSETTS, IS
OF ELM BARK. SUCH ROUGH,
COARSE BARK MUST HAVE ITS
OUTER SURFACE SHAVED THIN
AND SMOOTH WITH A KNIFE.
SOAKING MAKES IT PLIABLE
ENOUGH SO THAT IT WILL
NOT CRACK WHEN FOLDED.

SEEN FROM ABOVE

RIM CONTINUES IN HANDLE.

WITH THE BARK HELD TO
THE RIM WITH SPRING CLOTHESPINS,
THE MOISTENED LACING IS STARTED AT
THE ARROW. THE PARALLEL STITCH RUNS AROUND
THE RIM AND THEN THE HANDLE
IS BOUND.

$\frac{2}{3}$ X

70

BARK DIPPER

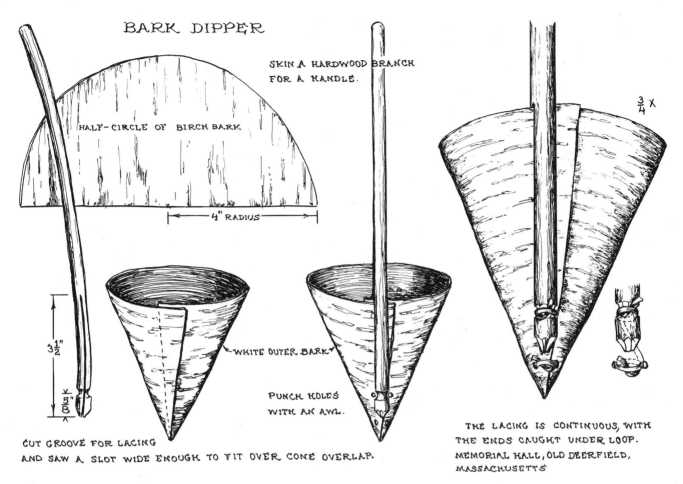

HALF-CIRCLE OF BIRCH BARK

SKIN A HARDWOOD BRANCH
FOR A HANDLE.

4" RADIUS

3½"

⅜"

CUT GROOVE FOR LACING
AND SAW A SLOT WIDE ENOUGH TO FIT OVER CONE OVERLAP.

WHITE OUTER BARK

PUNCH HOLES
WITH AN AWL.

¾ X

THE LACING IS CONTINUOUS, WITH
THE ENDS CAUGHT UNDER LOOP.
MEMORIAL HALL, OLD DEERFIELD,
MASSACHUSETTS

BARK BOWL, OR SAP BUCKET

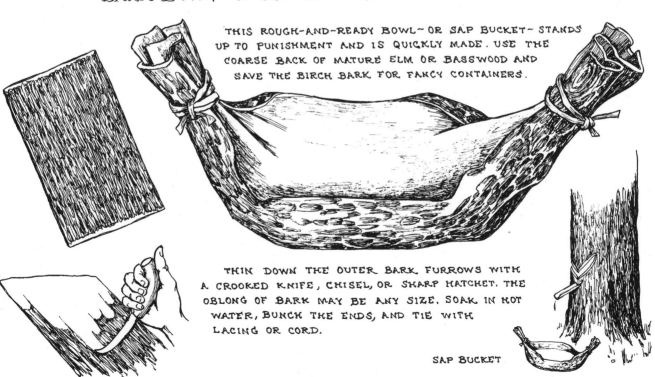

THIS ROUGH-AND-READY BOWL~ OR SAP BUCKET~ STANDS
UP TO PUNISHMENT AND IS QUICKLY MADE. USE THE
COARSE BACK OF MATURE ELM OR BASSWOOD AND
SAVE THE BIRCH BARK FOR FANCY CONTAINERS.

THIN DOWN THE OUTER BARK FURROWS WITH
A CROOKED KNIFE, CHISEL, OR SHARP HATCHET. THE
OBLONG OF BARK MAY BE ANY SIZE. SOAK IN HOT
WATER, BUNCH THE ENDS, AND TIE WITH
LACING OR CORD.

SAP BUCKET

71

BARK TRAIL KETTLE

THE WARRIOR HAD NO NEED TO CARRY WEIGHTY CROCKERY ON THE HUNT OR WARPATH.
ANY WHITE BIRCH NEAR THE CAMPSITE COULD BECOME A TEMPORARY COOKING KETTLE IN TEN
MINUTES. SEAMLESS AND WATERPROOF, IT COULD BE FILLED WITH WATER AND PLACED DIRECTLY ON
THE FIREPLACE COALS. THE INDIANS WERE CAREFUL NOT TO LET ANY FLAMES REACH ABOVE THE
WATERLINE; OTHERWISE THE UNPROTECTED BARK WOULD SURELY HAVE BURNED.
COOKING A STEW IN SUCH A BARK CONTAINER OVER LIVE COALS
WILL MAKE YOU A BELIEVER.

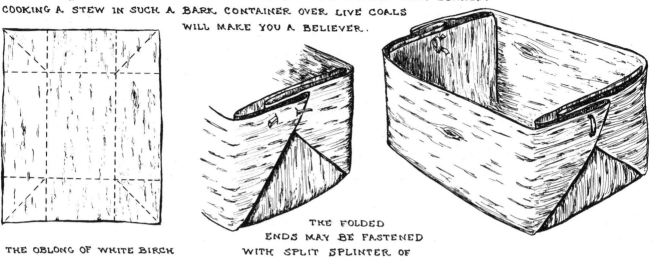

THE OBLONG OF WHITE BIRCH
IS FOLDED AS SHOWN. THE
CORNER SQUARES HAVE
SIDES OF EQUAL LENGTH.

THE FOLDED
ENDS MAY BE FASTENED
WITH SPLIT SPLINTER OF
LIVE HARDWOOD, OR ···

LOOPS OF LACING WORK WELL.

BARK BOWL OR TRAY

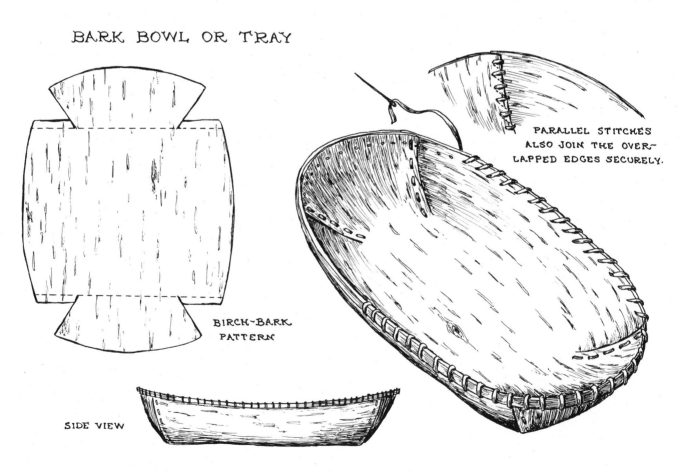

BIRCH-BARK
PATTERN

PARALLEL STITCHES
ALSO JOIN THE OVER-
LAPPED EDGES SECURELY.

SIDE VIEW

72

BARK TRAY OR DISH

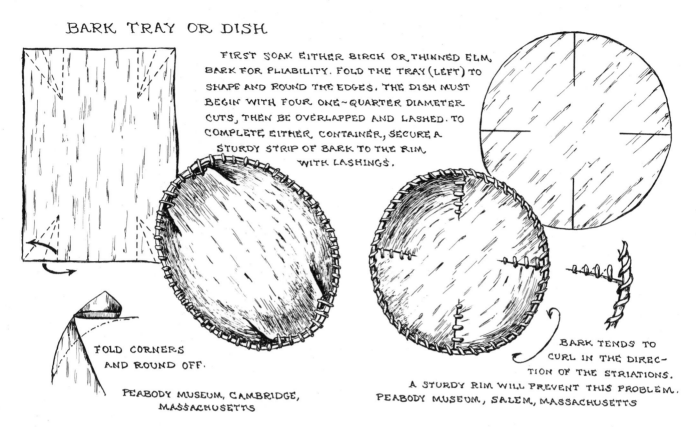

FIRST SOAK EITHER BIRCH OR THINNED ELM BARK FOR PLIABILITY. FOLD THE TRAY (LEFT) TO SHAPE AND ROUND THE EDGES. THE DISH MUST BEGIN WITH FOUR ONE-QUARTER DIAMETER CUTS, THEN BE OVERLAPPED AND LASHED. TO COMPLETE EITHER CONTAINER, SECURE A STURDY STRIP OF BARK TO THE RIM WITH LASHINGS.

FOLD CORNERS AND ROUND OFF.

PEABODY MUSEUM, CAMBRIDGE, MASSACHUSETTS

BARK TENDS TO CURL IN THE DIRECTION OF THE STRIATIONS. A STURDY RIM WILL PREVENT THIS PROBLEM. PEABODY MUSEUM, SALEM, MASSACHUSETTS

BIRCH-BARK BOX

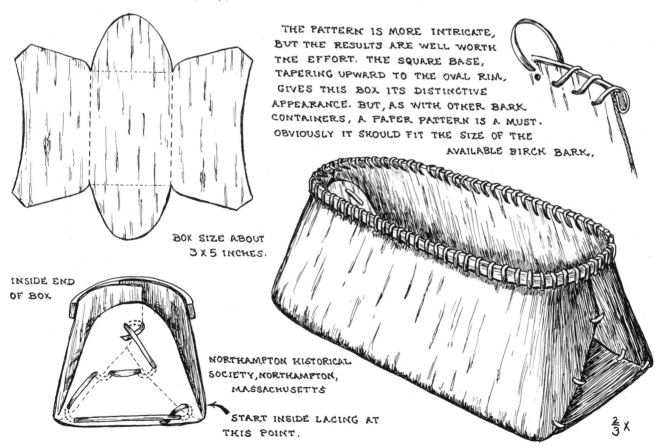

THE PATTERN IS MORE INTRICATE, BUT THE RESULTS ARE WELL WORTH THE EFFORT. THE SQUARE BASE, TAPERING UPWARD TO THE OVAL RIM, GIVES THIS BOX ITS DISTINCTIVE APPEARANCE. BUT, AS WITH OTHER BARK CONTAINERS, A PAPER PATTERN IS A MUST. OBVIOUSLY IT SHOULD FIT THE SIZE OF THE AVAILABLE BIRCH BARK.

BOX SIZE ABOUT 3 X 5 INCHES.

INSIDE END OF BOX

NORTHAMPTON HISTORICAL SOCIETY, NORTHAMPTON, MASSACHUSETTS

START INSIDE LACING AT THIS POINT.

$\frac{2}{3}$ X

73

CYLINDRICAL BARK CONTAINERS

Trinket Box ~ SMALL PIECES OF WHITE BIRCH BARK ARE JOINED FOR A HANDSOME EFFECT. THIS SPECIMEN IS LIKELY OF MAINE TRIBAL ORIGIN. BROWN AND WHITE QUILLWORK DECORATE THE TOP AND SIDES, BUT SCRAPED BARK DESIGNS ARE EASIER AND GIVE A PLEASING RESULT.

MEASUREMENTS AND DESIGN ADAPTED FROM TRINKET BOX ~ NORTHAMPTON HISTORICAL SOCIETY, NORTHAMPTON, MASSACHUSETTS

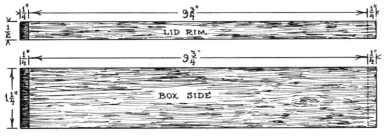

$\frac{1}{4}''$ LID RIM $9\frac{3}{4}''$ $\frac{1}{4}''$ $\frac{1}{8}''$

$\frac{1}{4}''$ BOX SIDE $9\frac{3}{4}''$ $\frac{1}{4}''$ $1\frac{1}{4}''$

$\frac{1}{4}''$ BOX LINER. PEEL TO ABOUT HALF-THICKNESS. FIT TO SIZE AFTER THE BOX SIDE AND PINE BASE ARE MADE. $8\pm$ $\frac{1}{4}''$ $1\frac{1}{2}''$

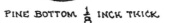

BEVEL $\frac{1}{4}$ INCH OF THE UNDER EDGE ON THE RIGHT OF RIM, SIDE AND LINER. THEN BEVEL THE UPPER SURFACE OF THE LEFT EDGE SO THAT THE ENDS OVERLAP. AS USUAL, THE DARK INNER BARK FORMS THE OUTER BOX SURFACE.

BIRCH-BARK TOP $2\frac{7}{8}''$

PINE BOTTOM $\frac{1}{8}$ INCH THICK $2\frac{7}{8}''$

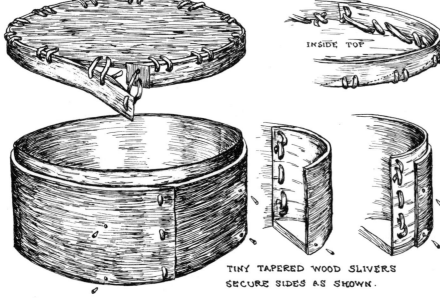

INSIDE TOP

TINY TAPERED WOOD SLIVERS SECURE SIDES AS SHOWN.

LACE THE LID AND THE BOX SIDES.

SECURE THE PINE BOTTOM TO THE LACED CYLINDRICAL SIDE WITH SPLINTERS OF HARDWOOD PLUGGED INTO AWL HOLES.

PLACE LINER INTO CYLINDER. BEVEL OVERLAP AND LACE. THE TAPERED SPLINTERS HOLD THE LINER TO THE INSIDE OF THE BOX. TRIM OFF PROJECTING SPLINTER ENDS.

DRAW THE DESIGNS AND SCRAPE OR PEEL THE BARK TO A LIGHT LAYER. THE DARK BACKGROUND IS UNTOUCHED.

MORE CYLINDRICAL CONTAINERS

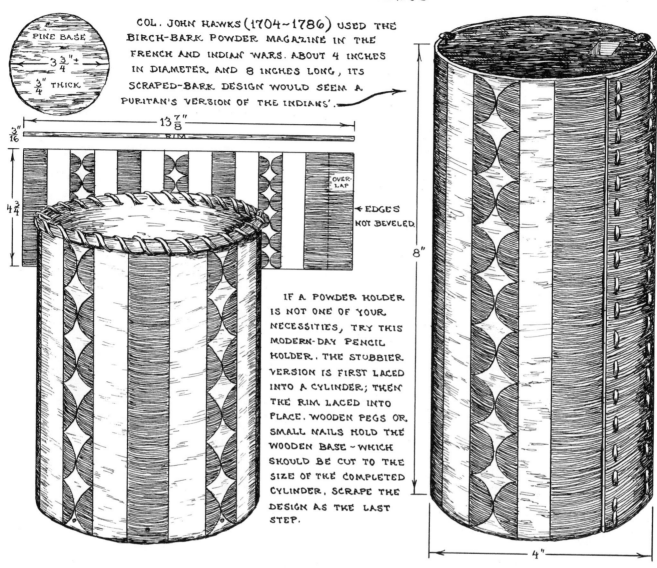

PINE BASE

3 3/4" ±

3/4" THICK

COL. JOHN HAWKS (1704~1786) USED THE BIRCH-BARK POWDER MAGAZINE IN THE FRENCH AND INDIAN WARS. ABOUT 4 INCHES IN DIAMETER AND 8 INCHES LONG, ITS SCRAPED-BARK DESIGN WOULD SEEM A PURITAN'S VERSION OF THE INDIANS'.

3/16"
13 7/8"
RIM

4 3/4"

OVER-LAP

← EDGES NOT BEVELED.

8"

IF A POWDER HOLDER IS NOT ONE OF YOUR NECESSITIES, TRY THIS MODERN-DAY PENCIL HOLDER. THE STUBBIER VERSION IS FIRST LACED INTO A CYLINDER; THEN THE RIM LACED INTO PLACE. WOODEN PEGS OR SMALL NAILS HOLD THE WOODEN BASE ~ WHICH SHOULD BE CUT TO THE SIZE OF THE COMPLETED CYLINDER, SCRAPE THE DESIGN AS THE LAST STEP.

4"

CYLINDRICAL CONTAINERS OF A DIFFERENT SORT

Arrow Quiver ~

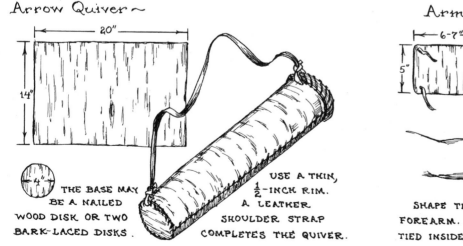

20"

14"

4"

THE BASE MAY BE A NAILED WOOD DISK OR TWO BARK-LACED DISKS.

USE A THIN, 1/2-INCH RIM. A LEATHER SHOULDER STRAP COMPLETES THE QUIVER.

Arm Guard ~

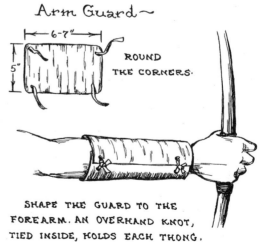

6-7"

5"

ROUND THE CORNERS.

SHAPE THE GUARD TO THE FOREARM. AN OVERHAND KNOT, TIED INSIDE, HOLDS EACH THONG.

CARVED UTENSILS

It is fortunate that important examples of woodenware have survived the centuries. The native nobility is well represented among the wooden bowls~Anne Walkkeed, queen of the Niantic tribe; Miamtonomo, chief of the Narragansetts; and Uncas, chief of the Mohegans. And there is an elm Wampanoag bowl~once thought to be owned by King Philip~that would do credit to any sachem.

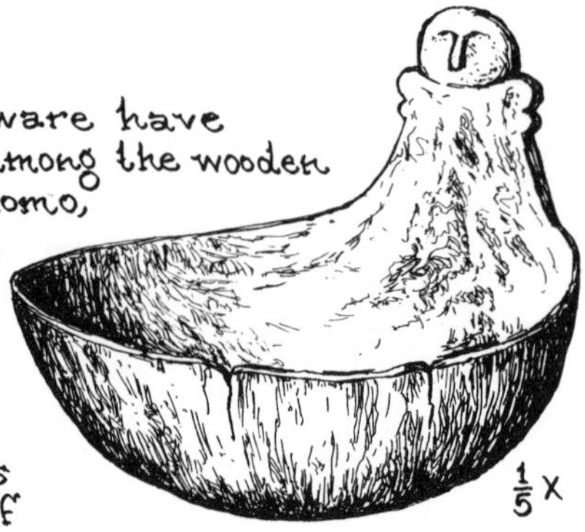

John Josselyn, in his <u>Two Voyages to New England</u>, mentions "dishes, spoons and trayes wrought very smooth and neatly out of the knots of wood." These hardwood burls~ the knobby growths formed by trees to heal wounds or insect assaults~ have a grain that tumbles in all directions. Excessive hardness made carving difficult, but early Indian craftsmen had an answer. The inside of the burl was carefully burned, then the char scraped free in the manner of the dugout canoe. This remarkable feat yielded, in some instances, a wall thickness of $\frac{1}{8}$ inch.

OWNED BY QUEEN ANNE WALKKEED, WITH OWL'S HEAD EFFIGY HANDLE. PEABODY MUSEUM, NEW HAVEN, CONNECTICUT

⅕ X

FROM THE GRAVE OF MIAMTONOMO. SLATER MUSEUM, NORWICH, CONNECTICUT

⅕ X

Historic Indians had the benefit of steel trade knives. Better yet, the crooked knife could gouge out the inner curves of the bowl. The hard steel could also carve the effigy handle that made the good spirits part of the container. In this regard, the pair of holes in the Wampanoag example may have represented spirit eyes rather than openings for a leather thong. Better burl producers included hardwoods such as maple, oak, birch, ash, elm, cherry, and hickory. Perhaps the earlier burning and scraping process acted as a sort of self~contained dry kiln. The rapid drying of the wood fibers by fire may have prevented the checking and cracking seen in air drying. But the scooping of the bowl with the crooked knife meant working with green wood. The hard, dry burls resisted any sort of carving. Bernard Mason, in his <u>Woodcraft and Camping</u>, states that the Indians roughed out the inside of the bowl with their knives while the wood was still green. Then, to prevent checking, they soaked the bowl in linseed oil or bacon fat and hung it up to dry. The bowl was later refined by further scooping and smoothing.

WAMPANOAG BOWL. PEABODY MUSEUM, CAMBRIDGE, MASSACHUSETTS

⅕ X

SUCCOTASH BOWL WHICH BELONGED TO UNCAS. SLATER MUSEUM, NORWICH, CONNECTICUT

⅕ X

REPRODUCING THE BURL BOWL

SINCE BURLS MAY HAVE INTERIOR ROT, SCRAPE OFF THE OUTERMOST BARK TIP TO BE SURE THE WOOD IS SOUND.
CUT THE RIM LEVEL WHILE ALLOWING FOR THE HANDLE PROJECTION. THEN CUT THE BOTTOM PARALLEL TO THE RIM. 

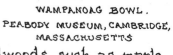

A TEMPORARY SCRAP-WOOD VISE WILL HELP HOLD THE BURL WHILE SAWING. THE BARK ACTS AS A CUSHION.

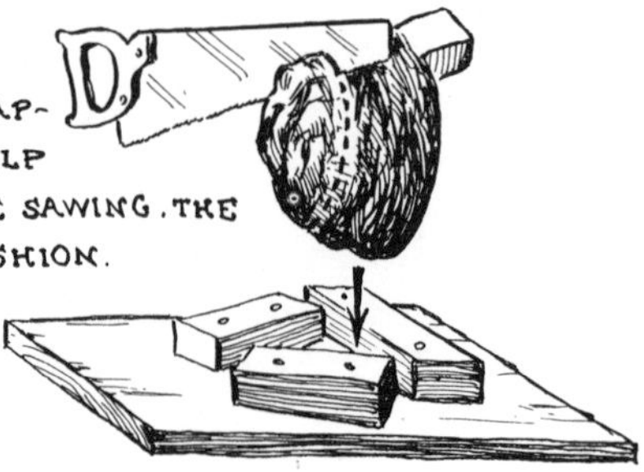

REPOSITION SCRAP-WOOD VISE. SCOOP OUT WOOD SHAVINGS TOWARD THE CENTER WITH A CROOKED KNIFE OR A GOUGE. KEEP TOOLS SHARP~ THIS IS TOUGH GOING.

BEFORE CARVING, YOU MAY WISH TO REMOVE THE BULK OF THE WOOD WITH A DRILL. MARK THE BIT WITH MASKING TAPE TO PREVENT TOO DEEP A PENETRATION. THE BEST BOWLS ARE $\frac{1}{4}$ - INCH THICK AT THE BOTTOM.

WHEN THE WALL AND BOTTOM ARE THINNED TO YOUR SATISFACTION, CARVE THE STYLIZED EFFIGY HANDLE. IT'S TIME TO STRIP OFF THE BARK AND TRIM WHERE NECESSARY.

IF THE WOOD IS UNFINISHED, WRAP IT IN A MOISTENED CLOTH OF LINSEED OIL. COVER THE WHOLE WITH A CLEAR PLASTIC WRAP. THIS WILL HOPEFULLY PREVENT CHECKING.

FINISH BY SOAKING FOR A DAY IN SALAD OIL, THEN DRY THOROUGHLY.

HARDWOOD BOWL

Burls~ especially the large sizes used for Indian bowls~ are not all that plentiful. A small burl is ideal for crafting a noggin. Meanwhile, consider a fresh chunk of hardwood. The Algonquian craftsman certainly did, for burls were by no means the only raw material used. Basswood, poplar, and the harder birch, maple, beech, and cherry carve well. Try a local firewood cutter for a freshly cut log. The ends must be sealed with such as varnish, shellac, or melted wax to pre~ vent checking.

MEASUREMENTS VARY WITH THE SIZE LOG THAT IS AVAILABLE, OF COURSE. 9-INCH LOG IS BUT AN EXAMPLE.

SPLIT A LOG 9 INCHES IN DIAMETER, 13 INCHES LONG.

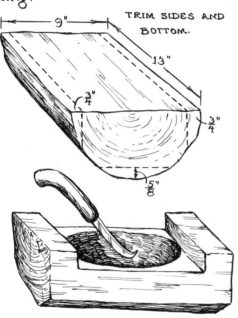

TRIM SIDES AND BOTTOM.

SCOOP OUT CENTER OF BOWL. DRILL HOLES IF YOU WISH - BUT DON'T LET ANY AIR THROUGH.

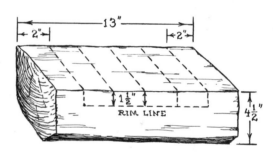

LEAVING 2 INCHES AT THE ENDS, SAW AND CHISEL OUT TO THE RIM LINE.

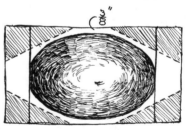

SAW OFF CORNERS. KEEP $\frac{3}{8}$ ~ INCH RIM.

SIDE VIEW WITH $\frac{3}{8}$ - INCH BOTTOM.

SAW OFF END CORNERS.

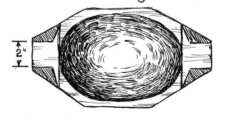

TRIM EFFIGY HANDLES TO 2 INCHES.

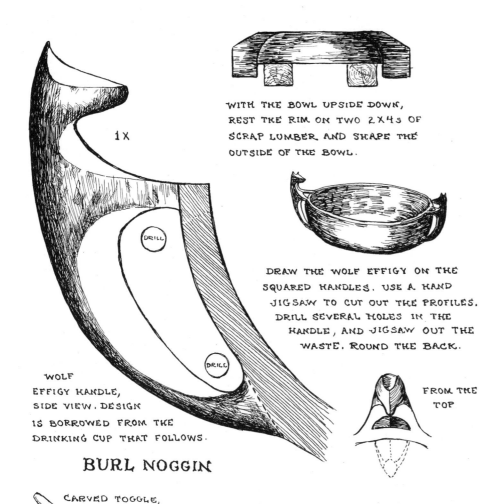

1X

WOLF
EFFIGY HANDLE,
SIDE VIEW. DESIGN
IS BORROWED FROM THE
DRINKING CUP THAT FOLLOWS.

WITH THE BOWL UPSIDE DOWN,
REST THE RIM ON TWO 2X4s OF
SCRAP LUMBER AND SHAPE THE
OUTSIDE OF THE BOWL.

DRAW THE WOLF EFFIGY ON THE
SQUARED HANDLES. USE A HAND
JIGSAW TO CUT OUT THE PROFILES.
DRILL SEVERAL HOLES IN THE
HANDLE, AND JIGSAW OUT THE
WASTE. ROUND THE BACK.

FROM THE
TOP

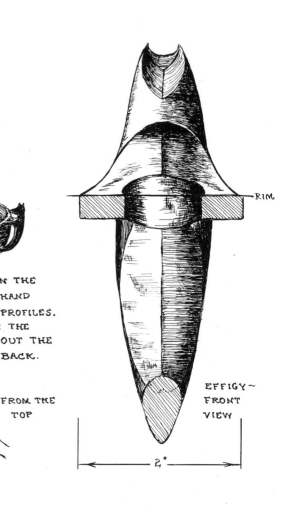

RIM

EFFIGY ~
FRONT
VIEW

2"

BURL NOGGIN

CARVED TOGGLE,
2 INCHES LONG

On the trail, the
warrior carried his
noggin with the toggle
tucked under his belt.
It was crafted in the same
way as the burl bowl.

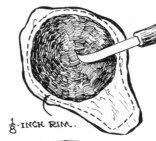

SAW THE BURL
FREE. DRILL A
SERIES OF HOLES
WHILE THE WOOD
IS FRESH. LEAVE
THE BARK IN PLACE
TO PROTECT THE
WOOD.

$\frac{1}{8}$-INCH RIM.

ALL $\frac{1}{3}$ X ±

DRILL GUIDE HOLES

SMALL PENOBSCOT NOGGIN 1X
PEABODY MUSEUM, CAMBRIDGE,
MASSACHUSETTS

THE AVERAGE NOGGIN IS 3 INCHES IN
DIAMETER. AFTER DRILLING, SCOOPING
OUT, REMOVING THE BARK, AND SMOOTHING
THE OUTSIDE OF THE FRESH BURL, SOAK
OVERNIGHT IN SALAD OIL. DRY AND
POLISH WITH A PIECE OF LEATHER, AS
RECOMMENDED BY MASON.

DON'T BE BASHFUL ABOUT USING A BLOCK
OF DRY HARDWOOD INSTEAD OF A BURL. MANY
INDIAN NOGGINS WERE MADE THIS WAY.

REMOVE BARK AND WHITTLE THE OUTSIDE
SMOOTH. DRILL A HOLE FOR THONG AND TOGGLE.

78

DRINKING CUP

Champlain, writing in 1608, tells of a Huron gathering where "Indians came to feast each bringing his wooden bowl and his spoon." This Nipmuc specimen must have been highly prized by its owner.

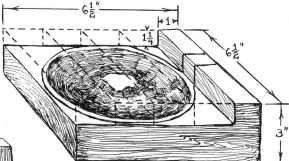

PROBABLE NIPMUC CUP ILLUSTRATED ON PAGE 259 OF CHARLES WILLOUGHBY'S ANTIQUITIES OF THE NEW ENGLAND INDIANS.

START WITH A SEASONED BLOCK OF HARDWOOD 6½ INCHES SQUARE AND 3 INCHES DEEP. THE HANDLE IS CARVED AFTER THE BOWL IS SHAPED. THE FRONT LEGS ARE NOT SEPARATED BY CARVING.

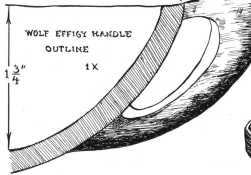

WOLF EFFIGY HANDLE OUTLINE

1 X

1¾"

1"

1¼"

SAW AND CHISEL OUT THE DOTTED-LINE SECTIONS. SCOOP OUT THE BOWL.

6½"

1

1¼

6½"

3"

SAW THE BOWL OUTLINE, ROUND THE UNDER SURFACE, AND CARVE THE HANDLE. OIL WITH REGULAR SALAD OIL AND THE CUP IS READY FOR USE.

SPOON

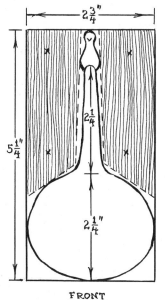

2¾"

2"

5¼"

2¼"

2¼"

FRONT

SIDE

THE BIRD'S TAIL HOOKS OVER THE RIM OF A BOWL.

IROQUOIS SPOON, NEW YORK STATE LIBRARY, ALBANY, NEW YORK. THE FIERCE MOHAWKS, PART OF THE IROQUOIS CONFEDERACY, MADE FREQUENT RAIDS AGAINST THE NEW ENGLAND TRIBES.

⅘ X

FINISH WITH SALAD OIL OR BACON GREASE, IF THE SPOON IS TO BE USED WITH FOOD.

SAW (USE A BAND SAW IF YOU HAVE ONE) ALONG THE DOTTED LINES. ROUGH-CUT THE SIDE FIRST, THEN TEMPORARILY NAIL BACK TOGETHER AT "X." CUT FRONT PATTERN. LEAVE THE BOWL SOMEWHAT SQUARE. SECURE IN A VISE AND CARVE OUT THE INSIDE OF THE BOWL.

LADLE

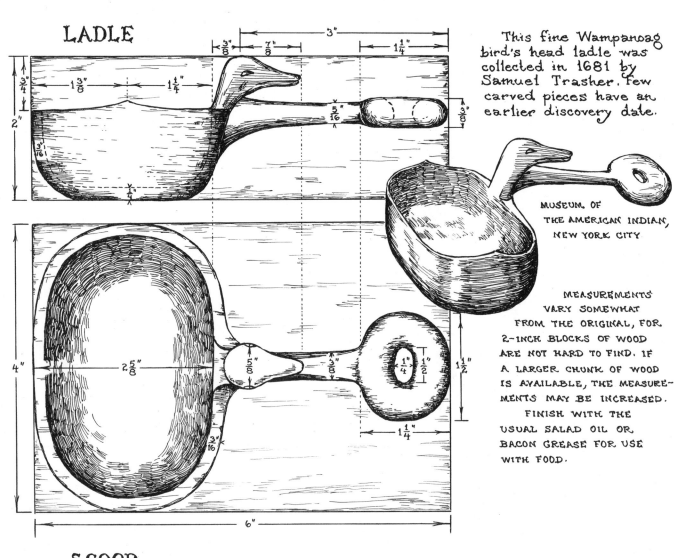

This fine Wampanoag bird's head ladle was collected in 1681 by Samuel Trasher. Few carved pieces have an earlier discovery date.

MUSEUM OF
THE AMERICAN INDIAN,
NEW YORK CITY

MEASUREMENTS VARY SOMEWHAT FROM THE ORIGINAL, FOR 2-INCH BLOCKS OF WOOD ARE NOT HARD TO FIND. IF A LARGER CHUNK OF WOOD IS AVAILABLE, THE MEASUREMENTS MAY BE INCREASED. FINISH WITH THE USUAL SALAD OIL OR BACON GREASE FOR USE WITH FOOD.

SCOOP

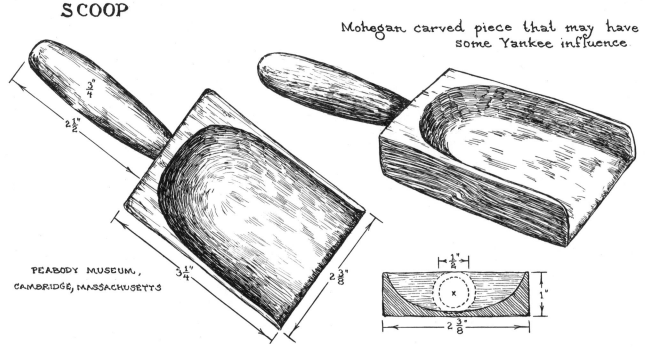

Mohegan carved piece that may have some Yankee influence.

PEABODY MUSEUM,
CAMBRIDGE, MASSACHUSETTS

80

METAL SPOONS

Some 5,000 years ago, the Late Archaic Indians were actually crafting crude metal tools. Pure copper nuggets were exported from the Great Lakes region to be fashioned into gouges, axes, knives, and such. But there was a problem, for repeated pounding created small cracks in the metal. The solution was to heat – or anneal – the copper periodically. After letting it cool, the tool could be shaped without these flaws.

Such metal tools were as scarce as they were prized. Although bog iron was available locally, the Indians were unable to smelt the raw material. Any quantity of workable metal was not to be had until the arrival of the early European traders and settlers. Any broken brass or copper pots were fair game for the Algonquian craftsmen. Sheet metals were popular trade items and probably used to shape the spoons shown here.

REPRODUCING SPOONS

USE THESE PATTERNS ON THIN SHEET BRASS OR COPPER. ROOFERS, METAL CRAFTSMEN AND SCHOOL METAL SHOPS USUALLY HAVE SMALL SCRAPS THAT ARE JUST RIGHT FOR THE PROJECT.

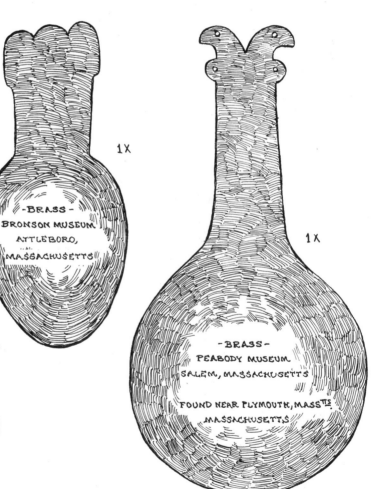

1X

-BRASS-
BRONSON MUSEUM
ATTLEBORO,
MASSACHUSETTS

1X

-BRASS-
PEABODY MUSEUM
SALEM, MASSACHUSETTS
FOUND NEAR PLYMOUTH, MASS.
MASSACHUSETTS

1X

-BRASS-
PEABODY MUSEUM
CAMBRIDGE, MASSACHUSETTS
FROM
GRAVE AT WINTHROP,
MASSACHUSETTS

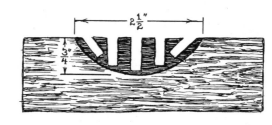

DRAW THE SPOON OUTLINE ON CARDBOARD, ADDING $\frac{3}{16}$ INCH TO THE BOWL CIRCUMFERENCE. THIS WILL ALLOW FOR THE CURVE OF THE BOWL. TRACE PATTERN ON THE METAL SHEET AND CUT WITH TIN SNIPS. ROUND OFF WITH A METAL FILE.

DRILL PILOT HOLES IN A PINE BLOCK. SCOOP OUT THE SPOON BOWL MOLD. THE WOODEN MALLET WILL HELP.

A LATHE MAKES SHORT WORK OF THIS MALLET, BUT A BROOM-STICK AND A SLAB OF HARDWOOD CAN BE WHITTLED TO SHAPE AND SANDED SMOOTH.

SLOT THE HANDLE, POUND THE HEAD HOME, AND DRIVE IN A WOODEN WEDGE TO SECURE IT.

CLEAN THE METAL WITH FINE STEEL WOOL. CENTER THE DISK OVER THE MOLD DEPRESSION. START WITH LIGHT, REGULAR, AND SHORT BLOWS AT THE CENTER OF THE DISK. SLIGHTLY ANGLE THE HAMMER TO STRETCH THE METAL TOWARD THE RIM.

GRADUALLY FORM CONCENTRIC CIRCLES WITH THE HAMMER. ROTATE THE BOWL AFTER EVERY FEW HAMMER STROKES TO KEEP THE STRETCHING UNIFORM. HAMMER MARKS SHOULD BE HARD TO SEE.

IF NECESSARY, STRAIGHTEN THE RIM OVER A CURVED HARDWOOD BLOCK. SHAPE IT WITH THE FLAT END OF THE MALLET.

ANNEALING

Although I found that the sheet-metal spoons needed no annealing, a thick piece might have want of it. If the metal no longer "gives" or stretches, it must be softened before continuing. Heat to a dull cherry red, using a blowtorch at low pressure with a spread flame. After several minutes, cool gradually to prevent hardening of the metal. Do not hammer until the metal is cold.

Annealing creates a metal scale which should be removed before pounding to prevent metal pitting. Dilute sulfuric acid (ten parts water to one part sulfuric acid in a glass jar) will clean it nicely, but it is safer to use steel wool and elbow grease.

GOURD CONTAINERS

It might be worthwhile checking the "Indian Garden" section (p.87) before reading on. Making gourd containers without gourds has little going for it.

Nature still provides the woodland Indians~ and those interested in such crafts~ with these light, waterproof, grown-to-shape containers. The fruits are known by their shape~ bottle, dipper, pipe, apple, orange, pear, and powder horn gourds are among the many varieties. Likely, the Indians prepared their gourds in the following way, with a few present~day exceptions.

Harvesting is best delayed until just before the first frost. Cut the dry brownish stems several inches from the fruit to prevent bruising. Each should be washed in warm, soapy water, then rinsed in clear water. Add a disinfectant to prevent spoilage from garden bacteria. Dry gently with a soft cloth, for any injury to the skin will invite rotting.

GOURD BOWL AND BOTTLE, BOTH OF MOHEGAN ORIGIN MUSEUM OF THE AMERICAN INDIAN, NEW YORK CITY.

IF THE GOURD IS CUT BEFORE DRYING, THE RIM WILL PUCKER INWARD AS IT DRIES~AND MAY DEVELOP MOLD.

The first week of drying sets the color and hardens the skin. Place the gourds on several layers of newspaper in a warm, dry spot~ preferably in the sunshine of a window. Turn the fruits daily. They must not touch one another. Replace any newspapers that have absorbed moisture. Also~ discard any fruits that shrivel or develop soft spots. They are sure targets for bacteria and mold that will then infect the remaining gourds.

The final drying takes about a month. Use a soft cloth, soaked with disinfectant, to wipe the gourds. Place on newspapers in a warm, dry, and dark place. Heat continues the drying, dryness helps prevent mold, and the darkness maintains the color.

The shape of the gourd suggests its use. Sketch the rim outline in pencil. Using a thin knife blade, cut down to within $\frac{1}{4}$ inch of the rim. Shave down to the rim for a smoother trim. Sand the edges and then consider an incised design. This may be as simple as the rings that encircle the Mohegan bowl, or you may wish to try some woodland designs. Cut a shallow "V" line with a knife or a V-parting carving tool. The incised design may be highlighted with colored pens, oil stain, or paint applied with a fine brush. The gourds may be left without finishing or you can use a paste wax~ well buffed~ for protection. If the gourd is to hold food or liquids, rub in vegetable oil~ but be careful not to smear soluble colors. Forget about shellac~ the surface will be glossy and may encourage rot from sealed-in moisture.

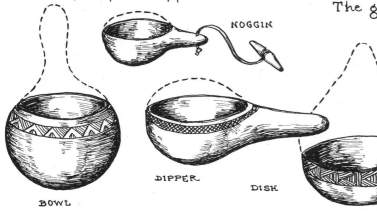

NOGGIN

DIPPER

DISH

BOWL

83

 # POTTERY

Handsome and practical cooking pots from common clay? It seemed nothing short of magic until migrating Adena Indians from Ohio brought the technique to New England about 500 BC. At first the bases of the pots were molded to a point~the better to secure them in the hearth while the fire was built around their walls. By A.D.1600, these bases were rounded. Pot necks were constricted and suspended by thongs to give a broad and even heat to the bottom.

Over these thousand years the basics of pot making really haven't changed; they are challenging yet simple enough for any of us to give pot making a try.

CLAY SOURCES AND QUALITIES

Local history books may reveal the sites of old brickyards~or keep a sharp eye along the eroded banks of streams or road cuts. Fill a bucket with as clean a clay as you can from the layered deposits.

Your raw clay will succeed or fail depending on the following:

PLASTICITY~When the clay is kneaded into a doughy, puttylike texture, a pencil-sized roll should bend around a finger without cracking. There should be little enough moisture so that it doesn't stick to one's hands. Sometime aging in the sun, wind, and frost for a month or two will give plasticity to an otherwise unworkable clay.

POROSITY~If a clay is very fine, gritty substances must be added to release the steam formed chemically in the heating process. Grit also helps reduce shrinkage of the clay and to withstand the abrupt firing and cooling in the native kiln. Ancient pot shards show the addition of ground pieces of old pottery, powdered shell, soapstone, limestone, or fine silt or sand from the wearing of stones in stream beds. The now-porous clay should not feel gritty, for too much temper makes it difficult to work.

FUSIBILITY~The best clay already has, as part of its makeup, a generous amount of fine quartz and feldspar particles. Their low melting point fuses the crystals into a hard and permanent substance. Sometimes these silicates were ground and added to that in the clay body.

COLOR~ Yellow, tan, red or brown~ all contain varying amounts of iron oxide. Depending on this amount, the clay will fire from tan to brick red.

PREPARATION

Break the chunks of clay into pieces and sun-dry them. Whack the pieces into powder with a mallet, but don't breath in that fine dust. Sift out any twigs or pebbles.

Temper may now be added for porosity ~ about 5 to 10 percent of the powdered clay to be used. Perhaps the handiest materials are pulverized soft bricks (orange in color and softer than the dark red brick that was baked nearer to the kiln fire) or a common flowerpot. Wear safety glasses for this chore.

Add enough water to the dry clay mixture to give a puttylike consistency. A sticky lump needs more clay powder ~ or more water, if it cracks easily when shaping. This will be evident on kneading the clay to remove remaining lumps and especially air pockets. This is a most important step, for trapped air will expand when heated. Since ceramic rubble isn't the object, work the clay ball for about twenty minutes with the heel of the palm. It's also helpful to cover the work surface with a piece of light canvas to prevent sticking.

MAKING THE POT

Start with a base mold that can be rotated as the work progresses. The Indian women often had several fired pot bases on hand for this purpose.

84

Sometimes the inside of a piece of gourd served as a mold. A porous base soaks up moisture. Today some potters use absorbent plaster-of-paris molds for this purpose. I've used plastic cereal and soup bowls ~ hardly porous, but there was enough shrinkage of the clay on drying to remove it without misery. At any rate, flatten a disk of clay; then smooth, thin, and shape to the base mold, much like a pie shell.

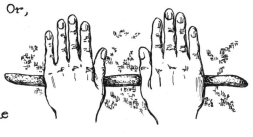

Coiling ~ Roll a ball of clay between the palms to make a sausage ~ about the thickness of your thumb. Or, if you wish, use a canvas-covered board to roll out the cylinder. Lay the coil on the rim of the clay base. Both clay surfaces should contain a like amount of moisture for joining. Use a single coil at a time and fuse the butt ends.

THE COIL SIZE VARIES WITH THE CURVE OF THE POT WALL, OR A CONTINUOUS COIL MAY BE USED IN SPIRAL FASHION.

BONDING THE COIL IS AN IMPORTANT STEP. PRESS DOWNWARD ON THE INSIDE AND UPWARD ON THE OUT~ SIDE FOR A STRONG POT WALL. THREE LAYERS OF COIL ARE ABOUT ALL YOU CAN MANAGE WITHOUT THE SIDES SLUMPING ~ BUT THEN YOU'LL PROBABLY NEED NO FURTHER COILING FOR A SMALL POT. SHAPE, THIN, AND SMOOTH AS YOU GO.

Larger pots should be dried an hour or so ~ but cover the rim with a damp cloth to keep it moist. (The Indian potter usually worked another pot along while the firming of the body took place.) More coils may then be added.

After the coils were joined, a wooden paddle was some~ times helpful for shaping, smoothing surface humps, and compacting the clay into a harder, more durable wall. It was twine~wrapped to prevent the clay from sticking, although the pot was dried for an hour or so to firm the wall for the paddling. Many excavated New England pot shards still show the cord impressions ~ and they do give a pleasing decorative touch.

A WATER~SMOOTHED STONE HELPED TO GIVE A SMOOTHER INSIDE.

Dry the pot in the shade for about a day; then ease it from the base mold. Any cracks may be filled with damp clay. Now is the time to scrape the walls to a thinness of $\frac{1}{4} - \frac{3}{8}$ inch ~ if the shaping left the walls too bulky. Use a table knife. Polish the surface ~ if not cord-marked ~ with the bowl of a spoon or a smooth stone. Use care and be sure the clay is leather hard. It is still fragile and needs support with your other hand. Any designs may be scratched into the surface at this time. Continue drying for several more days. The walls should not feel cool to the touch.

Designs ~ Since the later pots were more globular, they adapt better for modern

85

usage (see the pot comparison in The New England Indians, Globe Pequot, 1978). A slight basal flattening will prevent tipping. The designs of this period were scratched into the leather-hard surface with pronged sticks or chipped stones — or incised with a pointed flake.

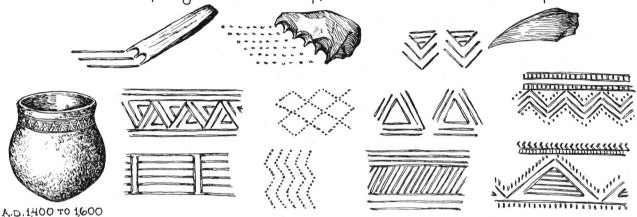

A.D. 1400 TO 1600

ABOUT A.D. 1600., IROQUOIAN INFLUENCES GAVE A MORE PRONOUNCED COLLAR WITH TWO TO FOUR RIM PEAKS. THE DECORATIONS ALSO CLOSELY RESEMBLED THOSE ON THE IROQUOIAN WARE.

1600 AND THEREAFTER.

Firing ~ The moment of truth. Your selection of clay will rise or fall on its fusibility. In addition, the porosity from added grit must be enough to withstand the rapid heating and cooling of the Indian kiln. (The long and gradual heating in a commercial kiln makes temper unnecessary.)

DIG A SHALLOW HOLE ABOUT 3 FEET IN DIAMETER. SPACE TIN CANS ON THE EARTH AND PLACE THE POTS UPSIDE DOWN ON THEM. SIDES SHOULD NOT TOUCH. ENCIRCLE WITH THIN SPLITS OF HARDWOOD AND PLACE SHORT PIECES OF WOOD UNDER POTS.

PROTECT THE POTS WITH A FEW PIECES OF TIN TO PREVENT FIRE STAINS. STACK SPLIT WOOD IN WIGWAM FASHION OVER THE TIN.

ON A WINDLESS DAY, LIGHT FIRE AROUND THE CIRCLE FOR EVEN BURNING. ADD WOOD AS NECESSARY FOR A BRISK, HOUR-LONG FIRE.

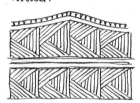

THEN BANK THE FIRE FROM THE BOTTOM UP WITH DAMP LEAVES, FRESH-CUT GRASS, AND WEEDS. FOLLOW WITH A FINAL COVER-ING OF VERY THIN SOD, LEAVING A SMOKE HOLE AT THE TOP. WITH THE HEAT CONCENTRATED, LET THE FIRE BURN OUT. AFTER A TOTAL OF ABOUT TWO HOURS FROM LIGHTING, REMOVE YOUR STILL-HOT CREATIONS CAREFULLY.

Now if you aren't of a chancy nature, commercial clays are available at craft stores. And there's bound to be a potter in the neighborhood who will fire your Indian pot. (Colored glazes were not used.) Or ~ consider some of the air-hardening clays or the plastic clay compounds that need only oven heating.

INDIAN GARDEN

Charles Willoughby, in his <u>Antiquities of the New England Indians</u>, observed that " good agricultural lands were necessary for the well~being of every community. The high, rocky shores of the central and eastern portion of Maine were not suitable for agriculture, but the fertile river valleys of the interior of this state, and throughout New England generally, had their well cultivated gardens wherein were grown corn, beans, pumpkins, squashes, artichokes, and tobacco."

STONE TRIANGULAR HOE

STONE STEM HOE   SEA-CLAM HOE

SHOULDER-BLADE HOE
FROM DEER, BEAR, OR MOOSE

Each family had one or more gardens. Trees were felled by burning and then chipping off the char(see"Dugout Canoes"section,p.43). Brush and weeds were also cleared by fire before the soil was turned over with hoes. Then, from planting to harvesting, it was all women's work.

CORN (Zea mays) New England Indians knew their most important crop as "Our Life Supporter." And so it was that despite its modest beginnings 6,000 years ago, the natives of southern Mexico cross bred grasses with tiny edible nubbins. The Caribbean Indians called it "mahiz," or maize. Sometime after A.D. 300, huskier relatives were introduced to New England. Fertilization and time produced five varieties of good eating~ sweet, dent, flint, flour, and pop corn.

SWEET CORN   DENT CORN   FLINT CORN   FLOUR, OR SOFT, CORN   POPCORN

SWEET CORN~ CONTAINS MORE SUGAR THAN OTHER VARIETIES, EATEN ROASTED OR BOILED ON THE COB.
DENT CORN~ MOST CORN GROWN COMMERCIALLY IS OF THIS VARIETY. WHEN THE CORN IS DRIED, THE STARCH INSIDE THE KERNEL SHRINKS, PRODUCING A DENT IN THE TOP.
FLINT CORN~ THE HARD SMOOTH KERNELS JUSTIFY THE NAME. THESE ARE THE MULTICOLORED EARS DESCRIBED BY THE COLONISTS, AND TODAY HUNG AS ORNAMENTAL CORN. ITS SHORT RIPENING PERIOD MADE IT POPULAR WITH THE NORTHERN NEW ENGLAND INDIANS.
FLOUR CORN~ ALSO CALLED SOFT CORN BECAUSE OF THE SOFT AND STARCHY KERNELS. FOR THIS

REASON, THE INDIANS COULD GRIND THEIR MEAL FROM IT WITH GREATER EASE.

POPCORN ~ THE SMALL, TOUGH~COATED KERNELS HAVE EITHER POINTED OR ROUNDED ENDS. ON HEATING, STEAM IS CREATED UNDER GREAT PRESSURE INSIDE, EXPLODING THE COVERING AND PUFFING OUT THE CONTENTS.

Since the kernels, or seeds, are encased in a husk, corn cannot reproduce itself. Therefore the Indian women helped nature along by planting the seeds about the last of April (when the leaves of the white oak were as large as a mouse's ears). Mounds of soil, about 3 feet apart, were heaped in rows. Fish and crushed horseshoe crabs fertilized the four seeds that represented the directions of travel. Bunched in this way, the wind could carry the tassel pollen to the female silk. In the weeks to come, the mound of earth was piled around the stalks to keep them upright.

HAND PLANTER.

$\frac{1}{4}$ X

STONE PLANTER ON STICK

SHARPENED STICK PLANTER WITH A BRANCH FOOTREST

Five days after the full moon, preparations were readied for the Green Corn Ceremony. Ground green corn became a ceremonial soup, dedicated to the spirits of growing things and believed to forestall famine. Meanwhile the men were hunting to supply the sacred broth with venison. For four days, gambling games, songs and dances, prayers, and the burning of tobacco were offered in thanks for the coming bounty.

As the corn matured, the green corn stalks were chewed, much like sugar cane, for the sweet juice. And at harvest time, the ears were boiled or roasted in the husks. The husk wrappings were stripped back, braided, and hung on poles to dry. The shelled kernels were stored in great woven grass baskets, well covered with mats, under 5 or 6 feet of sand. These grain barns were ready for the lean winter months.

THE FUNNEL~SHAPED CAVITIES OF THESE LOG MORTARS ALLOWED THE HEAVIER UNCRUSHED KERNELS TO GRAVITATE TO THE CENTER. THEY RECEIVED THE FULL FORCE OF THE STONE PESTLE AS THE SMALLER PARTICLES ROSE TO THE TOP.

BEANS

(Phaseolus vulgaris) Thanks to the constant weed chopping and fertilization, the corn stalks could reach a height of over 10 feet. All this vertical muscle was put to good use as bean-vine supports. Three or four kidney beans were planted in each hill. Colorful as Indian paints, the varieties included the red kidney beans, the mottled pinto beans, and the white navy beans. When cooked, the last type was better known to the colonists as Boston baked beans.

The kidney beans were usually picked only when they were completely ripe and hard. (String or snap beans and wax beans, by the way, are also a variety of kidney beans. They are simply picked at an early stage, when the seeds are partially formed.)

PUMPKINS

(Cucurbita pepo) The colonists called them pompions. The seeds were also planted in each hill. The lengthy vines spread out to occupy the ground between the mounds, well away from the shade of the corn and bean plants. Pumpkins were the Indians' chief food after corn.

88

SQUASH

(Cucurbita pepo) The word was shortened from the Massachusett "askōōtasquash." Squash seeds were also planted in hills. John Josselyn, in his New-England's Rarities, (1672), recorded the fruits as green or yellow, with some shapes resembling gourds and others round as an apple. Summer, acorn, and butternut squash would seem to fit these descriptions. Squash blossoms flavored many a stew well before harvest time.

SUMMER

ACORN

BUTTERNUT

JERUSALEM ARTICHOKES

(Helianthus tuberosus) They are neither from Jerusalem nor artichokes, but rather a close native relative to the sunflower. The sweet, crisp, and juicy tubers made the plant an important addition to the Indian garden.

The nubby roots grow to 3 or 4 inches in length. Since the stalks reach well over 6 feet, the tubers should be planted on the north side of the garden to prevent shading the other plants. Find your own tubers along ditches or meadows, or in a pinch, the grocery store may have a supply. The roots are harvested in the late fall when the leaves have dried. Any left behind will easily sprout the following spring.

SUNFLOWERS

(Helianthus annus) The giant sun-like heads are heavy with edible seeds. They were ground to provide oil for cooking and hairdressing.

HUSK TOMATO OR GROUND CHERRY

(Physalis pubescens) Colonial writers virtually ignored these early wild ancestors of the modern tomato. Yet they grew in plenty in our New England soil and were favored by both Indians and colonists. The settlers ate them fresh, dried, and in preserves and pies. (The red tomato, developed from the husk tomato through years of selective crossbreeding, was considered poisonous until the mid-nineteenth century.)

Each sweet yellow fruit is enclosed in a papery husk~much like miniature Japanese lanterns. They fall from the vines when ripe and are preserved for weeks by their unusual coverings. Be fore-warned~ungathered husk tomatoes will sprout the following year and may spread to crowd out other plantings. Give them their own corner. They will be one of your most fascinating crops.

GOURDS

(Curcurbita) The tiny yellow flowers of the genus Citrullus produce a wide range of small-bottle, spoon-, egg- and pear-shaped fruits. The genus Lagenaria, with its small white flowers and vines of up to 20 feet, grows large multishaped gourds. As relatives of the pumpkin and squash, cross~pollination among these three plants may yield renegade seeds. Probably the knowledgeable Indian women planted the pumpkin, squash, and gourds separately, each in different parts of the garden between the hills.

Although inedible, a mixture of both large and

89

small gourds will yield an unbelievable number of sizes, colors and shapes each suggesting its own use (see "Gourd Containers" p.83). Unlike their pumpkin and squash cousins, gourds prefer a fence for climbing rather than ramble about between the hills.

TOBACCO

(Nicotiana rustica and Nicotiana tabacum) The leaves were used for ceremonial offerings and medicinal purposes. Therefore the men alone tended and smoked this sacred plant, leaving the remainder of the gardening chores to the women. Only a small portion of the dried leaf was mixed with a variety of dry wild herbs. The nicotine content in the Indian's pipe was minimal.

John Josselyn noted the growing of tobacco in special beds in Maine~and the plant thrived elsewhere in New England. Along the Connecticut River~"Tobacco Valley"~the crop is still grown on a large scale. For a garden to be representative of Indian practices, a few plants should be grown in a special corner.

Cucumbers, muskmelons, and watermelons are not native to America. The English colonists imported the seeds, and most likely the Indians lost no time cultivating the new arrivals.

PLOTTING THE GARDEN PLOT

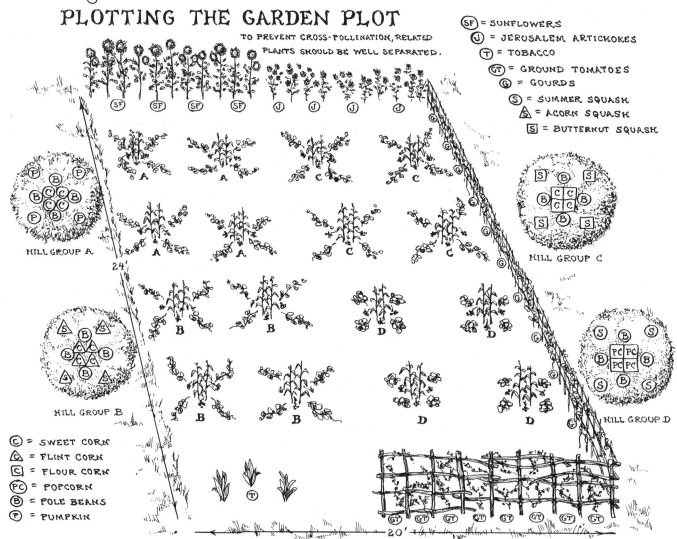

TO PREVENT CROSS-POLLINATION, RELATED PLANTS SHOULD BE WELL SEPARATED.

(SF) = SUNFLOWERS
(J) = JERUSALEM ARTICHOKES
(T) = TOBACCO
(GT) = GROUND TOMATOES
(G) = GOURDS
(S) = SUMMER SQUASH
(A) = ACORN SQUASH
(S) = BUTTERNUT SQUASH

HILL GROUP A

HILL GROUP C

HILL GROUP B

HILL GROUP D

(C) = SWEET CORN
(A) = FLINT CORN
(C) = FLOUR CORN
(PC) = POPCORN
(B) = POLE BEANS
(P) = PUMPKIN

24'

20'

PLANTING NOTES:

REFER TO THE SEED PACKETS FOR THE DEPTH OF PLANTING, DISTANCE BETWEEN SEEDS, AND
   THE BEST TIME FOR PLANTING IN YOUR SECTION OF NEW ENGLAND.
SINCE SUNFLOWERS AND JERUSALEM ARTICHOKES REACH CONSIDERABLE HEIGHTS, PLANT AT THE
   NORTH END OF THE GARDEN TO PREVENT THE SHADING OF OTHER PLANTS.
TOBACCO, A SACRED PLANT, SHOULD HAVE ITS OWN SPECIAL CORNER.
EACH HILL IS A STOREHOUSE OF CONCENTRATED NUTRITION. FOR THE BRISTLE OF CORN, BEANS,
   SQUASH, AND PUMPKINS, A SUBSTITUTE FOR THE INDIANS' FISH FERTILIZER MAY BE
   NECESSARY. LAYERS OF DECAYED MULCHED LEAVES, GRASS CLIPPINGS, SEAWEED, AND GARBAGE,
   ALTERNATING WITH A THIN LAYER OF SOIL, SHOULD BE PREPARED THE PREVIOUS SUMMER.
   HEAT, MOISTURE, AND AN OCCASIONAL MIXING TO PROVIDE AIR WILL YIELD A RICH, CRUMBLY
   AND DARK BROWN COMPOST FOR THE HILLS.
THE HILLS ACT AS DIRT ISLANDS TO PREVENT THE CROSS POLLINATION OF SQUASH, PUMPKINS, AND
   GOURDS. MONGREL SEEDS YIELD UNPLEASANT SURPRISES AT NEXT YEAR'S PLANTING.
IF SPACE IS LIMITED, REDUCE THE NUMBER OF HILLS AND NOT THE SPACE BETWEEN HILLS.
   SQUASH AND PUMPKINS NEED ELBOWROOM.
KEEP THE GROUND TOMATOES AND JERUSALEM ARTICHOKES TO THEIR OWN SECTIONS TO PREVENT
   THE NEED FOR RESEEDING THE REST OF THE GARDEN.
GOURD VINES GROW TO GREAT LENGTHS. PROVIDE A ROUGH WATTLE FENCE FOR SUPPORT
   AND TO ALLOW THE FRUIT TO HANG FREELY FOR SYMMETRICAL DEVELOPMENT.

WATTLE FENCE ~
POUND 4-FOOT STAKES, EACH ABOUT 1½ INCHES
IN DIAMETER, IN A ROW. LEAVE ABOUT 10 INCHES
BETWEEN THE UPRIGHTS. THEN, NEAR THE GROUND,
WEAVE FRESHLY CUT HORIZONTAL SAPLINGS, GRAPE-
VINES, OR BRANCHES BETWEEN THE STAKES. WORK
UPWARD WITH EACH WEAVING. THE TOP WEAVE MAY
BE SECURED WITH FRESH STRIPS OF SAPLING BARK
OR TWINE. SAPLINGS MAY HAVE WANT OF THINNING
TOWARD THE BUTT ENDS TO INCREASE FLEXIBILITY.

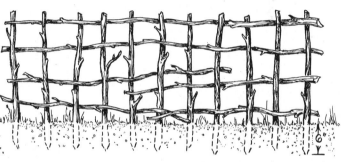

Actually, the hills in the original Indian gardens were placed irregularly
and not in the straight rows of the colonists and in our example~ but then
planting space was not at a premium with the Algonquians. Roger Williams gave
an indication of the family garden size when he wrote that "the women of
a family will commonly raise two or three heaps [of corn] of twelve, fifteene,
or twentie bushells a heap, which they drie in round broad heaps; and if
she have helpe of her children or friends, much more."

AFTER THE HARVEST

Fresh corn on the cob ~ no need for details for boiling this ageless summer
treat. But try roasted sweet corn, still in its husk, over the next campfire.
Green corn, boiled or roasted, was an Indian favorite. Early harvesting allowed
for a second planting

ROASTING CORN ~ DIG A SHALLOW TRENCH
AND FILL IT WITH ENOUGH DRIED STICKS TO
MAKE A HOT FIRE. REMOVE ONLY THE
OUTER HUSKS AND LAY A ROW OF CORN
DIRECTLY ON THE EMBERS. USING A FRESHLY CUT STICK, TURN EACH EAR WHEN THE INNER
HUSKS BECOME SCORCHED. CONTINUE THE ROTATION UNTIL THE HUSKS ARE COMPLETELY BROWN.
REMOVE THE HUSKS WHEN COOL ENOUGH.

91

Ripe corn was husked and dried in the sun on mats or bark sheets. Still on the cob, it was buried in a large basket with mats covering the top and sides. Shortly after landing on Cape Cod in 1620, Willoughby wrote, the Pilgrims found just such a cache and described one of the baskets as "round and narrow at the top, it held about three or four Bushels, which was as much as two of us could lift up from the ground, and was very handsomely and cunningly made." The kernels could be easily stripped from the cob with a hand, for winter eating.

Green, unripe corn was boiled on the ear and dried in the sun.

Nocake, or Nókehick, was defined by William Wood in this way: "It is Indian corn parched in the hot ashes, the ashes being sifted from it; it is afterwards beaten to powder and put into a leatherne bag trussed at the Indian's backe like a knapsacke, out of which they take three spoonful a day." Baked corn meal on the trail was known as "journey cake" or "jonny-cake."

BRIEFLY, THIS PARCHING PROCESS BEGAN WHEN THE FIRE WAS REDUCED TO HOT COALS. THEY WERE RAKED AWAY AND A ROW OF FRESH UNHUSKED CORN LAID ON THE HOT GROUND. DEAD ASHES WERE THEN RAKED OVER THE CORN, THEN THE WHOLE WAS COVERED WITH HOT COALS. A HOT FIRE WAS REBUILT AND THE EARS ROASTED FOR ABOUT FIFTEEN MINUTES. WHEN COOL ENOUGH, THE HUSKS WERE REMOVED, THE KERNELS WERE STRIPPED FREE AND POWDERED TO MEAL IN A MORTAR AND PESTLE.

Samp, or Nasàump was described by Roger Williams as "a kind of meale pottage, unparch'd. From this the English call their Samp, which is the Indian corne, beaten and boild." New Englanders know it today as hulled corn or hominy. Air-dried corn was used "unparch'd."

Flint corn was preferred to dent and sweet corn, for the hard kernel coverings (hulls) did not disintegrate in the removal process. Boiled hardwood ashes yielded an alkaline solution, known as lye, that could loosen the hulls. If too strong, this caustic solution could burn the skin~ and no doubt the women of the tribe were well aware of this risk.

A HALF-PINT OF HARDWOOD ASHES IN A GALLON OF WATER, WILL BE STRONG ENOUGH TO DO THE JOB. BOIL THE MIXTURE FOR FORTY-FIVE MINUTES. AFTER LETTING IT STAND FOR SEVERAL HOURS, POUR OFF THE LYE INTO A COOKING POT. THEN ADD THE AIR-DRIED KERNELS TO THE LYE AND BOIL THE MIXTURE FOR ABOUT FORTY-FIVE MINUTES. POUR OFF THE LIQUID (WITH CARE! DISCARD IT IN A HOLE AND COVER WITH DIRT) AND RINSE THE CORN WITH SEVERAL WASHINGS OF WATER. WHILE THE CORN IS STILL IN THE THE RINSE WATER, SEPARATE THE HULLS BY RUBBING THE KERNELS BETWEEN BOTH HANDS. THE HULLS SHOULD FLOAT TO THE SURFACE, WHERE THEY CAN BE SCOOPED OFF AND DISCARDED. SEVERAL MORE RINSES IN WATER SHOULD REMOVE ANY REMAINING LYE. DRAIN THE HULLED KERNELS AND SUN-DRY.

SIMPLE INDIAN COOKING

Little more than a brisk campfire can change the Indian garden harvest into some fine eating.

ASHCAKES

SCRAPE GREEN SWEET CORN FROM THE COB, MASH IN THE MORTAR, AND SHAPE INTO CAKES THAT RESEMBLE SMALL CORN EARS. SPRINKLE WITH FINE CORN MEAL AND WRAP EACH CAKE IN A FRESH CORNHUSK. BAKE IN THE ASHES, MUCH LIKE ROASTING FRESH CORN.

OR~ MIX CORN MEAL, SALT, AND WATER INTO A THICK PASTE. PAT INTO CAKES, WRAP IN FRESH HUSKS AND BAKE FOR ABOUT FORTY MINUTES, TURNING ONCE. SOMETIMES THE CAKES WERE PLACED ON THE HEARTHSTONES OR THE FLATTENED GLOBS WERE STUCK ON AN UPRIGHT RED-OAK BOARD FOR FIRESIDE BAKING. DRIED BERRIES WERE SOMETIMES MIXED INTO MEAL BEFORE BAKING.

JOURNEY CAKES

(jonny-cakes or johnnycakes) Flint or flour corn was ground to meal in a mortar. Lacking this, Kenyon's Grist Mill in Usquepaugh, Rhode Island, can supply the authentic flint corn meal - and has done so for three centuries.

POUR A CUP OF MEAL INTO A BOWL WITH A TEASPOON OF SALT AND A TABLESPOON OF MAPLE SYRUP OR HONEY. ADD ENOUGH BOILING WATER TO MAKE A STIFF DOUGH (A GLOB SHOULD DROP OFF THE MIXING SPOON WITH EASE). FRY SOME BACON STRIPS AND USE THE GREASE FOR SLOW-FRYING THE CAKES, 6 MINUTES TO A SIDE. FLANKED WITH THE CRISP BACON AND COVERED WITH MAPLE SYRUP, THE CAKES WILL MAKE A BREAKFAST TO REMEMBER.

POPCORN

Popped corn, gift-wrapped in buckskin, was presented by the Wampanoags to the Pilgrims at the first Thanksgiving. And about 1630, Governor Winthrop's journal took note of this corn treat. When the corn was "parched," he recorded that it turned inside out and was "white and floury within."

IT IS SAID THAT THE INDIANS SOMETIMES POPPED THEIR CORN BY RUNNING A STICK THROUGH THE COB AND HOLDING IT OVER THE FIRE. BETTER YET, WARM A HEAVY PAN OR HEAVY SKILLET. POUR IN $\frac{1}{4}$ CUP OF COOKING OIL, FOLLOWED BY ENOUGH KERNELS TO COVER THE BOTTOM OF THE PAN. COVER AND SHAKE GENTLY. REMOVE THE PAN FROM THE HEAT WHEN THE LAST POP IS HEARD, AND EMPTY THE CONTENTS INTO A LARGE BUTTERED BOWL. THE INDIANS FAVORED POURING HOT MAPLE SYRUP OVER THE POPPED CORN. WE KNOW IT TODAY AS CRACKER JACK.

SAMP PORRIDGE

A hot cereal or potato substitute.

COVER THE DRIED HULLED CORN WITH WATER OVERNIGHT. THE CORN WILL SWELL TO SEVERAL TIMES ITS SIZE, SO START WITH $\frac{1}{2}$ CUP OF CORN. DRAIN OFF THE WATER THE FOLLOWING DAY AND ADD $1\frac{1}{2}$ CUPS OF WATER, A TEASPOON OF SALT, AND A TEASPOON OF HONEY. BRING TO A BOIL, THEN SIMMER FOR SEVERAL HOURS. STIR OCCASIONALLY. ADD WATER AS NEEDED TO PREVENT BURNING AND TO MAKE A THIN PUDDING.

OR~ GRIND $\frac{1}{2}$ CUP OF DRY HULLED CORN IN THE MORTAR. BOIL $2\frac{1}{2}$ CUPS OF WATER IN A POT, THEN STIR IN THE MEAL AND A TEASPOON OF SALT AND A TEASPOON OF HONEY OR MAPLE SYRUP. IN ABOUT 20 MINUTES, THE WATER WILL HAVE BEEN ABSORBED BY THE MEAL AND THE PORRIDGE WILL BE READY FOR EATING WITH BUTTER.

SAMP CAKES

MAKE AN EXTRA BATCH OF BOILED SAMP PORRIDGE AND POUR INTO A GREASED PAN TO A DEPTH OF ABOUT $\frac{1}{2}$ INCH. CHILL OVERNIGHT, THEN CUT INTO CAKES. FRY IN BACON FAT AND EAT WITH BUTTER (AND THOSE STRIPS OF CRISP BACON, OF COURSE) OR SMOTHER IN MAPLE SYRUP.

SUCCOTASH

BOIL KIDNEY BEANS FOR SEVERAL HOURS WITH DICED PORK (BEAR FAT WAS PREFERRED, BUT YOU MAY JUST NOT HAVE ANY HANDY). ADD AN EQUAL AMOUNT OF FRESH SWEET CORN SCRAPED FROM THE COB. THE MOHEGANS ARE SAID TO HAVE THROWN IN THE STRIPPED COBS AS WELL, TO BOIL OUT THE REMAINING CORN MILK. BOIL FOR 20 MINUTES MORE TO GIVE A THICK STEW. ADD SEASONING.

EARLIER POTS (A.D. 300 TO 1600) HAD POINTED BOTTOMS TO REST IN THE GROUND. THE FIRE WAS BUILT AROUND THE BASE. AFTER THAT TIME, THE NECK OF THE POT WAS CONSTRICTED. FROM THIS, IT COULD BE SUSPENDED BY THONGS. MANY OF THE TRADITIONAL MEALS BEGAN IN SUCH CONTAINERS.

STEW

STRICTLY SPEAKING, ANY ADDITIONS TO THE SUCCOTASH MAKE IT A STEW. IT WAS A CATCHALL, AS GOOKIN EXPLAINED IN SOME DETAIL:

"THEIR FOOD IS GENERALLY BOILED MAIZE OR INDIAN CORN MIXED WITH KIDNEYBEANS, OR SOMETIMES WITHOUT. ALSO THEY FREQUENTLY BOIL WITH THIS POTTAGE FISH AND FLESH OF ALL SORTS, EITHER TAKEN NEW OR DRIED, AS SHADS, EELS, ALEWIVES OR A KIND OF HERRING, OR ANY OTHER SORT OF FISH. BUT THEY DRY MOSTLY THOSE SORTS MENTIONED. THESE THEY CUT IN PIECES, BONES AND ALL, AND BOIL THEM IN THE AFORESAID POTTAGE. I HAVE WONDERED MANY TIMES THAT THEY WERE NOT IN DANGER OF BEING CHOAKED WITH FISH BONES; BUT THEY ARE SO DEXTEROUS TO SEPARATE THE BONES FROM THE FISH IN THE EATING THEREOF, THAT THEY ARE IN NO HAZARD. ALSO THEY BOIL IN THIS FURMENTY ALL SORTS OF FLESH, THEY TAKE IN HUNTING ··· CUTTING THIS FLESH IN SMALL PIECES, AND BOILING IT AS AFORESAID. ALSO THEY MIX WITH THE SAID POTTAGE SEVERAL SORTS OF ROOTS, AND POMPIONS, AND SQUASHES, AND ALSO SEVERAL SORTS OF NUTS OR MASTS, AS OAK ACORNS, CHESTNUTS, WALNUTS: THESE HUSKED AND DRIED, AND POWDERED, THEY THICKEN THEIR POTTAGE THEREWITH."

CLAMBAKE

You'll need:

SOFT-SHELL CLAMS (STEAMERS) WITH QUAHOGS AND MUSSELS, $\frac{1}{2}^{+}$ POUND/PERSON
FLATFISH (SWORDFISH, FLOUNDER, MACKEREL) CUT INTO SMALL PIECES, $\frac{1}{2}$ POUND/PERSON
LOBSTER~ IF AFFORDABLE ~ PLUS LOBSTER FORKS
JERUSALEM ARTICHOKES OR SWEET POTATOES, 1/PERSON
SMALL WHITE ONIONS, PEELED, 2~3/PERSON
FRESH, UNHUSKED SWEET CORN, 2/PERSON
WATERMELON ON ICE
WINE, BEER, COFFEE~ OR INDIAN SUMAC DRINK
BUTTER, SALT, PEPPER, AND PICKLES
PLENTY OF PAPER NAPKINS~ IT'S JUICY EATING!
ASH CAKES OR CRACKERS
CHEESECLOTH BAGS FOR INDIVIDUAL SERVINGS
 (HARDLY AUTHENTIC!)
CLAM RAKE AND BASKETS
1 SEASHORE
SHOVEL AND RAKE
PLENTY OF HARDWOOD
FIRE PERMIT, IF REQUIRED
TARPAULIN OR HEAVY CANVAS

$\frac{1}{4}$ X $\frac{1}{2}$ X

STAGHORN SUMAC "LEMONADE" ~
COLLECT THE RIPE, RUBY-RED, AND
FUZZY BERRY CLUSTERS (POISON SUMAC
HAS WHITISH-GRAY DROOPING BERRIES).
CRUSH 10~15 RIPE BERRY CLUSTERS AND
DROP INTO SEVERAL QUARTS OF WATER.
STRAIN THE LIQUID THROUGH SEVERAL LAYERS
OF CHEESECLOTH. SWEETEN TO TASTE, CHILL,
AND SERVE.

CLAM BAKE TIMETABLE ~

THE DAY BEFORE THE BAKE, DIG THE CLAMS. SCOUT THE MUD FLATS AT LOW TIDE AND POUND THE BACK OF THE CLAM RAKE ON THE MUD. THE CLAMS SHOULD SHOW THEIR WHEREABOUTS BY SQUIRTING. SCRUB OFF THE SAND AND RINSE SEVERAL TIMES IN SEA-WATER. DISCARD ANY THAT FLOAT OR HAVE BROKEN SHELLS. COVER WITH FRESH SEAWATER AND ADD $\frac{1}{2}$ CUP OF CORN MEAL FOR EVERY 2 QUARTS OF WATER. LEFT STANDING OVERNIGHT, THE CLAMS WILL EXCHANGE INTERNAL GRIT AND WASTES FOR THE CORN. QUAHOGS ARE ALSO HARVESTED AT LOW TIDE. SOME USE A LONG-HANDLED QUAHOG RAKE, BUT YOU REALLY SHOULD TRY THE AGE-OLD WAY~ TREADING. BOTH FEET ARE TWISTED PARALLEL TO EACH OTHER, WORKING A PATH (USUALLY WHILE KNEE- OR WAIST-DEEP) DOWN TO ABOUT AN INCH BELOW THE SEABED SURFACE. THE QUAHOG IS ON END, AND THE FEEL OF THE ROUNDED EDGE IS UNMISTAKABLE. WASH IN SEAWATER. ALTHOUGH QUAHOGS ARE LESS APT TO BE GRITTY, THE CORN MEAL MAY BE ADDED, AS WITH THE CLAMS.
 FOUR HOURS BEFORE SERVING, GIVE EVERYONE A JOB ~ GUARANTEED TO BUILD AN

APPETITE :

DIG A HOLE IN THE SAND 1~2 FEET DEEP AND 2~3 FEET IN DIAMETER ~ DEPENDING ON THE SIZE OF THE BAKE. LINE WITH LARGE SMOOTH, AND FLAT ROCKS TO A DEPTH OF ABOUT 6 INCHES (THE ROCKS SHOULD NOT HAVE BEEN BAKED BEFORE). BUILD A HARDWOOD FIRE ON THE ROCK-LINED PIT, FEEDING IT AS NECESSARY FOR THE NEXT $2\frac{1}{2}$~3 HOURS.

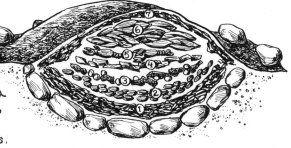

SEND OUT A SEARCH PARTY FOR MUSSELS. THEY GROW ON THE ROCKS AND ARE GATHERED AT LOW TIDE (THEY SPOIL IF NOT COOKED ON COLLECTION DAY). SCRUB WITH A STIFF BRUSH AND COVER WITH SEA WATER.

OUT GOES ANOTHER PARTY TO GATHER ABOUT 2 BUSHELS OF ROCK SEAWEED ~ THE KIND WITH SMALL RUBBERY AIR FLOATS THAT POP ON SQUEEZING. IT GIVES THE SALTWATER FLAVOR, PROTECTS THE FOOD FROM BURNING, AND PROVIDES THE MOISTURE FOR THE STEAM.

THE LAYERS ~ FROM BOTTOM UP ~
1. SEAWEED
2. CLAMS, QUAHOGS, MUSSELS
3. JERUSALEM ARTICHOKES, SWEET POTATOES, AND ONIONS
4. FLAT FISH (CHICKEN OR SAUSAGE IF YOU WISH)
5. LOBSTERS AND CRABS
6. CORN~ REMOVE OUTER HUSKS AND SILK
7. SEAWEED

AN HOUR BEFORE SERVING, RAKE THE EMBERS FROM THE PIT. LINE THE HOT ROCKS WITH 6 INCHES OF WET SEAWEED. ON THIS, PLACE THE LAYERS OF FOOD. SOME PREFER TO SEPARATE THE LAYERS WITH THE OUTER CORN HUSKS OR SEAWEED; OTHERS LIKE TO PACKAGE THE INDIVIDUAL SERVINGS IN CHEESECLOTH ~ PERHAPS THE SHELLFISH, FISH, ARTICHOKES, AND ONIONS~ FOR EASE IN DISTRIBUTING. AT ANY RATE, SPRINKLE IT ALL WITH A BUCKET OF SEA WATER AND COVER WITH WET CANVAS ANCHORED WITH ROCKS.

IT'S SERVING TIME IF THE CLAMS ARE OPEN AND THE LOBSTER IS BRIGHT RED AND THE LEGS PULL OFF EASILY. SERVE BEER, WINE, OR SUMAC "LEMONADE" WITH THE MEAL AND WATERMELON AND COFFEE FOR DESSERT; EXCEPT FOR THE SUMAC DRINK, THE BEER, WINE AND WATERMELON ARE COLONIAL ADDITIONS.

JERUSALEM ARTICHOKES

WASH WELL AND WRAP IN CORN HUSKS (OR HEAVY ALUMINUM FOIL). PLACE IN THE HOT COALS FOR 8 MINUTES, THEN TURN AND ROAST FOR 8 MINUTES MORE. BUTTER AND SALT AS ONE WOULD A POTATO.

HOT PUMPKIN SEEDS

PLACE THE RAW SEEDS IN A FOIL-LINED SHALLOW PAN. ADD 1 TABLESPOON OF VEGETABLE OIL FOR EACH CUP OF SEEDS, THEN SPRINKLE ON SALT AND GARLIC POWDER. BAKE FOR 10~15 MINUTES IN A 350-DEGREE OVEN. SEEDS WILL MAKE A POPPING NOISE WHEN READY.

SQUASH

COMPLETELY COVER THE WHOLE SQUASH WITH HOT CAMPFIRE COALS. AFTER 10 MINUTES, TEST THE SQUASH HIDE WITH A WOOD SPLINTER. KEEP TESTING UNTIL THE MEAT IS TENDER. IT'S READY TO EAT (THE INDIANS ATE THE SEEDS AND ALL) AFTER SEASONING.

🍁 MAPLE SUGARING

When winter snows gave way to the fresh smell of spring the Algonquian sugar-bush camps were alive with activity. According to Mohegan lore, the snow melt-off was the oil of the slain Great Celestial Bear that started the maple sap run. Certainly the sugar maples (Acer saccharum Marsh.) were the best known and most utilized, but the Indians had no hesitation about tapping the red maple (Acer rubrum L.) and its other relatives. Also occasionally adding their sap to the boiling kettle were the black birch (Betula lenta), yellow birch (Betula lutea), and the white birch (Betula papyrifera). The sap from these sweet-flowing trees would later flavor the Indian garden harvest.

SUGAR MAPLE

The warm days and frosty nights began in early March (not that New England's changeable weather had any set schedule to keep!) and continued about a month and a half. The clear, sweet sap flowed down a large "Y" that was slashed through the tree bark and out a spile inserted at its base. Frequently this spout was a stick with a pithy center ~ one that could be reamed without benefit of drilling. Stag-horn sumac and elderberry answered this need well. Other spiles were of curved slippery-elm branches with a "V" cut from their upper surface.

The "sugaring off" continued day and night. Toward dusk, when the sap flow had diminished, the collection buckets were carried in and added to the boiling kettle. If the bubbling became too rapid, it was stopped by whisking a branch of spruce through the froth. By early morning the sap had thickened to syrup and was ready for straining. Woven basswood mats ~ later a coarse burlaplike cloth ~ were used as filters. Then it was back to a slow heating in freshly scrubbed kettles. The thickening syrup was carefully stirred with a long paddle (of maple wood, naturally). At the proper moment, the molten sugar was poured into a basswood trough ~ crafted much like a small dugout canoe ~ and worked with the paddle to prevent lumping. The warm sugar was then packed into bark buckets for storage.

GRANULATING LADLE ¼ X

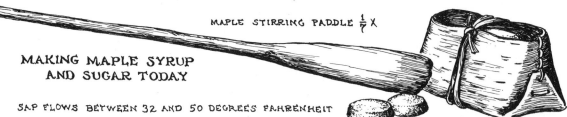

MAPLE STIRRING PADDLE ⅐ X

MAPLE SUGAR CAKES AND STORAGE BOX

MAKING MAPLE SYRUP AND SUGAR TODAY

SAP FLOWS BETWEEN 32 AND 50 DEGREES FAHRENHEIT TO PRODUCE THE LARGEST YIELD. BUT THE BEST, OR "FIRST RUN," SAP IS COLLECTED BETWEEN THE FIRST THAW AND THE SWELLING OF LEAF BUDS. THE SUGAR MAPLE BY ALL ODDS HAS THE HIGHEST SUGAR CONTENT.

ONE TAP
12"

TWO TAPS
18'

THREE TAPS
22"

A SINGLE TAP SHOULD BE ON THE SOUTH SIDE, WHERE THE SAP FLOWS BEST IN THE SUN'S WARMTH. FOR MORE THAN ONE TAP, PICK THE SIDES WITH THE MOST LIMBS, FOR MORE SAP IS DRAWN TO THEM. THE DIAMETER OF THE TREE DETERMINES THE NUMBER OF TAPS.

DRILLING ~ RATHER THAN SLASHING THE BARK INDIAN FASHION, USE A DRILL WITH A $\frac{7}{16}$ TO $\frac{1}{2}$-INCH BIT. DRILL ON A SLIGHTLY UPWARD SLANT TO A DEPTH OF ABOUT 2 INCHES. THE HOLE HEIGHT MAY VARY FROM 2 TO 3 INCHES ABOVE THE GROUND. A LOWER TAP WORKS BEST WHEN USING A COLLECTING BUCKET ON THE GROUND. CLEAN OUT THE HOLE WITH A JACKKNIFE.

SPILES OR SPOUTS – TRY THE STAGHORN (RED) SUMAC – IT'S EVERYWHERE.

THE PITHY CENTER OF A DRY
BRANCH REAMS OUT NICELY
WITH A RED-HOT, WOODEN-HANDLED
COAT HANGER WIRE. PUSH IT AS FAR
AS POSSIBLE, HEAT IT AGAIN, AND
ATTACK THE OTHER END OF THE
BRANCH. REPEAT UNTIL THE HOLE
IS OPENED TO ROUGHLY $\frac{1}{4}$ INCH
IN DIAMETER. TAPER ONE END

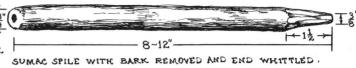

SUMAC SPILE WITH BARK REMOVED AND END WHITTLED.

PARTIALLY SPLIT SPILE WITH "V" GROOVE.

AS SHOWN AND TAP ONLY HALF WAY SO THAT THE FLOW OF THE SAP WILL NOT BE
STOPPED. ELDERBERRY PRODUCES DECENT SPILES AS WELL, AND BIRCH AND BALSAM WOOD ALSO
SEE SERVICE.

WHEN THE SUGARING SEASON IS OVER, THE SPILES ARE REMOVED. ALTHOUGH SOME
PLUG THE HOLES, THE TREE SHOULD HEAL THESE SMALL WOUNDS WITHOUT DIFFICULTY.

COLLECTING BUCKETS – SIMPLE BIRCH- OR ELM-BARK BUCKETS MAY BE CRAFTED AS SHOWN IN
THE "BARK CONTAINERS" SECTION P. 67. PROTECT THE SAP WITH A BARK
COVERING, LEAVING A GAP FOR THE SPILE DRIP.
LACKING BARK, WELL-SCRUBBED #10 TIN CANS OR
MOST ANY CONTAINER WILL DO. COVER WITH A
PIECE OF WOOD WITH A 4-INCH-SQUARE OPENING
TO CATCH THE DRIP AND TO KEEP OUT THE RAIN,
SNOW, TWIGS, AND OTHER FOREST DEBRIS.

BOILING KETTLE – THE INDIANS PRIZED THE LARGE CAST-IRON KETTLES TRADED FROM THE
COLONISTS. TODAY, A GALVANIZED WASHTUB OR A LARGE TURKEY-ROASTING PAN WILL
DO, BUT IT SHOULD HOLD AT LEAST FIVE GALLONS OF SAP. FOR OUTDOOR BOILING, THE
SIDES SHOULD BE HIGH ENOUGH TO PROTECT THE BOILING SAP FROM SMOKE OR SOOT.
OTHERWISE A DARK SAP WITH A POOR, SMOKY FLAVOR WILL REWARD YOUR EFFORTS.

IF AN INDOOR STOVE IS TO BE USED FOR THE BOILING, A LARGE SHALLOW PAN
WILL DO. SINCE THE SYRUP WILL SCORCH WHEN THE LEVEL IS DOWN TO ABOUT
$\frac{1}{2}$ INCH, TRANSFER IT TO A SAUCEPAN OR ADD MORE SAP. INDOOR BOILING DOES
HAVE ITS HORROR STORIES, BUT AT LEAST ONE SUGARING-OFF AUTHORITY,
MILTON WEND, ASSURES US THAT THE WALLPAPER WON'T UNPEEL IN YOUR LAP, THANKS
TO THE HUMIDITY RESISTANCE OF MODERN WALLPAPER PASTE.

FIREPLACE – BRICKS, ROCKS, OR CINDER BLOCKS MAKE A SUITABLE TEMPORARY FIRE-
PLACE. BUILD IT WITH SIDES CLOSE ENOUGH TO SUPPORT THE KETTLE. A
CHIMNEY IS A MUST TO SIDETRACK THE SMOKE. A 4-FOOT STOVEPIPE OR HOLLOW CEMENT
BLOCKS WILL DO IT. A HALF-CORD OF WOOD SHOULD BE MORE THAN ENOUGH FOR A
SMALL-SCALE SUGARING STINT.

MAPLE SYRUP – THIS IS THE TASTY THICKENED SAP THAT STOPS SHORT OF
BECOMING MAPLE SUGAR. FILL THE KETTLE WITH SAP TO ABOUT
TWO-THIRDS OF ITS DEPTH. STIR WITH A WOODEN PADDLE, AND ADD
FRESH SAP AS THE WATER EVAPORATES. THERE'S A GOOD DEAL
OF ADDING AHEAD, FOR IT TAKES ABOUT TEN GALLONS OF SAP
TO MAKE A QUART OF MAPLE SYRUP. IF THE BOILING
THREATENS TO FOAM UP AND OVERFLOW, TOSS IN A TINY DAB
OF BUTTER OR FAT OR PERHAPS A FEW DROPS OF CREAM.
THE FOAM WILL VANISH WITH THE SPEED THAT WOULD DO
CREDIT TO A MEDICINE MAN'S MAGIC.

AN "APRON" FORMS
WHEN THE MAPLE
SYRUP NEEDS NO
FURTHER BOILING.

THE END POINT OF SYRUP MAKING IS AT HAND WHEN THE SYRUP
FLOWS, OR "APRONS," FROM THE PADDLE OR SPOON. IT'S BACK TO THE BOILING IF SEPARATE
DROPS FORM INSTEAD. OR TEST WITH A DROP OF THE SYRUP BETWEEN THE THUMB
AND FINGER – IT SHOULD DRAW TO A THREAD.

AT THIS POINT, THE SYRUP MUST BE RID OF NITER, OR "SUGAR SAND" – WHITISH-GRAY
GLOBS OF LIME THAT PRECIPITATES TO GIVE A BITTER TASTE. IT WILL CAKE THE SIDES
ANY NITER THAT BUBBLES TO THE SURFACE SHOULD BE SKIMMED OFF. THERE ARE TWO WAYS
TO REMOVE THE REMAINING NITER FROM THE SYRUP:

1. FILTERING~USE SEVERAL LAYERS OF FLANNEL, FELT, OR A PIECE OF WORN BLANKET. FILTER INTO A LARGE POT OR CAN (A MILK CAN IS IDEAL, FOR THE FILTER CAN BE TIED TO THE NARROW NECK).

2. SETTLING~INSTEAD OF FILTERING, JUST LET THE SYRUP COOL IN THE KETTLE. THE CLEAR SYRUP CAN THEN BE POURED FREE OF THE SETTLED NITER. REHEAT THE SYRUP TO THE BOILING POINT.

WITH EITHER THE FILTERING OR THE SETTLING METHOD, POUR THE HOT SYRUP INTO CLEAN CANS (USED MAPLE SYRUP CONTAINERS, COFFEE CANS WITH PLASTIC LIDS, AND THE LIKE) WITH AS LITTLE AIR AS POSSIBLE. GLASS CONTAINERS ARE BEST FORGOTTEN~ IF THE SYRUP CRYSTALLIZES, THEY MAY BREAK.

GUM SUGAR, MAPLE TAFFY, OR MAPLE WAX~ THIS GUMMY SWEET WAS PRIZED BY THE INDIANS. WHEN A LONG, THIN STRING OF SYRUP RAN FROM THE PADDLE OR SPOON (BEFORE THE APRONING, WHEN THE SYRUP HAD GRAINED TO SUGAR), IT WAS POURED UNSTIRRED ONTO SNOW. WHEN COLD, THE GUM SUGAR WAS WRAPPED IN PACKETS OF BIRCH BARK. TODAY, IT IS POURED IN SMALL AMOUNTS ONTO SNOW AND THE GOLDEN GLOBULES EATEN WITH SOUR PICKLES TO BETTER APPRECIATE THE SWEET TREAT.

INDIAN "ICE CREAM CONE" WITH A BIRCH-BARK CONE HOLDING SNOW AND GUM SUGAR.

MAPLE SUGAR IS NOTHING MORE THAN SYRUP BOILED A BIT LONGER TO BECOME CRYSTALLINE. THIS WAS THE END RESULT OF THE INDIANS' SUGARING OFF AND COULD BE STORED WITHOUT SPOILAGE FOR THE COMING MONTHS.

NOW IF THERE IS NO SUGAR BUSH OR MAPLE GROVE HANDY, BUY SOME GRADE "B" SYRUP. THIS POOR GRADE WILL MAKE EXCELLENT SUGAR.~ONE PINT YIELDS A POUND OF SUGAR. POUR INTO A PAN TO A DEPTH OF ABOUT 1 INCH. BRING TO A BOIL AND THEN DECREASE THE HEAT TO PREVENT A BOIL- OVER. ON LOW HEAT, IT SHOULD TAKE ABOUT TEN MINUTES TO HAVE THE RIGHT CONSISTENCY FOR SUGAR. TO MAKE SURE, LIFT OUT THE WOODEN SPOON UNTIL INDIVIDUAL DROPS COME OFF. LET A DROP FALL INTO A GLASS OF COLD WATER. IT SHOULD FORM A FIRM, SLIGHTLY FLATTENED BALL AT THE BOTTOM. IF THE DROP FLATTENS OUT, TEST AGAIN IN A FEW MINUTES.

REMOVE IT FROM THE HEAT AND START STIRRING THE DARK STICKY GOO. THE MORE STIRRING, THE FINER THE SUGAR CRYSTALS AND THE LIGHTER THE COLOR. CONTINUE UNTIL THE SUGAR SETS, THEN REHEAT OVER A MEDIUM FLAME. IT WILL BECOME LIQUID AGAIN IN HALF A MINUTE OR SO. AFTER ANOTHER HALF-MINUTE OF HEATING AND STIRRING, POUR THE MOLTEN SUGAR DIRECTLY INTO MOLDS. LACKING SMALL BIRCH BOXES, THE MOLDS MAY BE OF ALUMINUM FOIL OR TIN. OR YOU MAY WISH TO POUR IT INTO A SHALLOW PAN AND CUT IT INTO SMALL BLOCKS AFTER COOLING~ IT TAKES ABOUT FIFTEEN MINUTES TO COOL. THE INDIANS FILLED BIRCH CONES AS A TREAT FOR THE YOUNGSTERS.

THE SUGAR REMAINS POURABLE FOR SEVERAL MINUTES; SO HAVE THE MOLDS READY. PRESERVATION OF THIS DELICIOUS SWEET IS NOT MUCH OF A PROBLEM.~ IT DISAPPEARS RAPIDLY. BUT IT'S BEST TO COVER THE CAKES WITH A CLEAR PLASTIC WRAP TO PREVENT DRYING OUT AND HARDENING. SOME OLD-TIMERS GLAZE THE CANDY WITH HOT SYRUP TO PRESERVE THE SOFTNESS.

SUGARING~OFF PARTIES ARE A NEW ENGLAND SPECIALTY. THE GUM SUGAR IS POURED OVER TUBS OF SNOW AND THE COLD STRIPS ARE CUT INTO SECTIONS. THESE ARE PICKED OFF THE SNOW WITH FORKS AND EATEN WITH SOUR PICKLES, DOUGHNUTS, AND COFFEE. IT'S ANOTHER OF OUR TRADITIONS THAT WE OWE TO THE ALGONQUIAN PEOPLE.

THE BUDS ARE SWELLING~ SUGARING IS OVER.

FIRE BY FRICTION

Fire was produced by several methods. The rubbing stick was mentioned by such early writers as Gyles and Josselyn as having limited use throughout New England. A bit cumbersome for the trail, the rubbing stick probably saw most of its service around the wigwam hearth.

To the uninitiated, producing a fire with wood alone borders on the impossible. (Skeptics hold that the best way to make a fire with two sticks is to be sure that one of them is a match.) But there is much to be said for using the raw materials of nature in the ancient way ~ a most satisfying way to make one's campfire from "scratch."

REPRODUCING THE RUBBING STICK

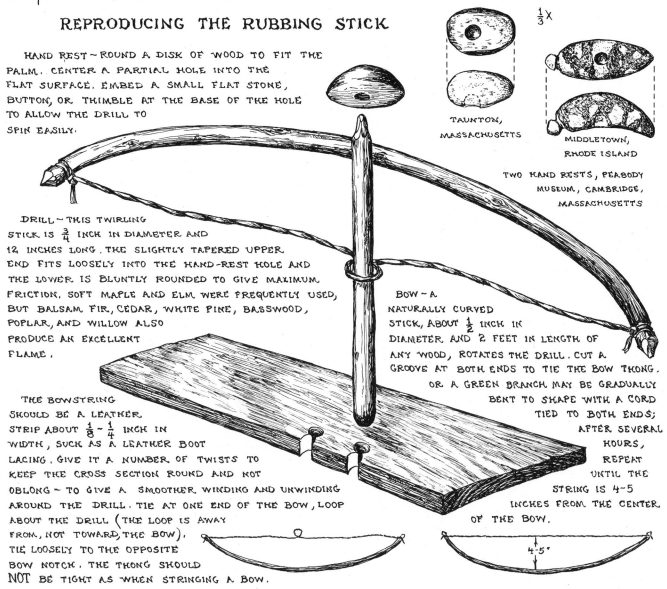

HAND REST ~ ROUND A DISK OF WOOD TO FIT THE PALM. CENTER A PARTIAL HOLE INTO THE FLAT SURFACE. EMBED A SMALL FLAT STONE, BUTTON, OR THIMBLE AT THE BASE OF THE HOLE TO ALLOW THE DRILL TO SPIN EASILY.

$\frac{1}{3}$ X

TAUNTON, MASSACHUSETTS

MIDDLETOWN, RHODE ISLAND

TWO HAND RESTS, PEABODY MUSEUM, CAMBRIDGE, MASSACHUSETTS

DRILL ~ THIS TWIRLING STICK IS $\frac{3}{4}$ INCH IN DIAMETER AND 12 INCHES LONG. THE SLIGHTLY TAPERED UPPER END FITS LOOSELY INTO THE HAND-REST HOLE AND THE LOWER IS BLUNTLY ROUNDED TO GIVE MAXIMUM FRICTION. SOFT MAPLE AND ELM WERE FREQUENTLY USED, BUT BALSAM FIR, CEDAR, WHITE PINE, BASSWOOD, POPLAR, AND WILLOW ALSO PRODUCE AN EXCELLENT FLAME.

BOW ~ A NATURALLY CURVED STICK, ABOUT $\frac{1}{2}$ INCH IN DIAMETER AND 2 FEET IN LENGTH OF ANY WOOD, ROTATES THE DRILL. CUT A GROOVE AT BOTH ENDS TO TIE THE BOW THONG. OR A GREEN BRANCH MAY BE GRADUALLY BENT TO SHAPE WITH A CORD TIED TO BOTH ENDS; AFTER SEVERAL HOURS, REPEAT UNTIL THE STRING IS 4-5 INCHES FROM THE CENTER OF THE BOW.

THE BOWSTRING SHOULD BE A LEATHER STRIP ABOUT $\frac{1}{8}$ ~ $\frac{1}{4}$ INCH IN WIDTH, SUCH AS A LEATHER BOOT LACING. GIVE IT A NUMBER OF TWISTS TO KEEP THE CROSS SECTION ROUND AND NOT OBLONG ~ TO GIVE A SMOOTHER WINDING AND UNWINDING AROUND THE DRILL. TIE AT ONE END OF THE BOW, LOOP ABOUT THE DRILL (THE LOOP IS AWAY FROM, NOT TOWARD, THE BOW), TIE LOOSELY TO THE OPPOSITE BOW NOTCH. THE THONG SHOULD NOT BE TIGHT AS WHEN STRINGING A BOW.

4-5"

FIRE BOARD ~ MAKE IT OF THE SAME WOODS AS THE DRILL. MEASUREMENTS SHOULD BE ROUGHLY $\frac{3}{8}$ TO $\frac{1}{2}$ INCH THICK, 1 FOOT LONG, AND 3 INCHES WIDE. DRILL SEVERAL SMALL HOLES $\frac{3}{8}$ INCH FROM THE EDGE OF THE BOARD. WHITTLE A ROUNDED "V" TO THE EXACT CENTER OF EACH HOLE. CONE THE HOLE SLIGHTLY AS A REST FOR THE BUSINESS END OF THE DRILL.

TINDER ~ THE INDIANS FAVORED SHREDDED RED-CEDAR BARK, WELL RUBBED BETWEEN THE

PALMS UNTIL IT WAS REDUCED TO FRAZZLED SHREDS. OTHER EXCELLENT SPARK-CATCHERS ARE SHREDDED WHITE CEDAR AND BIRCH BARK, THE INNER BARK OF CHESTNUT AND SLIPPERY ELM, DRY GRASS, AND MOSS. DRY-ROTTED WOOD MAY BE REDUCED TO POWDER FOR USE AS PUNK. SHREDDED ROPE MAKES A REASONABLE SUBSTITUTE. WHATEVER THE CHOICE, IT IS HELPFUL TO

TINDER NEST WITH CHARRED CLOTH CENTER. $\frac{2}{3}$X

MOLD THE TINDER INTO A SMALL NEST ~ WITH A BIT OF CHARRED CLOTH IN THE CENTER. FOR THE LATTER, TRY BURNING COTTON OR LINEN BEFOREHAND.

WHEN IT IS BURNING BRISKLY, SNUFF IT OUT QUICKLY BETWEEN TWO BOARDS OR BY TRAMPLING UNDER THE FEET. KEEP THE TINDER IN A WATERPROOF TIN BOX, SUCH AS AN OLD SHOE-POLISH CONTAINER, OR IN A COW-HORN TINDER BOX.

FIRE MAKING ~ CENTER THE NEST OF TINDER ON A DRY SLAB OF WOOD AND PLACE A FIRE-BOARD NOTCH DIRECTLY OVER THE TINDER. HOLD THE FIRE BOARD FIRMLY WITH THE LEFT FOOT WHILE KNEELING ON THE RIGHT KNEE. WITH THE HAND REST HELD IN THE LEFT PALM, THE ELBOW PRESSED FIRMLY AGAINST THE LEFT LEG TO KEEP THE WRIST STEADY, AND WITH THE BOW HELD IN THE RIGHT HAND, LONG AND SHORT STROKES SHOULD SHORTLY BRING A CURL OF SMOKE. PRESSING HARDER ON THE HAND REST SHOULD PRODUCE BLACK POWDER. GENTLY SET ASIDE THE BOW WHILE PICKING UP THE FIRE BOARD AND THE SLAB OF WOOD UNDERNEATH. THEN BLOW INTO THE NOTCH; THE SPREADING SPARK WILL SOON BURST INTO FLAME. IF IT'S STUBBORN, FOLD THE TINDER AROUND THE SPARK AND CONTINUE BLOWING.

STRIKE-A-LIGHT

The very workable rubbing stick was a second best where Algonquian fire-making sets were concerned. Throughout New England there is plentiful evidence of iron pyrites in ancient campsites. Indeed, Brereton, Gosnold, Morton, and Williams mentioned the percussion of these firestones. Brereton gave the specifics as observed near Buzzard's Bay: "They strike fire in this manner; everyone carrieth about him in a purse of tewed leather, a mineral stone ··· and with a flat emery stone ··· tied fast to the end of a little stick, gently he striketh on the mineral stone, and within a stroke or two, a spark falleth upon a piece of touchwood (much like our sponge in England), and with the least spark he maketh a fire presently."

Touchwood was an outgrowth of the black birch. As for the stones mentioned, they were probably iron pyrites and flint—although the striking of two lumps of iron pyrites could also yield a respectable spark. The same principle applied to the coveted colonial musket. The flint chip in the jaws was triggered forward, briskly striking the steel frizzen and throwing it up. The shower of sparks fell on the now-exposed powder in the pan, sending the flame through the touchhole to explode the powder-packed barrel. The bow and arrow were suddenly obsolete: a new use for the ancient flint and steel firemakers had arrived—for better or worse.

LOCK FROM THE MUSKET THAT KILLED KING PHILIP. MASSACHUSETTS HISTORICAL SOCIETY, BOSTON, MASSACHUSETTS

Starting a fire with the strike-a-light is unchanged

EARLY DOG LOCK MUSKET CIRCA 1630~1650
HAROLD PETERSON COLLECTION

through the centuries. A piece of flint, iron pyrites, quartz, or jasper produces sparks when struck with hardened iron-steel. An old file, broken off to a length of about 4-5 inches, works well.

FLINT CHIP

STRIKER~APTUCXET
TRADING POST,
BOURNE,
MASSACHUSETTS

ALL 1X.

WAMPANOAG STRIKER,
SEVENTEENTH CENTURY,
WARREN, RHODE ISLAND,
HAFFENREFFER MUSEUM.

LOOPED STEEL COLONIAL
STRIKER.

INDIAN MUSKET
FLINTS OF COLONIAL
MANUFACTURE

HOLD THE FIRE DIRECTLY ABOVE A NEST OF TINDER AND CHARRED CLOTH. A SHORT, BRISK, DOWNWARD STROKE OF THE FILE WILL SHOWER THE CLOTH WITH SPARKS. WHEN A SPARK CATCHES, BLOW GENTLY.

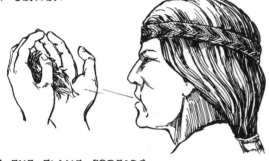

AS THE FLAME SPREADS, LOOSELY GATHER THE TINDER AROUND THE SPARK AND BLOW UNTIL THE NEST CATCHES FLAME.

IRON PYRITES
OR "FOOL'S GOLD"
(FeS_2), AS CRYSTALS,
GRAINS, OR IN MASSES. COLOR
IS YELLOW TO GREENISH BLACK.

TINDER HORN

Certainly the forest wise warrior could gather tinder as he needed it. Yet there was a real convenience in having this spark-catching material already prepared. Either way, dry tinder was a must. Horns from colonial cattle provided an answer, for any too small for a decent powder horn could make fine waterproof tinder holders. Certainly the early settlers were no strangers to them, and likely the native Americans as well. Dan Beard sketched the 1650 "Punk Horn" that follows.

A local veterinarian may have unwanted fresh horns after a dehorning session. And before any of these discards get too ripe, the inner pulp must be removed. Boil for a few minutes OUT~ DOORS, for the smell is enough to make you a social outcast with former friends and family alike. Tap the sides of the horn and the core should drop free~ or at least be removed with greater ease. The hollow horn, wet and still fragrant, should dry thoroughly on a tree branch or roof top for several days.

5±"   ½"k

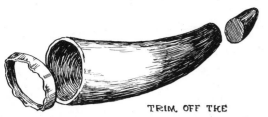

TRIM OFF THE ROUGH BUTT END WITH A HACK SAW AND THEN REMOVE ABOUT $\frac{1}{2}$ INCH OF THE TIP. SMOOTH BOTH ENDS BY RUBBING ON SANDPAPER THAT IS HELD FLAT ON A BOARD.

WHITTLE A PINE WEDGE TO FIT SNUGGLY INTO THE CAVITY. WITH THE END OF THE WEDGE HELD FIRMLY IN A VISE, DRILL A $\frac{1}{8}$-INCH HOLE CENTERED AT THE TIP END. CALCULATE THE CURVE OF THE HORN, FOR IT'S A POOR SURPRISE IF THE DRILL POINT APPEARS THROUGH THE SIDE OF THE HORN INSTEAD OF INTO THE HORN CAVITY.

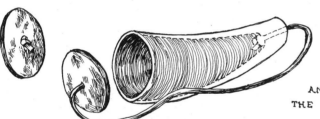

SINCE THE SIDES OF THE HORN MAY BE ROUGH AND UNEVEN, USE A WOOD RASP TO REMOVE ANY UNWANTED SURFACE. GLASS OR A WOOD SCRAPER WILL HELP REMOVE THE FILE MARKS. SMOOTH WITH COARSE TO FINE SANDPAPER.

THREAD A LENGTH OF LEATHER BOOT LACING THROUGH THE TIP, AND TIE A FIRM OVERHAND KNOT. SOAK THE KNOT AND PULL THE LACING BACK FIRMLY AGAINST THE END OF THE CAVITY.

PUNCH A SMALL HOLE THROUGH A DISK OF THICK SHOE LEATHER AND TIE ANOTHER KNOT. DAMPEN THE DISK AND PUSH IT INTO PLACE. THE PLUG SHOULD FIT SNUGGLY WHEN DRY. THE TINDER HORN SHOULD HOLD THE TINDER AND SOME PIECES OF CHARRED CLOTH ~ AND KEEP THE CONTENTS DRY.

STRIKE-A-LIGHT POUCH

Since the Indians had no pockets, pouches for small articles such as strike-a-lights, pipes, and tobacco served the purpose nicely. Buckskin pouches were often decorated with quillwork, paint, or wampum(beads) and hung from the neck by a thong or tucked under the belt.

SEW THE POUCH INSIDE OUT SO THAT STITCHING DOES NOT SHOW.

AN OLD HANDBAG MAY YIELD ENOUGH LEATHER FOR A DECENT POUCH. MEASUREMENTS ARE AVERAGE ~ ALTER AS YOU SEE FIT.

10"

-FOLD-

5"   5"

4"

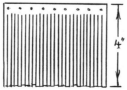

KNIVES

The Algonquian and his knife were constant companions. From the earliest days of the Paleo-Americans, survival in the New England countryside depended on its sharp edge. So common was this all-purpose tool that few of the early writers bothered to mention it. But Captain John Smith, when recording the Virginia Indians in 1612, gave some indication of the knife's versatility: "For his knife he hath the splinter of a reed to cut his feathers in forme. With this knife he will joint a Deare or any beast, shape his shooes, buskins, mantels &c."

The earlier stone knives were tools, not weapons. Finely chipped blades were sharp enough to cut meat and leather, while a coarsely flaked edge could be used for slashing off wood irregularities or sawing saplings of small diameter.

FLAKE

UP TO 2 INCHES IN LENGTH, THESE FLINT FLAKES WERE SOME-TIMES HAFTED. PALEO-AMERICAN-CERAMIC, 8500 B.C.~A.D.1676

ULU

SEMICIRCULAR SLATE. NOT CHIPPED BUT RATHER PECKED TO SHAPE AND GROUND SMOOTH. SOME, WITH HOLES, HAD LASHED HANDLES.
EARLY ARCHAIC, 5000~3000 B.C.

LEAF

SYMMETRICALLY CHIPPED EDGES. NO HANDLE NEEDED.
LATE ARCHAIC, 3000 B.C.~A.D. 300

STEMLESS

THE ROUNDED BASE WAS NOT HAFTED.
LATE ARCHAIC ~ CERAMIC, 3000 B.C.~A.D. 1676

ROUGHING KNIFE

STEM

NOTCHER

THE CHIPPED STEM WAS ALWAYS HAFTED.
LATE ARCHAIC~CERAMIC, 3000 B.C.~A.D.1676

ALTHOUGH EASILY CONFUSED WITH ARROW POINTS, THE KNIFE STEM WAS LARGER, TO FIT THE WIDTH OF THE HANDLE.

THE COARSELY CHIPPED EDGE WAS USEFUL FOR SAWING OR NOTCHING WOOD.
LATE ARCHAIC ~ CERAMIC, 3000 B.C.~A.D.1676

USED WITH A SLASHING MOTION, THE COARSE TEETH REMOVED BULGES FROM HANDLES. NO HAFTING REQUIRED.
LATE ARCHAIC ~ CERAMIC, 3000 B.C.~A.D.1676
ALL KNIVES ½ X

Not all prehistoric knives were of stone. The Lake Superior region was a treasure trove of copper nuggets. These surface finds were pounded into implements ~ but not without inter-mittent heating and cooling. Continued hammering without this annealing process would produce small cracks in the metal. A few nuggets ~ or the raw copper chunks ~ were brought into New England. They were highly prized rarities.

The native Americans knew nothing of working iron. Sixteenth-century explorers and traders first introduced the metal ~ from muskets and pots to hoes and knives. And when iron was combined with carbon, these same knife blades became exceptionally strong and held a fine cutting edge. Trade knives were high on the Algonquian "want list" and used for crafting most of the articles described on these pages. Unfortunately, the warrior also found it an efficient weapon in warfare.

KNIFE BLADES OF NATIVE COPPER FROM VERMONT WILLOUGHBY, P.114.

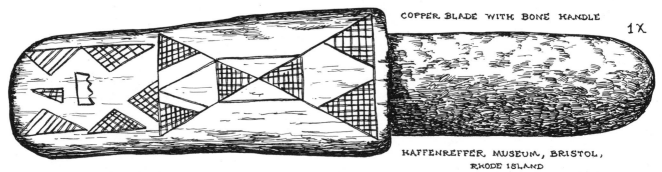

COPPER BLADE WITH BONE HANDLE

1X

HAFFENREFFER MUSEUM, BRISTOL, RHODE ISLAND

The only similarity between trade knives would seem to be their diversity. Each was as individual as the Algonquian who carried it. Perhaps local colonial blacksmiths accounted for many blade differences and the handles hafted according to the new owner's taste.

Yet some generalizing is possible. For example, eleven knives were retrieved from Burr's Hill, a seventeenth-century Wampanoag burial ground in Warren, Rhode Island. All have a straight top edge and a curved cutting edge. Those with handle fragments were either of bone or wood. Usually the bone was riveted to the tang. Wooden handles were often drilled to receive a narrow tang ~ much like that on a file.

LENGTH 9 INCHES, BLADE WIDTH 1 INCH, BONE AND STEEL

LENGTH 5½ INCHES, BLADE $\frac{5}{8}$ INCH BONE AND STEEL

THREE BURR HILL KNIFE STYLES WITH ROUGH MEASUREMENTS

LENGTH 7½ INCHES, BLADE WIDTH 1¼ INCHES, WOOD AND SHEET BRASS

REPRODUCING THE KNIFE

COMMERCIAL HACK SAW KNIFE

REMEMBER ~ A KNIFE CAN BE A FAITHFUL FRIEND OR A FEARFUL ENEMY, DEPENDING ON ITS CAREFUL OR CARELESS USE.

Worn-out blades had a second lease on life, for Indian and Yankee alike were make-do-or-do-without experts. And don't overlook worn-out blades from handsaws, knives, and power lawn mowers.

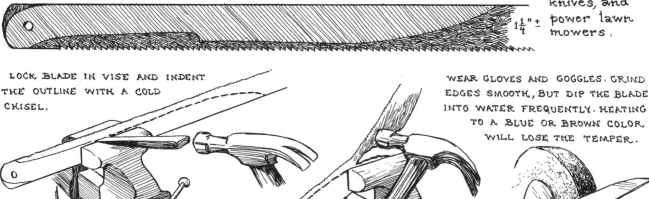

1¼"±

LOCK BLADE IN VISE AND INDENT THE OUTLINE WITH A COLD CHISEL.

WEAR GLOVES AND GOGGLES. GRIND EDGES SMOOTH, BUT DIP THE BLADE INTO WATER FREQUENTLY. HEATING TO A BLUE OR BROWN COLOR WILL LOSE THE TEMPER.

BREAK OFF EXCESS, CLAMPING VISE BELOW THE CENTER OF IMPACT.

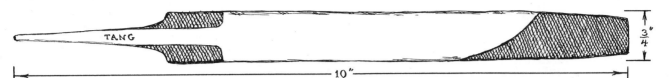

A fine trade knife can be crafted from a tired file of this size. But first, the metal must be softened, or annealed, by heating it to a cherry red and then cooling it gradually. The Indian's campfire is a second-best to the blacksmith's forge or a welder's oxyacetylene torch. And for small blades, a butane torch or a plumber's gasoline torch may supply enough heat to remove the temper.

WEAR SAFETY GOGGLES. GRIND GROOVES ON BOTH SIDES OF THE BLADE POINT AND BREAK IT OFF WITH A HAMMER.

GRIND DOWN TO THE KNIFE OUTLINE. NO NEED TO OCCASIONALLY COOL IT IN WATER, OF COURSE, FOR THE BLADE MUST REMAIN ANNEALED IN THE GRINDING PROCESS. ONCE SHAPED, THE FILE GROOVES ARE GROUND OFF, THINNED, AND THEN SMOOTHED. GRIND THE CUTTING EDGE AS SHOWN WITH THE SAW BLADE KNIFE. BUFF TO A MIRROR FINISH WITH TRIPOLI COMPOUND OR FINE METAL SANDPAPER.

THE ANNEALED BLADE, SOFT ENOUGH FOR GRINDING TO SHAPE BUT CERTAINLY NOT FOR USE, MUST BE TEMPERED. THE METAL IS REHEATED AND WILL GO THROUGH VARIOUS COLOR CHANGES. A FAINT STRAW COLOR WILL FIRST APPEAR, THEN CHANGE TO STRAW, ORANGE, AND FINALLY CHERRY RED. FOR THE KNIFE, THE BLADE SHOULD BE HEATED TO AN OVERALL STRAW COLOR — AND NO MORE. THIS WILL GIVE A STRONG BUT NOT-TOO-BRITTLE CUTTING EDGE. IF A FAINT STRAW COLOR BEGINS TO SHOW IN ONE SPOT AND NOT ELSEWHERE, SHIFT THE BLADE OR RAISE IT FOR A MORE EQUAL HEAT DISTRIBUTION. WHEN THE BLADE IS STRAW (BRONZE) COLOR, DOUSE IT INTO A BUCKET OF WATER TO HOLD ITS TEMPER.

HAFTING THE FILE KNIFE TANG ~

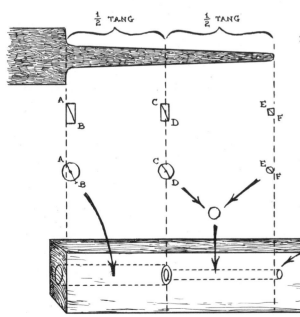

BEFORE SHAPING THE HARDWOOD BLOCK FOR THE HANDLE, DRILL THE TANG HOLE AS SHOWN. PROTECT THE BLADE WITH MASKING TAPE, AND CLAMP IN A VISE. THE HANDLE IS TAPPED ON SECURELY AND THE WOOD CARVED TO THE DESIRED SHAPE.

MEASURE TANG CROSS SECTIONS BETWEEN OPPOSITE EDGES AB, CD, AND EF.

DRILL MUST BE UNDERSIZE FOR A TIGHT FIT. THEREFORE USE A DRILL WITH THE DIAMETER OF AB MINUS $\frac{1}{64}$ INCH FOR THE FRONT HALF OF THE TANG.
DRILL THE BACK HALF OF THE TANG HOLE WITH A DRILL HALF THE AVERAGE OF CD AND EF $(CD + EF \div 2)$.

EXTEND THE SMALLER DRILL HOLE $\frac{1}{8}$ INCH LONGER THAN THE TANG.
IF $\frac{7}{8}$ INCH OF THE TANG DOES NOT FIT EASILY INTO THE HANDLE, TWIST THE TANG TO REMOVE A BIT MORE WOOD.

HAFTING THE BONE HANDLE ~ The steel of hack saw blades, hand saws, knives, and rotary lawn-mower blades are, of course, high carbon and hard tempered. The trade knife depends on these qualities for its fine cutting edge. But this hard steel must have two holes for securing the handle. It should be annealed or softened if a drill point is to make any sort of impression. No need to heat the entire handle ~ only where the holes are to be made.

CUT THE HEAD FROM A NAIL AND FLATTEN THE POINT BY GRINDING WITH THE NAIL SECURED IN THE DRILL, PRESS ON THE HOLE MARK, RUN DRILL AT HIGH SPEED UNTIL THE HEAT GENERATED TURNS THE SPOT BLUE. DO THE SAME FOR THE SECOND HOLE MARK, AND THE STEEL IS SELECTIVELY SOFTENED. CLEVER!

NOW DRILL THE MARKS AT LOW SPEED WITH A HIGH-SPEED TWIST DRILL, USING THE SAME SIZE AS THE RIVETS TO BE USED.

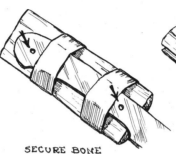 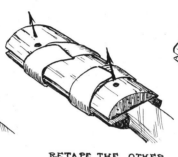 

USE A HACKSAW TO SAW TWO PIECES FROM AN OLD BONE.

SECURE BONE TO METAL WITH MASKING TAPE AND DRILL DOWN THROUGH METAL HOLES.

RETAPE THE OTHER PIECE OF BONE AND DRILL, STARTING THROUGH THE PREVIOUSLY DRILLED HOLES.

DRILL A SLIGHT DEPRESSION AT EACH HOLE SO THAT BRASS WASHERS WILL FIT FLUSH TO THE SURFACE.

HOLD THE WASHERS WITH PLIERS AND DRILL SMALL CONES. THE RIVET WILL MASH INTO IT.

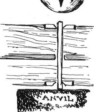

USE A BRASS NAIL OR A PIECE OF BRASS WELDING ROD THAT FIT THE WASHERS AND DRILLED HOLES SNUGGLY. WITH A WIRE CUTTER, SNIP TO GIVE A LENGTH THAT PROJECTS A BIT ABOVE THE WASHERS. BOTH ENDS WILL FLATTEN INTO THE WASHER TO HOLD IT SECURELY. ALTERNATE EASY BLOWS WITH A BALL PEEN HAMMER ~ FIRST ONE SIDE, THEN THE OTHER.

FILE OR GRIND OFF BONE EDGES TO THE METAL HANDLE EDGE.

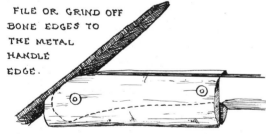

THEN ROUND THE HANDLE TO YOUR LIKING. THE RIVET AND WASHERS MAY BE FILED FLAT.

---- POSSIBLE OUTLINE

GRINDING THE CUTTING EDGE ~

GRIND A GENTLY CURVED BEVEL ONE-THIRD OF THE BLADE DIPPING IN WATER FREQUENTLY TO GUARD AGAINST LOSING THE TEMPER. THEN GRIND A FLAT BEVEL THE LAST $\frac{1}{4}$ INCH TO GIVE A SHARP EDGE. HONE OFF ANY BURRS.

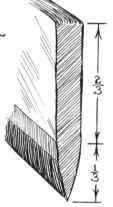

BONE HANDLES WITH DESIGNS ARE RARE. THIS SPECIMEN WEATHERED THE CENTURIES. BRONSON MUSEUM, ATTLEBORO, MASSACHUSETTS.

TWO HANDLE CONSIDERATIONS ~

1. FERRULES ~ METAL COLLAR REINFORCEMENTS ~ WERE SOMETIMES FOUND ON TRADE KNIVES. THIS

 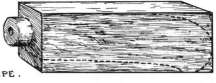

DECORATIVE ADDITION STARTS WITH A SMALL PIECE OF BRASS PIPE. MAKE IT OVAL BY SQUEEZING IN A VISE. CENTER OVER THE TANG HOLE AND TAP WITH A HAMMER. TO MAKE A FAINT IMPRESSION. USE THIS TO CARVE A PROJECTION TO FIT THE FERRULE. BEVEL THE INSIDE OF THE FERRULE AND TAP INTO PLACE. DRIVE HOME THE KNIFE TANG AND CARVE THE HANDLE.

2. TO MAKE A WOODEN HANDLE INSTEAD OF BONE, FOR A SAW BLADE TRADE KNIFE ~

DIVIDE THE HANDLE BLOCK, BUT MAKE ONE HALF WIDER TO ALLOW FOR THE TANG THICKNESS. TRACE THE TANG ON THE WIDER SECTION.

CARVE OUT ENOUGH WOOD SO THAT THE TANG LIES FLUSH. APPLY EPOXY GLUE TO THE TANG AND THE TWO HANDLE HALVES. CLAMP.

IF THE KNIFE HAS NEED OF A BRASS COLLAR, AS SHOWN IN 1, ATTACH IT BEFORE GLUING THE TANG IN PLACE.

(SINCE I KNOW OF NO EXAMPLES OF TRADE KNIFE GUARDS, THEY HAVE NOT BEEN INCLUDED.)

KNIFE SHEATHS

In 1623, the Plymouth Colony sent Miles Standish to settle a dispute at Wessagusset (Weymouth). For his trouble, he was confronted by a menacing knot of warriors, sharpening their knives and making gestures less than friendly. One, an Indian named Pecksuot, towered over the smaller Standish, insulted him roundly, and threatened him with a knife that hung from his neck by a cord. To make an exciting slice of history much too short, Standish managed to isolate Pecksuot, grabbed the Indian's knife, and dispatched his enemy after a wild tussle.

Knives were frequently carried in this fashion ~ actually in a suspended sheath. The warrior also wore the knife at the waist, secured with the belt running over the sheath and through a slot on its side. With the sheath next to the body and under a snug belt, it was probably the safest and most convenient way to wear a knife.

There is a fascinating painting at the Rhode Island School of Design in Providence. This portrait of Ninigret, sachem of the Niantics, is the only surviving seventeenth

century painting of a New England sachem. I have sometimes wondered if the object that Ninigret wore in his belt was a sheathed knife.

Most Indian sheaths enclosed the entire knife, leaving only the butt of the handle exposed. With this in mind, fold a piece of paper and place the back of the knife inside and against the fold. Mark along the cutting edge through both pieces of paper. The knife should fit rather snuggly along its length, except for an inch or so of the handle protruding. Transfer the pattern to a piece of heavy tanned leather (sometimes rawhide was used as an inner sheath, then covered with a decorated buckskin outer sheath).

ALTHOUGH THE INDIAN WOULD PASS A LEATHER THONG THROUGH THE SLITS AND TIE THE SHEATH TO HIS CLOTHING OR SUSPEND IT FROM THE NECK, THE SLITS CAN BE MADE WIDE ENOUGH FOR A BELT.

THIS INDIAN BELT SHEATH IS CARRIED NEXT TO THE BODY, WITH THE BELT OVER THE SHEATH AND PASSED THROUGH THE SLOT.

PERHAPS THIS SHEATH HAS NO PLACE IN A BOOK ON INDIAN HANDCRAFTS, FOR ITS ANCESTRY IS UNCERTAIN AT BEST. IT IS SIMPLY OFFERED AS AN EFFICIENT KNIFE CARRIER THAT IS NOT UNLIKE THE NATIVE AMERICAN DESIGNS.

CROOKED KNIFE

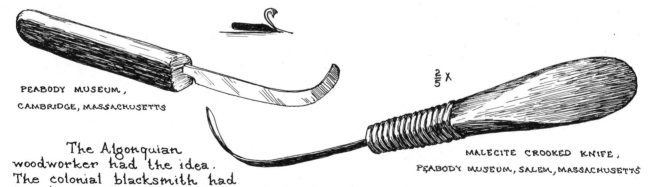

PEABODY MUSEUM, CAMBRIDGE, MASSACHUSETTS

MALECITE CROOKED KNIFE, PEABODY MUSEUM, SALEM, MASSACHUSETTS

The Algonquian woodworker had the idea. The colonial blacksmith had the discarded files and forging tools. From them all came a most remarkable tool—the crooked knife. This combination draw knife and gouge could shave down anything from a bow to snowshoe frames or scoop out samp bowls and dugout canoes. It was drawn or pulled toward the body and with no more risk than whittling with an ordinary knife. The blade was beveled on the upper edge only, leaving the flat underface in contact with the wood.

The handles may be just as unusual. Unlike those sketched above, most were curved to fit the palm. Therefore each handle was made specifically

108

for right- or left-handers. And since the Indian made his own handle for a blade shaped to his liking, no two crooked knives were the same.

The crooked knife is crafted as it was three hundred years ago, and you should find this unusual tool to be just as handy as did the New England Indians.

CRAFTING THE CROOKED KNIFE

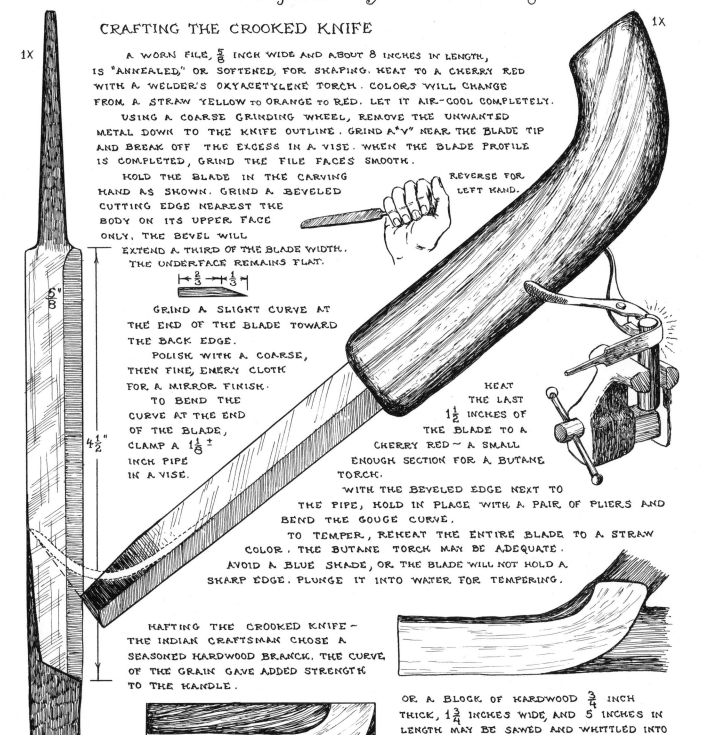

1X

1X

A WORN FILE, $\frac{5}{8}$ INCH WIDE AND ABOUT 8 INCHES IN LENGTH, IS "ANNEALED," OR SOFTENED, FOR SHAPING. HEAT TO A CHERRY RED WITH A WELDER'S OXYACETYLENE TORCH. COLORS WILL CHANGE FROM A STRAW YELLOW TO ORANGE TO RED. LET IT AIR-COOL COMPLETELY.

USING A COARSE GRINDING WHEEL, REMOVE THE UNWANTED METAL DOWN TO THE KNIFE OUTLINE. GRIND A "V" NEAR THE BLADE TIP AND BREAK OFF THE EXCESS IN A VISE. WHEN THE BLADE PROFILE IS COMPLETED, GRIND THE FILE FACES SMOOTH.

HOLD THE BLADE IN THE CARVING HAND AS SHOWN. GRIND A BEVELED CUTTING EDGE NEAREST THE BODY ON ITS UPPER FACE ONLY, THE BEVEL WILL EXTEND A THIRD OF THE BLADE WIDTH. THE UNDERFACE REMAINS FLAT.

REVERSE FOR LEFT HAND.

$\vdash \frac{2}{3} \dashv \vdash \frac{1}{3} \dashv$

GRIND A SLIGHT CURVE AT THE END OF THE BLADE TOWARD THE BACK EDGE.

POLISH WITH A COARSE, THEN FINE, EMERY CLOTH FOR A MIRROR FINISH.

TO BEND THE CURVE AT THE END OF THE BLADE, CLAMP A $1\frac{1}{8}$ ± INCH PIPE IN A VISE.

HEAT THE LAST $1\frac{1}{2}$ INCHES OF THE BLADE TO A CHERRY RED ~ A SMALL ENOUGH SECTION FOR A BUTANE TORCH.

WITH THE BEVELED EDGE NEXT TO THE PIPE, HOLD IN PLACE WITH A PAIR OF PLIERS AND BEND THE GOUGE CURVE.

TO TEMPER, REHEAT THE ENTIRE BLADE TO A STRAW COLOR. THE BUTANE TORCH MAY BE ADEQUATE. AVOID A BLUE SHADE, OR THE BLADE WILL NOT HOLD A SHARP EDGE. PLUNGE IT INTO WATER FOR TEMPERING.

HAFTING THE CROOKED KNIFE ~ THE INDIAN CRAFTSMAN CHOSE A SEASONED HARDWOOD BRANCH, THE CURVE OF THE GRAIN GAVE ADDED STRENGTH TO THE HANDLE.

OR A BLOCK OF HARDWOOD $\frac{3}{4}$ INCH THICK, $1\frac{3}{4}$ INCHES WIDE, AND 5 INCHES IN LENGTH MAY BE SAWED AND WHITTLED INTO SHAPE. DRILL THE TANG HOLE AS SHOWN IN "HAFTING THE FILE KNIFE TANG," P.105.

$\frac{5}{8}$"

$4\frac{1}{2}$"

The crooked knife has no equal for removing unwanted wood. Worked as a one-handed draw-knife, it will handily remove clean lengthy strips. There is no danger of gouging too deeply, for the single beveled blade shaves upward toward the surface of the wood. The curved end has an admirable scooping action. But all this comes with practice. The blade should be held perpendicular to the wood - and most important, drawn toward the body. Better control and efficiency make the crooked knife a much safer tool to use than the ordinary jackknife.

SHAVING

GOUGING

 # FALSE-FACE MASK ~ IROQUOIS

FALSE FACE
BEFORE SEPARATION
FROM TREE TRUNK

When it came to neighbors, the New England Indians had want of something better. To the west ~ specifically the Albany, New York, region~ lived the Mohawk, that fierce and merciless easternmost tribe of the Iroquois Confederacy. Eyewitnesses of the period left little doubt that the Mohawk warriors had made few friends during their incursions through Algonquian territory.

Father Druilletes, the Jesuit priest, noted in 1650 that "all the Nations of Savages which are in New England hate the [Mohawk] and fear lest he will exterminate them."

William Wood, in New England's Prospect of 1634, enlarged on this. "These [Mohawks] are a cruel bloody people which are wont to come down on their poor neighbors with more than brutish savageness, spoiling their corn, burning their houses, slaying men, ravishing women; yea very cannibals they were, sometimes eating on a man, one part after another, before his face and while yet living, in so much that the very name of a Mohawk would strike the heart of a poor Aberginian dead, were there not hopes at hand of relief from the English to succor them."

The nightmarish Iroquois False Faces are here presented as a reminder of the terror that the Mohawks created throughout the New England tribes. Although purely decorative and not of Algonquian origin, the masks make an interesting project for testing the crooked knife.

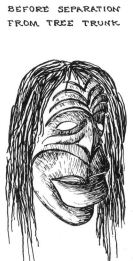

110

Actually, these wooden masks were considered to have curative powers over illness or injury. False Face members gathered about the sick bed to dance, shake rattles, or perhaps blow ashes from the fire upon the patient. Once cured, the patient automatically became a False Face member. He searched out a suitable tree, such as the easily worked basswood. After burning tobacco and offering prayers, he carved the face into its living wood. It was then chiseled free, hollowed out with the crooked knife, and finally painted.

No one face was like the others, but each had the magical qualities of the original False Face. According to legend, this supernatural being brought on the wrath of the Great Spirit because of his boastful ways. False Face was sentenced to an eternity of healing the sick and injured.

A FINE EXAMPLE OF THE IROQUOIS FALSE FACE IS ON DISPLAY AT THE AMERICAN INDIAN ARCHAEOLOGICAL INSTITUTE AT WASHINGTON, CONNECTICUT. WITH OR WITHOUT THE CROOKED KNIFE, THE WOODEN MASK MAKES A FINE CARVING PROJECT.

11"

7"

4"

SPLIT A WHITE PINE LOG, 8 INCHES IN DIAMETER, IN HALF. AFTER DEBARKING, SKETCH THE OUTLINE AND ROUGH OUT WITH A CHISEL, GOUGE, AND KNIFE. WHEN REFINED, THE BACK MAY BE SCOOPED OUT WITH THE CROOKED KNIFE OR LEFT SOLID IF THE MASK IS NOT TO BE WORN.

IF THE INDIAN BEGAN CARVING THE TREE IN THE MORNING, THE MASK WAS PAINTED RED. IF STARTED IN THE AFTERNOON, BLACK (OR IN THE CASE OF OUR MASK, DARK BROWN) WAS USED.

USE TIN SHEARS TO SHAPE THE THIN BRASS EYES. NAIL WITH BRASS TACKS.

"V" GROOVE FOREHEAD AND CHEEKS. THESE WILL BE PAINTED WHITE.

HAIR~ UNWIND HEMP ROPE INTO STRANDS AND SOAK IN HOT WATER TO STRAIGHTEN (NO CURLY HAIR FOR THIS MASK!).

IF A PINE LOG IS DIFFICULT TO LOCATE, GLUE A SANDWICH OF $\frac{3}{4}$-INCH PINE BOARDS. USE A JIGSAW OR SABER SAW TO SHAPE THE OUTLINES AS SHOWN. CLAMP SECURELY.

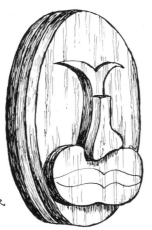

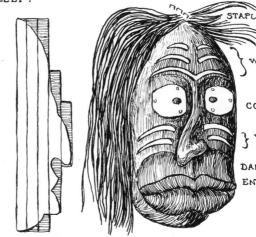

STAPLE HAIR

WHITE

COPPER

WHITE

DARK BROWN ENTIRE FACE

INDIAN BROOM

The origins of the Indian, or birch-split, broom have become clouded through the years. The early settlers gave full credit to the Indians, then enthusiastically set about making copies for their own use. Indeed, the Indian broom became one of the earliest American industries in New England at the turn of the nineteenth century.

The technique has remained unchanged through the years. Since a strong metal blade is a must, it would seem that the Algonquians required trade knive before attempting such a project. It took a full day of patience to whittle a 4-foot Indian broom for sweeping. There were smaller brooms - down to 6 inches for beating eggs and cream - while those twice that size did service for scouring maple sugar kettles.

Yellow birch seems to be preferred, with the runners-up being hickory, ash, black beech, and witch hazel. In any event, the wood was worked freshly cut. Annular rings could be split free and slivered before the wood dried out. And equally important, the slivers were pried free and NOT whittled, or the broom would end up as a pile of shavings.

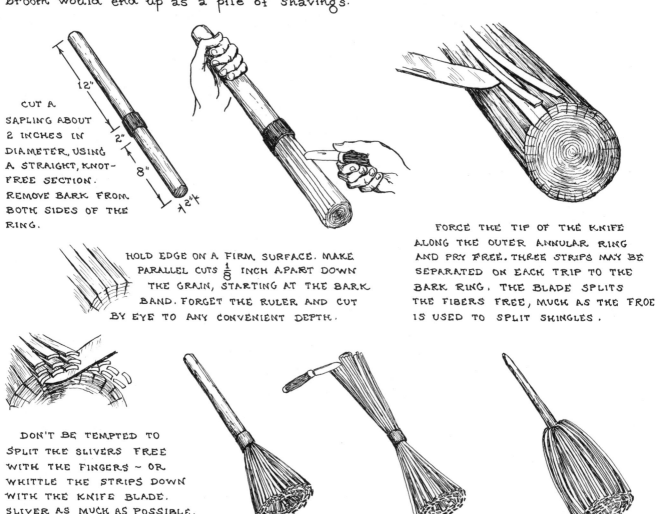

CUT A SAPLING ABOUT 2 INCHES IN DIAMETER, USING A STRAIGHT, KNOT-FREE SECTION. REMOVE BARK FROM BOTH SIDES OF THE RING.

HOLD EDGE ON A FIRM SURFACE. MAKE PARALLEL CUTS $\frac{1}{8}$ INCH APART DOWN THE GRAIN, STARTING AT THE BARK BAND. FORGET THE RULER AND CUT BY EYE TO ANY CONVENIENT DEPTH.

FORCE THE TIP OF THE KNIFE ALONG THE OUTER ANNULAR RING AND PRY FREE. THREE STRIPS MAY BE SEPARATED ON EACH TRIP TO THE BARK RING. THE BLADE SPLITS THE FIBERS FREE, MUCH AS THE FROE IS USED TO SPLIT SHINGLES.

DON'T BE TEMPTED TO SPLIT THE SLIVERS FREE WITH THE FINGERS - OR WHITTLE THE STRIPS DOWN WITH THE KNIFE BLADE. SLIVER AS MUCH AS POSSIBLE.

THEN CUT OUT THE SMALL CORE REMAINING IN THE CENTER. REVERSE THE BROOM AND REPEAT THE PRY-STRIP PROCESS. LEAVE ENOUGH WOOD FOR A DECENT HAND GRIP. BEND DOWN THE PLIABLE SLIVERS FROM THE HANDLE END.

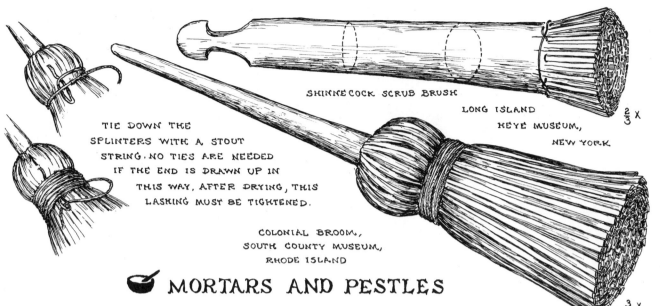

SHINNECOCK SCRUB BRUSH

LONG ISLAND
HEYE MUSEUM,
NEW YORK

TIE DOWN THE
SPLINTERS WITH A STOUT
STRING. NO TIES ARE NEEDED
IF THE END IS DRAWN UP IN
THIS WAY. AFTER DRYING, THIS
LASHING MUST BE TIGHTENED.

COLONIAL BROOM,
SOUTH COUNTY MUSEUM,
RHODE ISLAND

MORTARS AND PESTLES

The Paleo~American Indians (10,500~7,000 years ago) used any handy round stone against a flat rock to crush their roots, tubers, and berries. When the Late Archaics (5,000 years ago to A.D. 300) discovered that soft soapstone (steatite) could be pecked in the shape of a bowl, a useful mortar soon followed. Pulverized roots, seeds, nuts, berries, and bone marrow could then be added to another newcomer, the soapstone stew pot.

By A.D. 300, agriculture and ceramics had revolution~ ized life in New England. Plentiful garden crops filled the baked clay pots, and bigger and better mortars were needed. A scooped-out hardwood log was the answer for making meal from the corn harvests. Ninety-five percent of these mortars were without ornamentation. The remaining ones, many from Mohegan craftsmen, were nicely carved.

LATE ARCHAIC STEATITE
MORTAR AND PESTLE $\frac{1}{4}$ X

Mortars were made from hardwoods, and oak was preferred. Black gum (pepperage) and apple were those listed in <u>Folk Medicine of the Delaware and Related Algonkian Indians</u>. It's author, Gladys Tantaquidgeon mentioned in <u>Indian Notes</u> of 1930 that the Wampanoag tribe on Martha's Vineyard used sassafras for small mortars. An exception was one made from a ship's spar from colonial days ~ presumably pine.

LOG MORTAR $\frac{1}{7}$ X
BRONSON MUSEUM.

These small mortars averaged 9 inches in height, 5$\frac{1}{2}$ inches in diameter, and a rim width of $\frac{3}{4}$ inch. Larger mortars were 17 to 20 inches in height, 12 inches in diameter, and had a cavity depth of 12 inches. Some reached the considerable height of 36 inches.

CHECKING OF MANY HARDWOODS MAY BE A
REAL PROBLEM. APPLE, BEECH, BIRCH, CHESTNUT,
LOCUST, OAK, WALNUT, AND
SASSAFRAS MAY ALL DEVELOP
CRACKS THAT SPLIT THE WOOD
AS IT DRIES. ASH, BASSWOOD,
BUTTERNUT, CEDAR, CHERRY, ELM, AND MAPLE,
AS WELL AS WHITE PINE (A SOFT WOOD), CHECK TO A
LESSER DEGREE. A GOOD BET IS A STORM-FELLED TREE. THE LEAVES HASTEN THE DRYING PROCESS
AND THE TRUNK CHECKS LESS THAN DRYING GREEN CHUNKS. SAW OUT A PIECE OF THE PROPER
DIAMETER, STRAIGHT AND FREE OF KNOTS AND LIMBS.

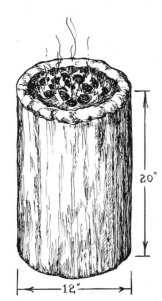

THE INDIANS USED THE QUAHOG SHELL, STONE SCRAPER, OR GOUGE ~ AND LATER THE CROOKED KNIFE ~ TO REMOVE THE CHAR BEFORE FURTHER BURNING.

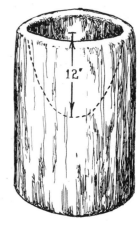

WET CLAY OR MUD WAS DAUBED AROUND THE RIM TO PREVENT BURNING. TODAY, BRIQUETTES HELP THE CENTER BURNING. MOISTEN THE MUD EDGE PERIODICALLY.

CARVED MOHEGAN MORTAR

PESTLES WERE PECKED TO SHAPE FROM SCHIST OR SANDSTONE. ABOUT 6 INCHES PROJECTED FROM THE MORTAR RIM FOR A SECURE HAND GRASP. TODAY, A HARDWOOD PESTLE IS PREFERRED. THE TEETH OF THE INDIANS WERE OFTEN WORN DOWN FROM THE GRIT GROUND FREE FROM STONE MORTARS AND PESTLES.

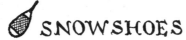 SNOWSHOES

DAVIDSON P83.

It's possible ~ just possible ~ that the Paleo-American hunters wore snowshoes to invade the American continent. After all, they were in use in Asia before America was peopled. Once over the iced~in Bering Strait and into Alaska, the snowshoe would have permitted hunting on the receding glaciers. Floundering mastodons, mammoths, musk-ox, beaver, elk, and deer could be tracked, surrounded, and dispatched.

These ancient snow feet gradually became known eastward. Probably of solid wood, they generally had a toe hole, crossbars to reinforce the underside, and side frames. Each tribe adapted the wooden plank to its own liking, resulting in a variety of sizes and shapes. Although this slow and awkward winterwear may still be found, the bear paw that followed was far and away the better answer to the drifting snows of New England.

Early on, the bear paw was simply a round or oval frame that was bent from a branch with the ends lashed together. The filling was of rawhide strips ~ sometimes strips of bark or pieces of vine ~ woven in an un~ systematic way and attached

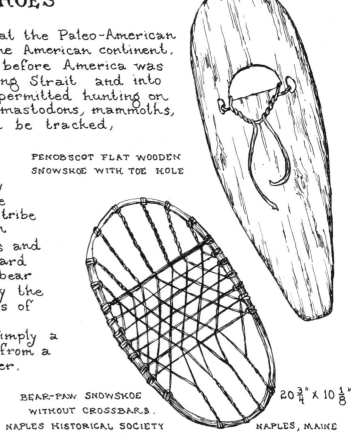

PENOBSCOT FLAT WOODEN SNOWSHOE WITH TOE HOLE

BEAR-PAW SNOWSHOE WITHOUT CROSSBARS. NAPLES HISTORICAL SOCIETY

20¾" X 10⅛"

NAPLES, MAINE

114

BONES FOR STRETCHING
RAWHIDE ~ PENOBSCOT,
MUSEUM OF NATURAL HISTORY,
NEW YORK CITY

$\frac{1}{2}$ X

to the frame by wrapping. The earliest bear paws had no toe-hole (that was a later development) and was lashed firmly to the foot. Worn as big flat shoes, each had to be lifted and lowered as occurs with ordinary walking.

The invention of the toe-hole allowed the snowshoe to be dragged instead of the exhausting raising of each shoe. Thongs were secured to the ball of the foot to the toe hole, then brought behind the heel. In this way the heel could be raised while the toes were lowered while walking.

Other niceties accompanied the change. The rawhide filling that supported the foot was usually woven in a hexagonal ("lattice" or "cane chair") pattern. Cross-bars of wood ~ at first not mortised into the frame ~ lent sturdiness to the shoe. Often the rear of the frame was pointed to give a sort of rudder that was dragged when the shoe was lifted.

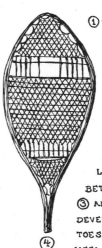

IN GENERAL, THE NEW ENGLAND SNOWSHOE HAD THESE CHARACTERISTICS:

BEARPAW OR POINTED HEEL FRAMES OF A SINGLE BENT STRIP OF WOOD, NEVER TWO-PIECE FRAMES.

ROUNDED TOE (OCCASIONALLY PENOBSCOTS HAD SQUARE TOES).

TOE HOLE (LACKING IN THE WAMPANOAG SHOES).

HEXAGONAL RAWHIDE WEAVE (THE WAMPANOAGS ALONE HAD A RECTANGULAR WEAVE). ALL WEAVES WERE WRAPPED

WOODEN NEEDLE WITH
RAWHIDE ~ PENOBSCOT
MUSEUM OF NATURAL HISTORY,
NEW YORK CITY

AROUND THE FRAME. EXCEPT FOR THOSE OF THE WAMPANOAG, NIPMUC, AND MASSACHUSETT TRIBES, THE TOE AND HEEL SECTIONS WERE FILLED WITH FINE RAWHIDE, ATTACHED TO A SELVAGE THONG.

BEAR PAWS HELD A SINGLE MORTISED CROSSBAR, THE POINTED HEELS HAD TWO, AND THE WAMPANOAG SHOES HAD THREE CROSSBARS. ALL THE SNOWSHOES WERE FLAT WITH NO UPTURNED TOES.

PENOBSCOT

WAMPANOAG
(CONJECTURAL)

MASSACHUSETT / NIPMUC

ABENAKI

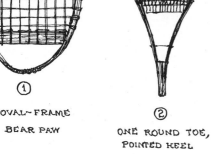

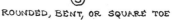

① OVAL ~ FRAME
BEAR PAW

② ONE ROUND TOE,
POINTED HEEL

③ ROUNDED, BENT, OR SQUARE TOE

④ BENT TOE

① THE BEAR PAW IS THE EARLIEST SHOE WITH ONE-PIECE FRAME, RECTAN-GULAR WEAVING AND NO TOE HOLE.

② DEVELOPED FROM THE BEAR PAW, IT HAS A ONE-PIECE FRAME ROUNDED TOE, TOE-HOLE, AND HEXAGONAL WEAVE LIMITED TO THE CENTER BETWEEN THE CROSSBARS.

③ AND ④ ARE LATER DEVELOPMENTS, WITH SHARPER TOES AND FILLED TOE AND HEEL SPACES WITH WEAVING TIED TO A SELVAGE THONG.

115

RECONSTRUCTING THE SNOWSHOE

THE FRAME

Live wood is flexible ~ so much so that it may be bent into a curve without breaking and then dried to hold its shape. Choose the right sapling, have a snowshoe mold ready for shaping, and the big winter shoes will be ready for the netting in several weeks.

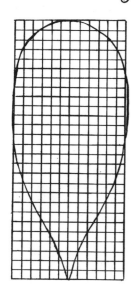

CUT TWO FORMS FROM ¾-INCH SCRAP WOOD. EACH SQUARE = 1 INCH.

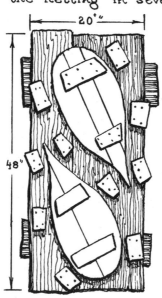

20"

48"

NAIL THE TWO FORMS TO A PIECE OF PLYWOOD OR SEVERAL LENGTHS OF WOOD, NAILED TOGETHER BY SEVERAL CROSSPIECES BEHIND.

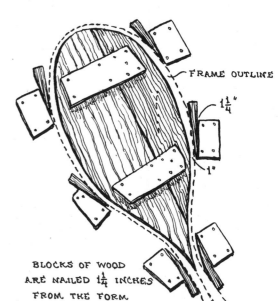

FRAME OUTLINE

1¼"

1"

BLOCKS OF WOOD ARE NAILED 1¼ INCHES FROM THE FORM WHERE THE WEDGES ENTER. TWELVE WEDGES ARE NEEDED. THE OPPOSITE END OF EACH BLOCK IS 1 INCH FROM THE FORM.

¾"

¾"

WITH THE TWO FORMS PREPARED, SEARCH OUT SEVERAL STRAIGHT, KNOT-FREE ASH OR HICKORY SAPLINGS. A LENGTH OF AT LEAST 7 FEET FOR EACH FRAME IS NEEDED. SQUARE DOWN TO ¾ INCH WITH A DRAWSHAVE OR CROOKED KNIFE. OR ~ SELECT A TREE OF 4~5 INCHES AT THE BUTT END. SPLIT DOWN THE CENTER WITH CHISELS.

CUT CROSS FIBERS FREE.

WITH THE DRAWSHAVE OR CROOKED KNIFE, TRIM BOTH SPLIT SURFACES FLAT. CLAMP A ¾-INCH STRIP OF WOOD AND PENCIL EACH EDGE.

THIS FACE WILL BECOME THE OUTER SURFACE OF THE SNOWSHOE FRAME. WHEN SQUARED, THE STAVE WILL BE ¾ X ¾ INCHES X 7⁺ FEET.

116

|← 12" →| |← 16" →| |← 12" →|

END   CENTER   END

WITH TWO LENGTHS OF FRESHLY CUT ASH OR HICKORY, EACH 7⁺ FEET
LONG AND SQUARED TO 3/4 INCH, PROCEED AS
FOLLOWS:

LOCATE THE FRAME'S INNER FACE (THAT
NEAREST THE BARK AND OPPOSITE TO THE
SPLIT LOG FACES). MARK THE INNER FACE
AS SHOWN ABOVE AND SHAVE THE TWO ENDS
AND CENTER TO GIVE EASIER BENDING.
GRADUALLY BEND THE FRAME TO REST INSIDE
THE FORM BLOCKS AND DRIVE IN THE WEDGES.
THE FRAME IS NOW SNUG AGAINST THE SHOE FORM.
DRY FOR SEVERAL WEEKS.

STEAMING OR
SOAKING THE
STAVES MAY
HELP THE
BENDING.

|← 9 1/4" →| |← 6" →|
TOE CROSSBAR   HEEL CROSSBAR
|← 10 3/8" →| |← 5 3/8" →|

CROSSBARS ~ SPLIT OUT FOUR PIECES 1 3/8 INCHES
WIDE AND 5/16 INCH THICK. PLACE EACH IN
POSITION BEHIND THE FRAME AND MARK. ADD
1/4 INCH TO FIT INTO FRAME. MAKE A SERIES
OF DRILLED HOLES 3/16 INCH IN DIAMETER AND
1/4⁺ INCH DEEP. CUT AWAY THE WOOD BETWEEN AND
FIT THE CROSSBARS. WHEN SNUG, DRILL HOLES AT THE TAIL AND PUSH THROUGH
A FINISH NAIL THAT EXTENDS 1/8 INCH ON BOTH SIDES. BEND BOTH PROJECTIONS WITH A HAMMER
FOR A SECURE CLOSURE.

TIDY UP THE SHOE BY SANDING THE FRAME AND SLIGHTLY ROUNDING THE EDGES.
THE CROSSBARS SHOULD ALSO BE ROUNDED. APPLY SEVERAL COATS OF A RUGGED SPAR VARNISH.

LACING THE FRAME

STARTING THE LACING

SPLICING

TWO LENGTHS
OF LACING JOINED
TOGETHER

For centuries, rawhide lacing was the
made-to-order filling for snowshoe frames. Strips
from green dehaired hides were tough and durable
enough to challenge the sturdiest snowstorms.
Woven wet, the netting would shrink on drying to
give a webbed support second to no other
material~that is, until neoprene lacing upstaged
the natural product. Made of synthetic rubber
sandwiching tough nylon fibers, this modern
substitute outwears the old rawhide three to
one, takes less lacing know-how, refuses to
ice up, will not rot, and needs no varnish to
prevent stretching and sagging.

Therefore, in the face of tradition,
neoprene will be used in the following
directions. Start with 5/16 - 1/2 inch X 13 yards
of neoprene for each shoe of the Massachusett/
Nipmuc style. Since lacing can be a frustrating
experience, the added effort of filling the more
northern shoes with a selvage thong and weaving will
not be discussed here.

MARK OFF THE FRAME MEASUREMENTS AS SHOWN. START BY
MAKING A SLIT NEAR THE END OF THE LACING. FEED THE LACING
THROUGH AND SNUG AROUND THE FIRST MARK. KEEP LACING TIGHT.

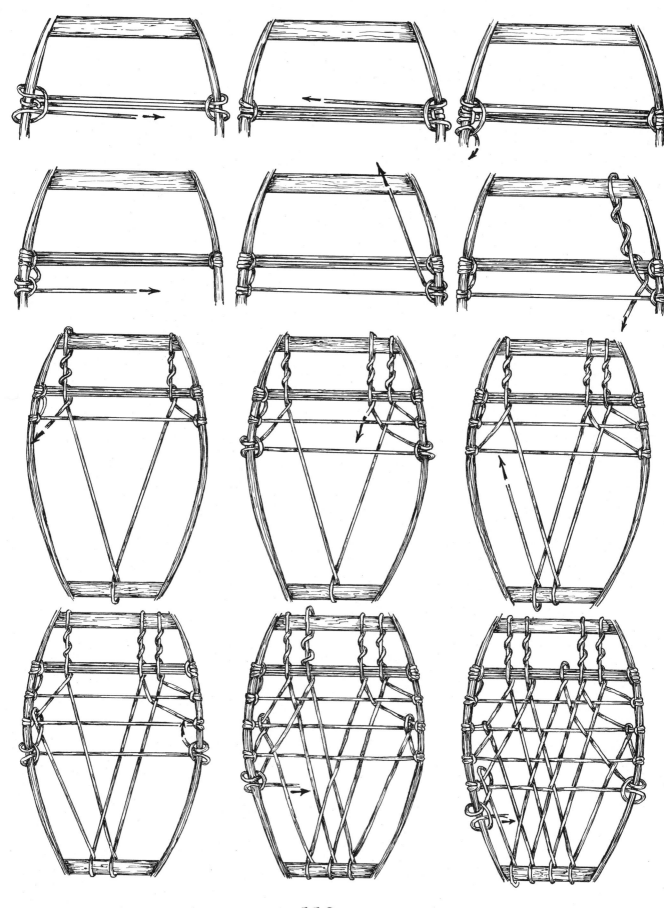

118

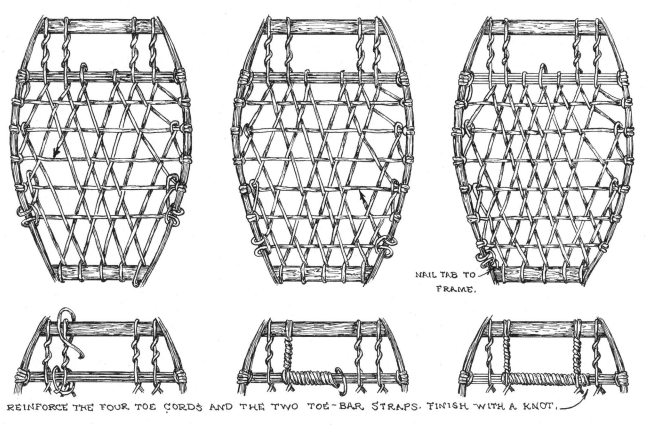

NAIL TAB TO FRAME.

REINFORCE THE FOUR TOE CORDS AND THE TWO TOE-BAR STRAPS. FINISH WITH A KNOT.

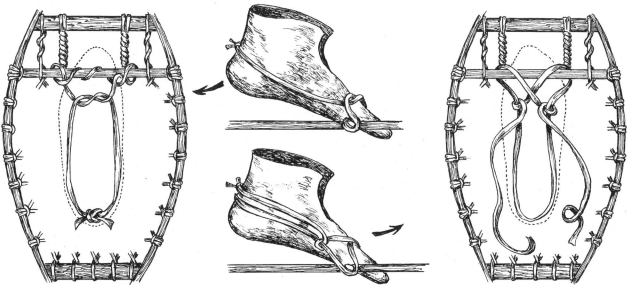

IROQUOIS ~ DAVIDSON SPECIMEN

OLD MAINE HARNESS, COURTESY OF
CLIFFORD G. ANDERSON, CUMBERLAND
CENTER, MAINE

INDIAN TIE HARNESS ~ PROPERLY TIED, THE FOOT
SHOULD NOT SLIDE FORWARD TO COLLECT BLISTERS. THE TIE
SHOULD ALSO BE LOOSE ENOUGH NOT TO CHAFE THE TOP OF THE MOCCASIN. A TWIST OF THE
FOOT SHOULD SHAKE THE SNOWSHOE FREE. BUCKSKIN OR ROPE MAY BE USED.

We have chosen the one-piece frame with a round toe and pointed heel and the hexagonal filling only between the toe and heel crossbars as characteristic of the earlier New England snowshoes. The lack of netting in the toe or heel spaces seems to make this type no less efficient than the later selvage toe and heel filling.

119

Some feel the former is more useful on crusted snow, while others give strong arguments for its general versatility. Your handcrafted snowshoes will let you draw your own conclusions.

USE~ Since both shoes are the same, there is no right or left. Briefly, the dragging tail acts as something of a rudder. Only the toe of the snowshoe is lifted, and then only a thumb's width above the surface of the snow. This is much less tiring than lifting the entire snowshoe. The knees are slightly bent, with the body swinging alone in a side-to-side motion.

An experienced snowshoer is known by his or her snow tracks. The shoe tracks will be close together~ accomplished by bringing the rear shoe forward, close to the inner ankle.

STEAMING THE WOOD

To backtrack just a bit~ live green ash or hickory, readied by nature for bending, may be difficult to come by. A local lumberyard may be able to supply these woods, usually air-dried and planed to a $\frac{3}{4}$-inch thickness. From the plank, several 7-foot (or slightly longer) lengths are cut $\frac{3}{4}$ inch wide. Each stave will therefore be 7 feet X $\frac{3}{4}$ inch X $\frac{3}{4}$ inch. Try to have the grain straight down the length to give the frame maximum strength. Shave the center and tail sections as shown previously, have the shoe molds and wedges ready for action, and the wood is ready for steaming. Only the penetration of the fibers with hot moisture will give enough pliability for bending.

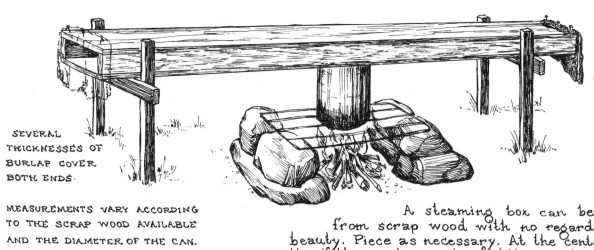

SEVERAL THICKNESSES OF BURLAP COVER BOTH ENDS.

MEASUREMENTS VARY ACCORDING TO THE SCRAP WOOD AVAILABLE AND THE DIAMETER OF THE CAN.

CENTER

RAISE THE STAVES OFF THE STEAM-BOX FLOOR WITH PIECES OF WOOD AT EACH END.

A steaming box can be made from scrap wood with no regard for beauty. Piece as necessary. At the center of the bottom, cut a circle slightly smaller than a #10 tin can (or any like-size container). Fill the can with water and refill as necessary. Rest the center of the box on the can. Pound in end supports to allow contact between can rim and the bottom of the box. An hour of steaming should do the trick. Bend the wood to shape on the snowshoe molds without delay.

120

KING PHILIP'S "TOMAHAWK"

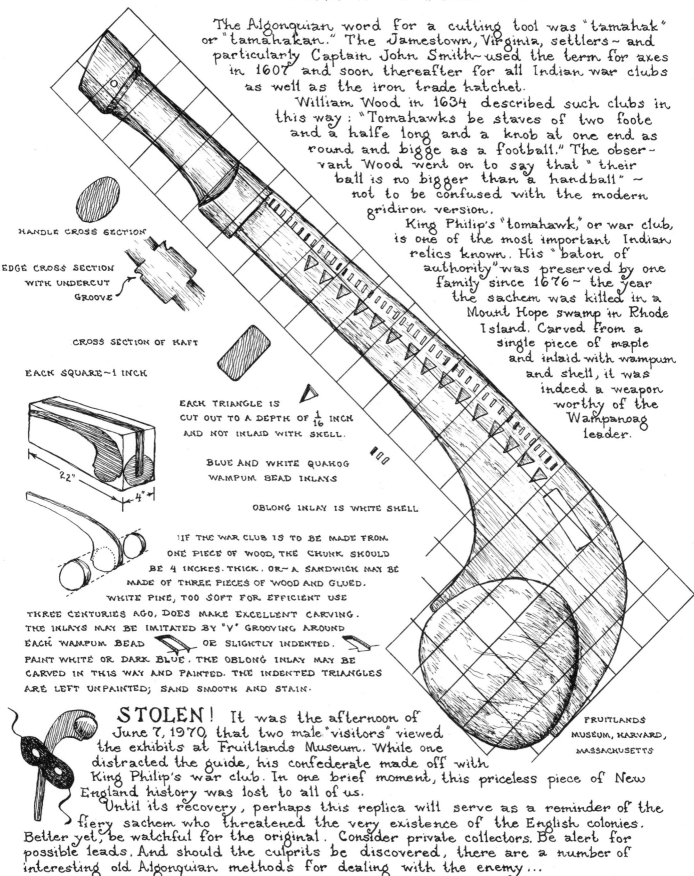

The Algonquian word for a cutting tool was "tamahak" or "tamahakan." The Jamestown, Virginia, settlers ~ and particularly Captain John Smith ~ used the term for axes in 1607 and soon thereafter for all Indian war clubs as well as the iron trade hatchet.

William Wood in 1634 described such clubs in this way: "Tomahawks be staves of two foote and a halfe long and a knob at one end as round and bigge as a football." The observant Wood went on to say that "their ball is no bigger than a handball" ~ not to be confused with the modern gridiron version.

King Philip's "tomahawk," or war club, is one of the most important Indian relics known. His "baton of authority" was preserved by one family since 1676 ~ the year the sachem was killed in a Mount Hope swamp in Rhode Island. Carved from a single piece of maple and inlaid with wampum and shell, it was indeed a weapon worthy of the Wampanoag leader.

HANDLE CROSS SECTION

EDGE CROSS SECTION WITH UNDERCUT GROOVE

CROSS SECTION OF HAFT

EACH SQUARE ~ 1 INCH

22"

4"

EACH TRIANGLE IS CUT OUT TO A DEPTH OF $\frac{1}{16}$ INCH AND NOT INLAID WITH SHELL.

BLUE AND WHITE QUAHOG WAMPUM BEAD INLAYS

OBLONG INLAY IS WHITE SHELL

IF THE WAR CLUB IS TO BE MADE FROM ONE PIECE OF WOOD, THE CHUNK SHOULD BE 4 INCHES THICK. OR ~ A SANDWICH MAY BE MADE OF THREE PIECES OF WOOD AND GLUED. WHITE PINE, TOO SOFT FOR EFFICIENT USE THREE CENTURIES AGO, DOES MAKE EXCELLENT CARVING. THE INLAYS MAY BE IMITATED BY "V" GROOVING AROUND EACH WAMPUM BEAD OR SLIGHTLY INDENTED. PAINT WHITE OR DARK BLUE. THE OBLONG INLAY MAY BE CARVED IN THIS WAY AND PAINTED. THE INDENTED TRIANGLES ARE LEFT UNPAINTED; SAND SMOOTH AND STAIN.

FRUITLANDS MUSEUM, HARVARD, MASSACHUSETTS

STOLEN! It was the afternoon of June 7, 1970, that two male "visitors" viewed the exhibits at Fruitlands Museum. While one distracted the guide, his confederate made off with King Philip's war club. In one brief moment, this priceless piece of New England history was lost to all of us.

Until its recovery, perhaps this replica will serve as a reminder of the fiery sachem who threatened the very existence of the English colonies. Better yet, be watchful for the original. Consider private collectors. Be alert for possible leads. And should the culprits be discovered, there are a number of interesting old Algonquian methods for dealing with the enemy...

CHILDREN'S TOY

Indian children were free spirits. Backed by the encouragement of a loving family, they explored the streams and woodlands at will. Nature provided the playground, and the countless raw materials were ready to become playthings~ with the help of a child's imagination.

CATTAIL DUCK

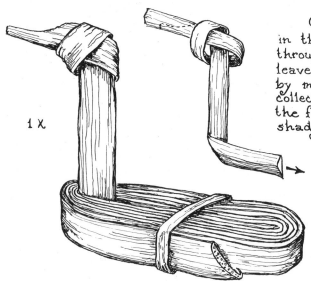

1 X

Cattails grow in great plenty in the damp and marshy areas throughout New England. The leaves reach their full growth by midsummer and may be collected from that time well into the fall. Dry the leaves in a shady spot for several days to preserve the delicate green color. Each will shrink to two-thirds of its width. To give some contrast, part of the white base~that portion attached to the other leaves~ will form the outermost part of the body. Its thickness makes it especially buoyant.

The dried leaves should be soaked for an hour or so. Cut off the last 6 inches of the base and save for tying the body. Measure up 30 inches (the less sturdy pointed tip is not so usable) and cut.

Now for the head. The overhand knot, tightened and flattened, seemed to work well for my flock of ducks. But a simpler and easier head is illustrated in the Forty-fourth <u>Annual Report of the</u> <u>Bureau of American Ethnology.</u> That version is folded flat and trimmed as shown here.

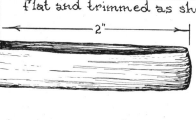

1 X

2"

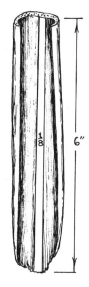

⅛

6"

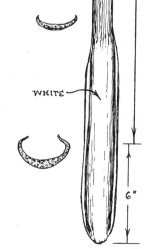

30"

¾ ±

WHITE

6"

Whatever the choice, the bend should be toward the flat side of the leaf. Another fold at the base of the neck starts the body. Fold again about 2 inches from the neck. Then it's just a matter of winding until the body is finished.

Tie with an ⅛-inch strip from the severed leaf base. Or a strip of inner basswood bark will answer the need nicely. Too much soaking may leave the tie loose as the leaf dries.

CATTAIL DOLL

CATTAIL STEM

As with the toy ducks, gather and dry the cattails. Split the leaves down the center ~ thinner strips shape the head a bit easier. After soaking the leaves, cut to a length twice as long as the doll. Bend in half without creasing. The strips go side to side as well as front to back. Tie the neck when the head is well rounded. Bend and insert a short piece of cattail stalk for the arms. Tie the waist to secure the arms.

CORNHUSK DOLL

If it's difficult to think that fresh corn on the cob could have a bonus, look no further than its wrapping. For centuries, Indian parents used the husks to make dolls for the youngsters.

SELECT THE INNER HUSKS NEAREST THE COB AND DRY ON A NEWS-PAPER. ALSO DRY SOME OF THE INNER WHITE AND THE OUTER BROWN CORN SILK FOR HAIR. THE DRY, OAT-COLORED HUSKS, NOW CURLED AND TWISTED, ARE SOAKED IN WARM WATER FOR AN HOUR OR SO. BLOT OFF ANY EXCESS MOISTURE WITH A TOWEL. THE HUSKS WILL NOW BE PLIABLE ENOUGH TO SHAPE WITHOUT SPLITTING AND WILL KEEP THEIR SHAPE WHEN DRY.

WITH SCISSORS, CUT OFF THE THICK BUTTS AND THE THIN TOPS OF SIX SWEET CORNHUSKS. THE LENGTHS WILL RANGE FROM 6 TO 8 INCHES.

FORGET FRESH HUSKS THAT ARE NOT DRIED. THE TIES WILL LOOSEN WITH DRYING AND MILDEW MAY FOLLOW.

BEGINNING $\frac{3}{4}$ INCH FROM THE NARROW ENDS, TIE THE OVERLAPPING, SLIGHTLY DAMP HUSKS WITH STRING.

PENOBSCOT, MAINE, CORN-HUSK DOLL WITH CORN-SILK HAIR. CIRCA 1880. PEABODY MUSEUM, CAMBRIDGE, MASSACHUSETTS

123

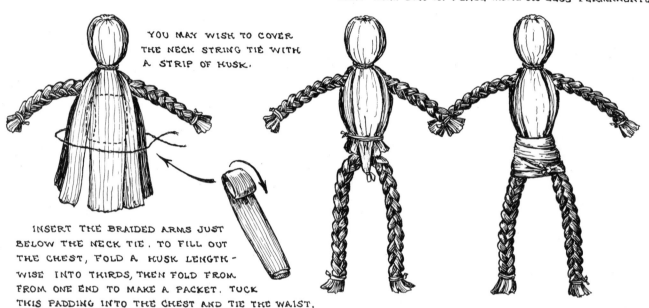

BRING DOWN EACH HUSK OVER THE $\frac{3}{4}$-INCH TIE ~ LIKE PEELING A BANANA. THE LAST ONE TO TURN SHOULD BE THE SMOOTHEST, FOR IT WILL BECOME THE FACE. MOLD IT AROUND THE OTHER HUSKS AND TIE THE NECK.

TEAR OFF SIX HUSK STRIPS ABOUT $1\frac{1}{4}$ INCHES IN WIDTH AND $9\frac{1}{2}$ INCHES IN LENGTH. THE LENGTHWISE VEINS MAKE THIS QUICK AND EASY. ALSO TEAR OFF FOUR STRIPS $\frac{1}{4}$ INCH IN WIDTH, FOLD AND USE TO TIE THE BRAIDED ENDS.

ROLL THREE OF THE $1\frac{1}{4}$-INCH STRIPS, TIE NEAR ONE END AND BRAID. THIS WILL BECOME THE ARMS. REPEAT FOR THE LEGS.

WHEN THE LIMBS ARE ATTACHED TO THE BODY, PLACE THEM IN THE DESIRED POSITIONS. THEY WILL DRY IN PLACE MORE OR LESS PERMANENTLY.

YOU MAY WISH TO COVER THE NECK STRING TIE WITH A STRIP OF HUSK.

INSERT THE BRAIDED ARMS JUST BELOW THE NECK TIE. TO FILL OUT THE CHEST, FOLD A HUSK LENGTHWISE INTO THIRDS, THEN FOLD FROM FROM ONE END TO MAKE A PACKET. TUCK THIS PADDING INTO THE CHEST AND TIE THE WAIST.

CUT OFF THE PROJECTING HUSKS BELOW THE WAIST TIE TO ABOUT $\frac{3}{8}$ INCH, EXCEPT FOR THE FRONT AND BACK FLAPS. USE THESE TO TIE THE BRAIDED LEGS IN PLACE. THEN BIND THE HIPS WITH ANOTHER STRIP OF HUSK.

THREE OR FOUR GOOD HUSKS ARE TIED WITH STRING, THEN FOLDED DOWN FOR A SKIRT.

A SHAWL-LIKE MANTLE FILLS OUT THE SHOULDERS. A FOLDED STRIP OF HUSK BINDS IT TO THE WAIST.

MOISTEN THE DRY CORN SILK AND TWIST OR BRAID INTO HAIR. SEW IN PLACE. IT'S A BIT FRAGILE, AND SO THIN BRAIDED HUSK STRANDS MAY BE USED.

FACE? RARELY DRAWN, BUT RED-DOT CHEEKS SOMETIMES WERE PAINTED IN.

1 X

TOY AX

The stone ax did service
in clearing campsites and
leveling trees up to 6 inches in
diameter for house poles, bed
planks, platforms, and stockades.
If severing wood fibers with
a sharpened stone was
difficult at best, it was
well-nigh impossible when
it came to larger trees.
Felling had to be done
by fire and a gradual
chipping away of
the char with the
ax. The "Dugout
Canoe" section (p.43)
does have this
procedure in
a bit more
detail.

1 X

CERAMIC DOLL

Grass, pine needles, willow
twigs, green summer leaves and those
colored from brisk autumn days, bark
from the slippery elm or birch ~ and
even clay ~ were crafted into dolls.
Possibly this ceramic toy was molded
by a mother at the end of a clay-pot-
making day.
See the "Pottery" section (p. 84)
for suggestions.

THE CENTER
BRANCH OF A THREE-PRONGED STICK
WAS SEVERED AND THE OUTER
BRANCHES TRIMMED.

The adult ax was carefully pecked to shape with a
pointed rock, and smoothed with an abrading stone of quartz
or quartzite; then the cutting edge was ground.
Just like dad's, this toy ax was made in the same way.
Although a bit too small for pecking, a small stone may be
shaped with a coarsely textured stone. While the ax was usually
lashed with rawhide, this smaller version was probably lashed with
sinew. Hemp string or thin basswood strips could be used. The head may
be further secured by several tightened loops over the top.

⚙ GAMES

DICE GAME

The dice game was second only to football (also called
lacrosse or hockey). Roger Williams described it in this
way: "They have a kind of Dice which are
Plumb stones painted, which they cast in a
Tray with a mighty noyse and
sweating."
Williams goes on
to mention the
many hundreds

1 X

1 X

ABOUT FORTY PINE SLIVERS
WERE USED AS COUNTERS. 1 X

that flocked to the gaming house: "This Arbor or Play house is made of long poles set in the earth, foure square, sixteen or twentie foot high, on which they hang great store of their stringed money, have great stakings, towne against towne, and two chosen out of the rest by course to play the *Game* at this kinde of Dice in the midst of all their Abettors, with great shouting and solemnity."

FIVE OR MORE OF THE BONE DISKS WERE PLACED IN A SHALLOW BOWL, DESIGN SIDE DOWN. THE BOWL WAS STRUCK ON THE GROUND WITH ENOUGH FORCE TO MAKE THE DISKS JUMP AND TURN OVER. THE SCORING DEPENDED ON THE NUMBER OF DESIGNS THAT WERE FACE UP AFTER A SINGLE JARRING OF THE BOWL. THE SCORE WAS KEPT WITH THE COUNTING STICKS.

~ SCORING ~
ALL BLACK OR ALL WHITE = A DOUBLE GAME.
3 AND 2 = A SINGLE GAME, AND
4 AND 1 COUNTED NOTHING.

Now Roger Williams took a dim view of this sort of thing. This poem followed his description:

"Our *English* Gamesters scorne to stake
  Their clothes as *Indians* do
Nor yet themselves, alas, yet both
  Stake soules and lose them to.

Oh fearfull Games! the divell stakes
  But Strawes and Toyes and Trash,
(For what is *All*, compar'd with Christ,
  But Dogs meat and Swines wash?

Man stakes his Jewell~darling soule
  (His owne most wretched foe)
Ventures and loseth all in sport
  At one most dreadfull throw."

NOT TO SERMONIZE, BUT I'M WITH MR. WILLIAMS. GAMES ARE ONE THING, GAMBLING ANOTHER. A NEW ENGLAND CONSCIENCE PROPERLY AVOIDS THE WAMPUM!

PIN GAME

The target was perforated leather, a rolled cone of moose hair, or a bundle of wrapped cedar twigs. Connecting this and an 8-inch spear of wood or bone was a foot-long cord. Sometimes a bundle of cedar twigs acted as a counterweight. The game was played throughout New England.

WHEN A PENOBSCOT YOUNG MAN COURTED A MAIDEN, HE WOULD PRODUCE THE GAME AND PLAY UNTIL HE MISSED. IT WAS THEN THE MAIDEN'S TURN. IF SHE CONTINUED THE GAME TO THE END, IT WAS A SURE SIGN THAT SHE FOUND HIS COMPANY PLEASING. BUT IF SHE HANDED IT BACK AFTER A SUCCESSFUL THRUST, SHE OBVIOUSLY WISHED TO BE RID OF HIS COMPANY. NO WONDER THEY CALLED IT THE LOVER'S GAME.

$\frac{1}{2}$ X

$\frac{1}{2}$ X

$\frac{1}{2}$ X

PASSAMAQUODDY, MAINE, EXAMPLE, PEABODY MUSEUM, CAMBRIDGE, MASSACHUSETTS

SNOW SNAKE

When snowflakes came to New England, the snow snake was not far behind. The warrior who could hurl his highly polished ash or hickory stick the farthest distance won all the other snow snakes. But by spring, all were discarded for fear that they would turn into real snakes.

1~2"   6~10'   6"

SELECT A SAPLING 1~2 INCHES IN DIAMETER, AND 6~10 FEET IN LENGTH. PLANE THE UPPER HALF FLAT, AVOIDING THE LAST 6 INCHES OF ONE END. THIS BECOMES THE HEAD. THE LOWER HALF MAY BE LEFT AS IS OR SLIGHTLY FLATTENED.

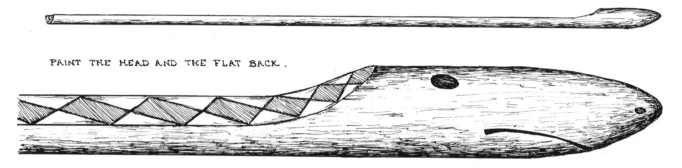

PAINT THE HEAD AND THE FLAT BACK.

A STRAIGHT RUNWAY ~ OR RATHER, SNAKEWAY ~ WAS NEEDED FOR THE THROW. A UNIFORM GROOVE COULD BE MADE BY SIMPLY DRAGGING A LOG THROUGH THE SNOW. SOMETIMES WATER WAS SPRINKLED IN THE TROUGH TO GIVE A SLICK FROZEN SURFACE.

TEAMS OF SIX COMPETED TO SKID THE SNAKE THE GREATEST DISTANCE. THE THROW WAS MADE BY HOLDING THE TAIL OF THE SNAKE WITH THE INDEX FINGER. THE THUMB AND OTHER FINGERS HELD THE SNAKE PARALLEL TO THE GROUND. IN A CROUCHED POSITION, THE THROWER HURLED THE STICK FORWARD WITH AN UNDERHAND SWEEP, MUCH AS IN MODERN-DAY BOWLING. OR ~ THE SNOW SNAKE COULD BE THROWN DOWN THE TROUGH, MUCH LIKE SKIPPING A STONE ON THE WATER.

SOAPSTONE PIPES

Out of the Ohio valley came a filtering of the Adena people, bringing with them a host of new ideas for better living. By A.D. 200~300, clay pots had made the old soapstone bowls obsolete, and the Indian gardens that began peppering the country-side filled these pots with good things to eat.

MASSACHUSETTS

* MILLBURY
WESTFIELD* * WILBRAHAM
WINSTED * * PEOPLE'S STATE FOREST
BAKERVILLE* * NEW HARTFORD   *PROVIDENCE
                     OAKLAWN*
BRISTOL*   R.I.
CONNECTICUT

A FEW STONE-BOWL QUARRY LOCATIONS

On a much lesser scale, some soap-stone (steatite) quarries continued to supply a limited amount of the soft stone for pipe making. It was another Adena idea, and smoking became so popular that Roger Williams thought fit to make note of it: "for generally all the men throughout the Countrey have a *Tobacco-bag*, with a *pipe* in it, hanging at their back: sometimes they make such great *pipes*, both of *wood* and *stone*, that they are two foot long, with men or beasts carved so big or massie, that a man may be hurt mortally by one of them."

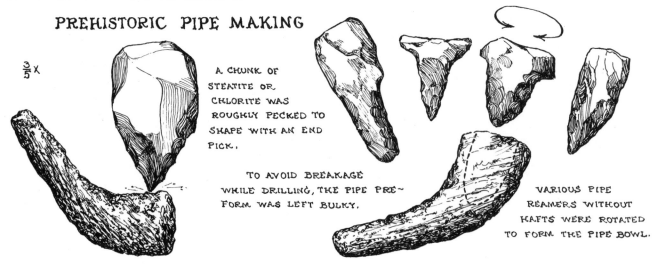

PLATFORM PIPE

STRAIGHT PIPE

ELBOW PIPE

BOWL PIPE

THE STRAIGHT PIPE WAS EARLIEST, FOLLOWED BY THE PLATFORM, THEN THE ELBOW (THE LATER, THE MORE UPRIGHT THE BOWL), AND THEN THE BOWL PIPE.

A "GREAT" PIPE

SOAPSTONE PIPE, BELIEVED TO BE FROM MASSASOIT'S GRAVE AT BURR'S HILL, WARREN, RHODE ISLAND. IT WAS CRAFTED WITH COLONIAL STEEL TOOLS DURING THE FIRST HALF OF THE SEVENTEENTH CENTURY. THE EFFIGY MAY BE A MOUNTAIN LION OR WOLF. A REPLICA, WITH OTHER BURR'S HILL FINDS, IS DISPLAYED AT THE HAFFEN-REFFER MUSEUM OF ANTHROPOLOGY, BRISTOL, RHODE ISLAND. THE ORIGINAL CAN BE SEEN AT THE HEYE MUSEUM OF THE AMERICAN INDIAN, NEW YORK CITY.

PREHISTORIC PIPE MAKING

A CHUNK OF STEATITE OR CHLORITE WAS ROUGHLY PECKED TO SHAPE WITH AN END PICK.

TO AVOID BREAKAGE WHILE DRILLING, THE PIPE PRE-FORM WAS LEFT BULKY.

VARIOUS PIPE REAMERS WITHOUT HAFTS WERE ROTATED TO FORM THE PIPE BOWL.

128

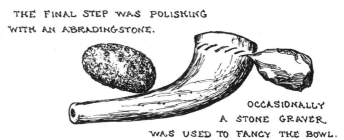

THE STEM WAS DRILLED, FOR THE MOST PART, WITH A TAPERED HARDWOOD DRILL OF $\frac{1}{8}$ TO $\frac{1}{16}$ INCH DIAMETER. THE EXPERIMENTS BY WILLIAM FOWLER, USING FINE SILICA SILT WITHOUT WATER, PROVED THAT THE GRITTY WOOD DRILL TIP WAS THE METHOD USED FOR STEM DRILLING. STONE DRILLS WERE TOO THICK FOR THE JOB. OUR ADMIRATION GOES TO MR. FOWLER, ONE OF NEW ENGLAND'S MOST KNOWLEDGEABLE AND PRACTICAL ARCHAEOLOGISTS. HIS EXPERIMENTS ON COUNTLESS ALGONQUIAN HANDCRAFTS HAVE GIVEN US INVALUABLE INSIGHT INTO THE USE OF INDIAN ARTIFACTS.

WITH THE TEDIOUS AND RISKY BUSINESS OF DRILLING COMPLETED, A FLAKE SCRAPER THINNED AND SMOOTHED THE PECKED SURFACE OF THE PIPE.

THE FINAL STEP WAS POLISHING WITH AN ABRADINGSTONE.

OCCASIONALLY A STONE GRAVER WAS USED TO FANCY THE BOWL.

REPRODUCING A BOWL PIPE

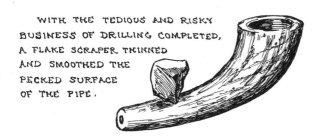

It took a skilled and determined hand to drill a soapstone pipe stem. But an easier pipe-making method was discovered sometime after A.D. 1200, and it grew in popularity well into the colonial historical period. A hollowed wooden stem could be inserted into the bowl ~ and it had many advantages. Of course there was no stone stem to drill or break, the short stem hole into the bowl could be made quickly with an ordinary stone drill, and it could be disassembled for travel. Known as the Micmac type, it became the everyday smokestick in New England and southeast Canada.

Freshly quarried soapstone is soft enough to carve with a knife. Yet it will harden when exposed to the air, giving the

PEABODY MUSEUM, CAMBRIDGE, MASSACHUSETTS

1X

MAINE PIPE
PEABODY MUSEUM, CAMBRIDGE, MASSACHUSETTS

1X

CONNECTICUT VALLEY PIPE, AMHERST COLLEGE MUSEUM, AMHERST, MASSACHUSETTS

1X

MAINE PIPE. PEABODY MUSEUM, CAMBRIDGE, MASSACHUSETTS

$\frac{1}{8}$-INCH HOLE

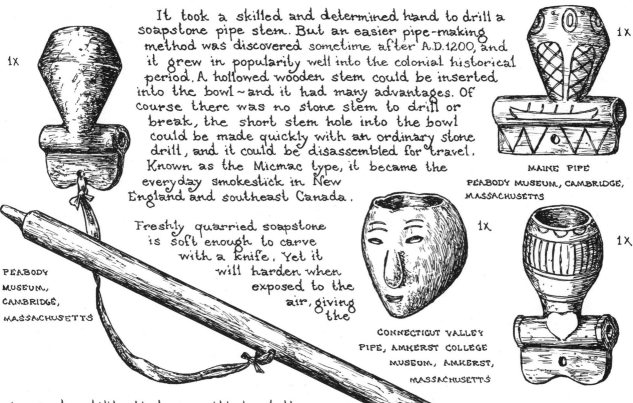

pipe a durability that can withstand the heat of the burning tobacco. Avoid weathered surface pieces that may crumble or easily split.

Quarried soapstone may be ordered in $1\frac{1}{2}$-inch-thick pieces ~ or in block pieces for the carving of effigy figures, if pipe-making is not for you. The Vermont Soapstone Company (Perkinsville, Vermont 05151) has good quality stone for sale. Although slightly more hardened than fresh stone, broken soapstone bed warmers can be whittled quite handily. Check flea markets and antique shops for bargain pieces. Specimens will be grayish in color, but the finished pipe will develop a fine black sheen with handling and polishing.

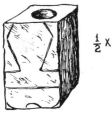

SCRATCH THE DESIGN ON THE BROAD FACE. HACK SAW THE ROUGH CUBE TO SIZE. THE BOWL CAVITY IS THEN BORED OR DRILLED.

USE A METAL DRILL OR OLD BIT. WOOD DRILLS WILL DULL.

SAW THE ROUGH OUTLINE. MARK THE DRILL DEPTH WITH TAPE AND DRILL THE STEM INSERTION.

WITH JACKKNIFE AND METAL FILE, SHAPE THE FINAL DESIGN. POLISH WITH EMERY CLOTH AND THEN FINE STEEL WOOL. WAX WILL GIVE A HANDSOME FINISH.

SELECT A STRAIGHT, DRY BRANCH WITH A PITHY CENTER. ASH, WITCH HAZEL, AND STAGHORN SUMAC ANSWER THE NEED. HEAT A CLOTHES HANGER WIRE AS HOT AS POSSIBLE, AND PUSH IT INTO BOTH ENDS. REHEAT AND CONTINUE UNTIL A $\frac{1}{8}$-INCH HOLE IS COMPLETED. SHAPE STEM TO TO FIT THE STEM HOLE IN THE BOWL, AND SLIGHTLY FLATTEN THE MOUTH END.

PUMP DRILL

The ancient chipped drill point had its problems. Necessarily thick to prevent breakage, it produced a rather large hole, conical in shape. Usually both sides of the object had to be drilled. Another pair of hands were needed to hold the object being drilled, for the craftsman had to use both palms to rotate the hafted wooden stem. It was slow, hard, blister-raising work.

And then the pump drill was introduced to America by the Spaniards (one of the very few advancements from a people whose chief business was plundering). The steel point could produce a small, cylindrical hole. It could be worked effortlessly with one hand while the other steadied the object to be drilled. Because of its low speed, the bit cut through bone, stone, and shell quite handily. And it was simple to make. In short order, the Indian craftsmen were turning out native ornaments, wampum, and pipes in a fraction of the time.

MAKING A NO~FRILLS PUMP DRILL

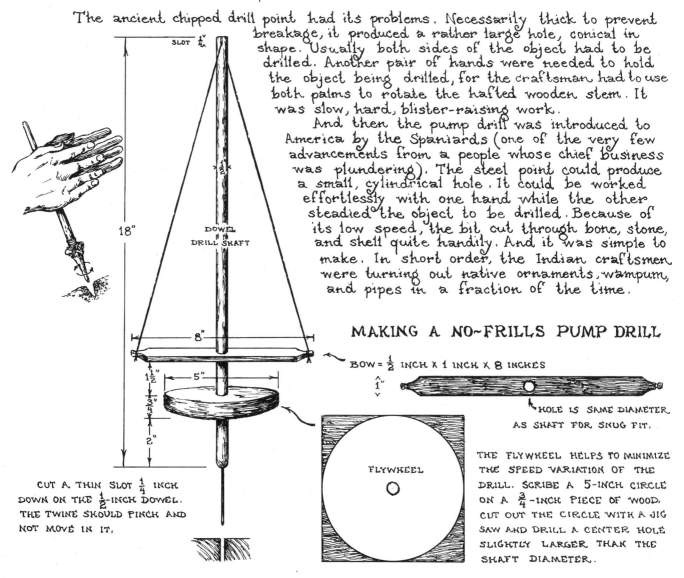

BOW = $\frac{1}{2}$ INCH X 1 INCH X 8 INCHES

HOLE IS SAME DIAMETER AS SHAFT FOR SNUG FIT.

FLYWHEEL

THE FLYWHEEL HELPS TO MINIMIZE THE SPEED VARIATION OF THE DRILL. SCRIBE A 5-INCH CIRCLE ON A $\frac{3}{4}$-INCH PIECE OF WOOD. CUT OUT THE CIRCLE WITH A JIG SAW AND DRILL A CENTER HOLE SLIGHTLY LARGER THAN THE SHAFT DIAMETER.

CUT A THIN SLOT $\frac{1}{4}$ INCH DOWN ON THE $\frac{1}{2}$-INCH DOWEL. THE TWINE SHOULD PINCH AND NOT MOVE IN IT.

Before the drill is assembled, consider the bit. It should be high-carbon steel~hard enough to penetrate soft stone or shell. Test any steel rod possibles of the desired diameter on an electric grindstone. A shower of bright, sharply exploding sparks will show your choice of steel was a good one.

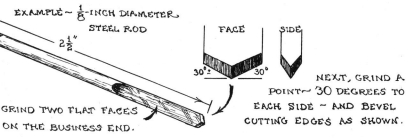

THIS END WILL BE INSERTED INTO THE SHAFT. TO ANCHOR SECURELY, GRIND FOUR SLIGHTLY TAPERED FACES.

WHEN GRINDING THE ROD TO SHAPE, DOUSE FREQUENTLY IN WATER TO PRESERVE THE TEMPER. HOLD WITH PLIERS~IT GETS HOT.

EXAMPLE ~ $\frac{1}{8}$-INCH DIAMETER STEEL ROD

2 $\frac{1}{2}$"

GRIND TWO FLAT FACES ON THE BUSINESS END.

FACE   SIDE

30°   30°

NEXT, GRIND A POINT~ 30 DEGREES TO EACH SIDE ~ AND BEVEL CUTTING EDGES AS SHOWN.

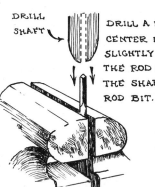

DRILL SHAFT

DRILL A HOLE DEAD CENTER IN THE SHAFT~ SLIGHTLY SMALLER THAN THE ROD DIAMETER. TAP THE SHAFT OVER THE ROD BIT.

And why not use an ordinary drill from an electric drill? It cuts only in a clockwise direction, and our drill must rotate both clockwise and counterclockwise as the bowstring winds and unwinds.

But if you have a worn electric drill bit of the right diameter~say, $\frac{1}{8}$ inch or so -reverse it and grind the point on the round end (as with the steel rod). Insert it in reverse in your electric drill. Drill into the end of the drill shaft~well centered~and leave it embedded.

ASSEMBLY
The drill shaft~the 18-inch dowel (or the tapered straight spindle from an old chair) with its bit and slotted top is ready for the flywheel. Glue the flywheel 1½ inches from the bit end. When dry, slip the bow down the shaft. Tie one end of the bow with a strong string or fish line (the earlier Indians used a thin leather thong). With the bow 1½ inches from the fly- wheel, pull the string taut and lock it in the slotted top. Tie to the other end of the bow~ both lengths of string will be equal.

DRILLING
Rotate the bow until the string is wound around the shaft. An easy downward thrust starts the drill spinning. Ease off on the bow as it nears the flywheel. The string will rewind and the drill point will rotate in the opposite direction.

A well-balanced flywheel and a centered bit will give a very satisfying whirrrr. And you are ready to tackle some of the projects in the "Ornaments" section that follows.

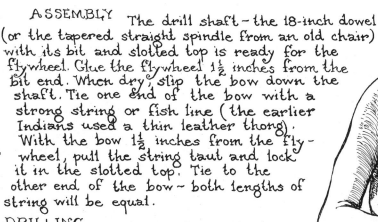

1½

DRILLED BEADS

Time was when only sachems and other influential New England tribe leaders wore a few beads for decoration. And small wonder. These valued decorations must have taken hours on end for a skilled craftsman to perforate and smooth to shape. (Perhaps you recall the drilling methods described in earlier pages.)

Beads were of two shapes ~ discoid and cylindrical. As for the first, the thin disks were easier to drill. The cylindrical beads were fairly husky ~ as was the hole that ran their length. And characteristic of these prehistoric beads, the hole was drilled from both ends to give tapered openings.

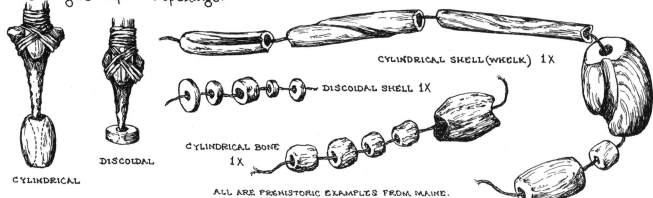

CYLINDRICAL SHELL (WHELK) 1X

DISCOIDAL SHELL 1X

CYLINDRICAL BONE 1X

CYLINDRICAL

DISCOIDAL

ALL ARE PREHISTORIC EXAMPLES FROM MAINE.

This was the state of the art prior to 1627. Then steel awls from European traders became plentiful. Perhaps they were used as bits in the pump drill or rotated between the palms. At any rate, the Narragansetts and Pequots soon became expert at drilling fine holes in quahog shells. There was certainly no scarcity of this shellfish at seaside. The core of the whelk also continued to be used. The new small beads were cylindrical and averaged less than $\frac{1}{4}$ inch in length and about $\frac{1}{8}$ inch in thickness ~ small enough to be woven into handsome belts, collars and neck ornaments, gaiters, bracelets, and headbands or for adding decoration on bags, wallets, or clothing. Less eye-catching but handsome nonetheless were the hair or ear decorations, necklaces or bracelets that were simply strung on fiber twine.

SHELL WAMPUM 1X

FILLET OF WAMPUM BEADS X 2

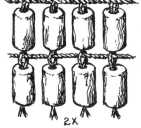

2X

WAMPUM BELT CONSTRUCTION

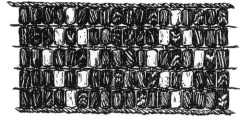

PENOBSCOT WAMPUM BELT SECTION 1X

Roger Williams observed that "their white they call *Wômpam* (which signifies white): their black *Suckáuhock* (*Súcki* signifying blacke.)." He went on to say that the white was fashioned from "the core of the periwincle" (whelk) and was worth half as much as the black. The white portion of the quahog served the same purpose. The difference in value was understandable, for the black (purplish black to a light purple) beads could only be obtained from a small section of the quahog shell.

The wampum was turned out in such volume and so eagerly sought that these small cylindrical beads became the money of the day Indians and colonists alike used them as the medium of exchange. Speaking of the "most rich" Narragansetts, William Wood said that "the northern, eastern, and western Indians fetch all their coin from these southern mintmasters. From hence they have most of their curious pendants and bracelets."

REPRODUCING DRILLED BEADS

$\frac{1}{3} \sim \frac{1}{2} X$

BEAD BLANKS

The quahog shell was cracked into workable pieces, ready for the pump drill. At this point my admiration spans the centuries to those old "mintmasters." Quahog seems to drill about as well as a china plate. However, the bit seems to bite better into freshly harvested shells than the more weathered covers. My best try was the disk bead, but the pile of cracked lime castoffs was impressive. You'll find that bone and soapstone are much more workable.

PORTION OF WHELK CORE 1 X

WHELK ~ Both the knobbed and channeled varieties are found from Cape Cod southward. Crack off the remaining outer casings (with care, for the outer curved face makes a fine pendant) to reach the core. Nibble off any shell fragments to free the core. It may now be hacksawed into bead lengths. Fortunately, the slightly softer core center drills a bit easier.

CHANNELED WHELK $\frac{1}{2} \sim \frac{1}{3}$ X

SECTION BONE

BONE ~

AFTER DRILLING, HACKSAW INTO SEGMENTS.

1X

Freshly cooked lamb or raw beef bone take to the drill nicely. Old dried beef bones are considerably harder but may be worked without too much difficulty. Strips of bone were cut in the same manner as in the "Bone Points" section, p.19), but today any Indian would probably opt for a hacksaw ~ as we have.

If your pump drill needs a rest, consider the small wing bones of the duck, goose, or chicken. Boil until white, push out the marrow, and cut in lengths of $\frac{1}{2} \sim \frac{1}{4}$ inch. The ends are tapered with a file.

SOAPSTONE ~ stone beads were something of a rarity. Grain and color gave an interesting contrast when strung with beads of shell, bone, or copper. Retrieve the hacksaw and cut bars of soapstone (see "Stone Pipes" section, p.128) $\frac{1}{4}$ X $\frac{1}{4}$ inch on cross section. Larger and heavier beads might be a bit too weighty for comfort. Cut the bars to bead length.

1X

DRILLING

The pump drill and the Indian vise make fine companions. The vise is nothing more than a partially split stick, bound firmly to prevent an extension of the crack. Insert the bead blank and temporarily lash the two split ends. The vise is held in one hand, the drill in the other.

SHAPING THE BEADS

THE ANCIENT WAY ~

GROOVED RUBBING STONES WERE OF COARSELY GRAINED GRANITE, QUARTZ, PEGMATITE, OR CONGLOMERATE. FINER-GRAINED POLISHING STONES WERE ARGILLITE, SCHIST, AND SANDSTONE. THREAD THE BEADS, APPLY PRESSURE AT BOTH ENDS OF THE BEAD COLUMN UNTIL SMOOTH AND UNIFORM.

MAKE A MODERN GROOVED GRINDSTONE OF SANDPAPER. PRESSURE THE ENDS OF THE DISKS COLUMN WHILE HOLDING THE THREADED STRING TAUT WITH THE FINGERS.
~OR~
THREAD THE BEADS ON A STIFF WIRE. SMOOTH ON A GRINDSTONE, ANGLING THE BEADS TO PREVENT RAPID SPINNING. PUSH THE BEADS TOGETHER WITH BOTH THUMBS TO ALLOW SLOW ROTATION FOR EVEN GRINDING.

COPPER BEADS

Since the Late Archaic days, minimal amounts of pure copper nuggets were imported from the Great Lakes region (see "Metal Spoons"). Some were pounded into barrel-like beads. European traders changed all that with their plentiful sheet copper and brass. Long thin strips could be hammered around a wooden form that was then removed or left around an elder wood base and the pith removed.

BRONSON MUSEUM, ATTLEBORO, MASSACHUSETTS

More popular were the small rolled copper beads that averaged between $\frac{3}{8}$ and $\frac{5}{8}$ inch in length. The demand was so great for these shiny metal ornaments that the Dutch began shipping in quantities of rolled beads. Indian-made beads differed from these with uneven rolls and slightly varied lengths.

CRAFTING ROLLED BEADS ~ Sources might include roofers' and carpenters' flashing scraps or thin strips of copper or brass weather stripping.

PINCH OVERLAPPING EDGES WITH NEEDLE-NOSED PLIERS.

CUT SQUARES AND START THE ROLL WITH NEEDLE-NOSED PLIERS.

PRESS EDGE SLIGHTLY INTO "Q-TIP" WOOD TO PREVENT TURNING.

HAMMER OR PLIERS COMPLETE BEAD SHAPE.

FILE EDGE FLAT WITH "Q-TIP" IN PLACE, THE "Q-TIP" IS THEN REMOVED.

PENDANTS

William Wood told of the Indians' "natural pride which appears in their longing desire after many kind[s] of ornaments, wearing pendants in their ears, as forms of birds, beasts and fishes, carved out of bone, shells, and stone". Like pendants also graced many a beaded necklace.

Pendants were often of ocean-smoothed oval pebbles. More easily inscribed were the soft soapstone or such sedimentary stones as sandstone and shale, or metamorphic stones such as slate. If necessary, the pendant shape was ground to size. After being polished with fine silica sand on a damp piece of buckskin, the design could be engraved with a hard stone flake from the arrow point chipping process.

CONCORD RIVER, MASSACHUSETTS
1X

SUDBURY, MASSACHUSETTS
$\frac{2}{3}$X

TIVERTON, RHODE ISLAND
$\frac{2}{3}$X

PLYMOUTH, MASSACHUSETTS
$\frac{2}{3}$X

HOLLISTON, MASSACHUSETTS
$\frac{2}{3}$X

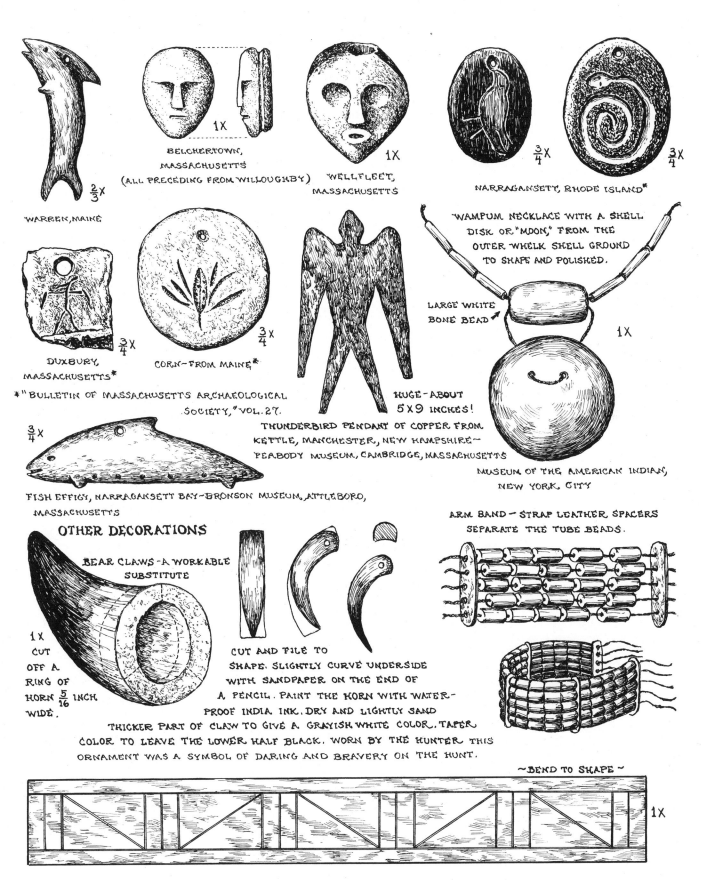

BELCHERTOWN,
MASSACHUSETTS
(ALL PRECEDING FROM WILLOUGHBY)

1X

WELLFLEET,
MASSACHUSETTS

1X

¾X

NARRAGANSETT, RHODE ISLAND*

¾X

WARREN, MAINE

⅔X

WAMPUM NECKLACE WITH A SHELL
DISK OR "MOON," FROM THE
OUTER WHELK SHELL GROUND
TO SHAPE AND POLISHED.

LARGE WHITE
BONE BEAD →

1X

DUXBURY,
MASSACHUSETTS*

¾X

CORN—FROM MAINE*

¾X

*"BULLETIN OF MASSACHUSETTS ARCHAEOLOGICAL
SOCIETY," VOL. 27.

HUGE—ABOUT
5X9 INCHES!

THUNDERBIRD PENDANT OF COPPER FROM
KETTLE, MANCHESTER, NEW HAMPSHIRE—
PEABODY MUSEUM, CAMBRIDGE, MASSACHUSETTS

MUSEUM OF THE AMERICAN INDIAN,
NEW YORK CITY

¾X

FISH EFFIGY, NARRAGANSETT BAY—BRONSON MUSEUM, ATTLEBORO,
MASSACHUSETTS

OTHER DECORATIONS

BEAR CLAWS—A WORKABLE
SUBSTITUTE

1X
CUT
OFF A
RING OF
HORN 5/16 INCH
WIDE.

CUT AND FILE TO
SHAPE. SLIGHTLY CURVE UNDERSIDE
WITH SANDPAPER ON THE END OF
A PENCIL. PAINT THE HORN WITH WATER-
PROOF INDIA INK. DRY AND LIGHTLY SAND
THICKER PART OF CLAW TO GIVE A GRAYISH WHITE COLOR. TAPER
COLOR TO LEAVE THE LOWER HALF BLACK. WORN BY THE HUNTER THIS
ORNAMENT WAS A SYMBOL OF DARING AND BRAVERY ON THE HUNT.

ARM BAND—STRAP LEATHER SPACERS
SEPARATE THE TUBE BEADS.

~BEND TO SHAPE~

1X

PRINCESS KINIGRET'S BRACELET OF SHEET BRASS OR COPPER FROM CHARLESTON, RHODE ISLAND—
RHODE ISLAND HISTORICAL SOCIETY, PROVIDENCE

BIBLIOGRAPHY

Note: *MAS* refers to the Bulletin of the *Massachusetts Archaeological Society,* Bronson Museum, Attleboro, Massachusetts.

Adrosko, Rita J. *Natural Dyes and Home Dyeing.* New York: Dover, 1971.

Angier, Bradford. *How to Live in the Woods on Pennies a Day.* Harrisburg, Penn.: Stackpole Co., 1972.

—*Living off the Country.* Harrisburg, Penn.: Stackpole Co., 1963.

Bailey, L. H. *The Garden of Gourds.* New York: Macmillan, 1937.

Barber, Joel. *Wild Fowl Decoys.* Windward House, 1934. Reprint. New York: Dover, 1954.

Barton, George H. "Unique Artifacts from Maine." *MAS* 24, No. 2 (January 1963): 25.

Beard, Dan. *American Boys Handy Book of Camp-Lore and Woodcraft.* Philadelphia: Lippincott, 1920.

—*Do It Yourself.* Philadelphia: Lippincott, 1925.

Biggar, H. P., ed. *Works of Samuel de Champlain.* Translated by John Squair. Vols. 1–4. Toronto: The Champlain Society, 1925.

Bolton, Reginald Pelham. *Indian Life of Long Ago.* New York: Schoen Press,1934.

Brereton, John. *Account of Gosnold's Voyage.* Massachusetts Historical Society Collections, 3rd Series, Vol. 8. Boston: 1843.

—*A Brief and True Relation of the Discovery of the North Part of Virginia,* 1602. Tracts appended from Massachusetts Historical Society Collections. Boston, 1843.

Brevoort, James Carson. *Verrazzano the Navigator.* Albany, N.Y.: Argus Company, 1874. Extracted from the American Geographical Society of New York for 1873.

Brewington, M. V. "The Log Canoe Builder and His Canoe." *The Chronicle of the Early American Industries Association, Inc.* 15 (June 1962): 13–15.

Brookshow, Doreen. *Pottery Craft.* London: Frederick Warne & Co., 1967.

Burrage, Henry S., ed. *Early English and French Voyages: Original Narratives.* New York: Scribner's, 1906. Chiefly from Hakluyt, 1534–1608.

Church, Colonel Benjamin. *Diary of King Philip's War 1675-76.* Published for the Little Compton Historical Society. Chester, Conn.: Pequot Press, 1975.

Couch, Osma Palmer. *Basket Pioneering.* New York: Orange Judd Publishing Co., 1933.

Cox, Doris, and Barbara Warren Weismann. *Creative Hands.* New York: John Wiley & Sons, 1945.

Creekmore, Betsey B. *Traditional American Crafts.* New York: Hearthside Press, 1968.

Cumming, W. P., R. A. Skelton, and D. B. Quinn. *The Discovery of North America.* New York: American Heritage, 1971.

Cunnington, C. Willett, and Phillis Cunnington. *Handbook of English Costume in the Eighteenth Century.* London: Faber & Faber, Ltd., 1964.

Davidson, Daniel Sutherland. "Snowshoes." *Memoirs of the American Philosophical Society.* Vol. 6. Philadelphia, 1937.

de Champlain, Samuel. *Voyages of Samuel de Champlain.* Translated from the French by Charles Pomeroy Otis. Vols. 1–3. Boston: The Prince Society, 1880. Reprint. New York: Burt Franklin, 1966.

Densmore, Francis. *How Indians Use Wild Plants for Food, Medicine, and Crafts.* Forty-fourth Annual Report, Bureau of American Ethnology. Reprint. New York: Dover, 1974.

Dodge, Ernest S. "Some Thoughts on the Historic Art of the Indians of Northeastern North America." *MAS* 13, No. 1 (October 1951): 3–5.

Drake, Samuel Gardner. *Biography and History of the Indians of North America.* 5th ed. Boston Antiquarian Institute, 1837. Reprint. Boston, 1851.

Duff, James. *Bows and Arrows.* New York: Macmillan, 1927.

Earle, Alice Morse. *Home Life in Colonial Days.* New York: Macmillan, 1898.

Eastman, Charles A. *Indian Scout Craft and Lore.* New York: Dover, 1974.

Ellis, Asa. *The Country Dyer's Assistant.* Brookfield, Mass.: E. Merriam & Co., 1798.

Erb, Elmer T. "Fire: The First Scientific Tool of Man." *MAS* 31, No. 3–4 (April 1970): 20–23.

Feder, Norman, curator. "Colors in Indian Arts; Their Sources and Uses." Leaflet 56. Denver: Denver Art Museum, March 1933. Reprint, 1975.

Forbes, Allan. *Other Indian Events of New England.* Vol. 2. Issued by State Street Trust Company of Boston in Commemoration of its Fiftieth Anniversary. Boston: Walton Advertising & Printing Co., 1941.

Fowler, William S. "Aboriginal Grinding Equipment." *MAS* 31, No. 1-2 (October 1969): 19–25.

—"Ceremonial and Domestic Products of Aboriginal New England." *MAS* 27, No. 3-4 (April 1966): 33–68.

— "Classification of Store Implements of the Northeast." *MAS* 25, No. 1 (October 1963): 1–17.

— "Eating Practices in Aboriginal New England." *MAS* 36, No. 3–4 (April 1975): 111.

— "Hafting Atlatl Weights." *MAS* 30, No. 2 (January 1969): 15–17.

— "Hafting Stone Implements." *MAS* 34, No. 3-4 (April 1973): 1–12.

—"The Making of Wing Atlatl Weights." *MAS* 36, No. 1-2 (October 1975): 19–21.

—"Metal Cutouts of the Northeast." *MAS* 34, No. 3-4 (April 1973): 24–30.

— "Procurement and Use of Bark." *MAS* 37, No. 1–2 (October 1975): 15–19.

—"Some Sources of New England Flints." *MAS* 32, No. 3–4 (April 1971): 23-26.

— "Stone Importation in Prehistoric Massachusetts." *MAS* 1, No. 2 (January 1950): 29–35.

—"Stone Pipe-Making." Report of the Narragansett Archaeological Society of Rhode Island (June 1978): 1–10.

— "Stone Pipes." *MAS* 27, No. 3-4 (April 1966): 45–47.

—"A Study of Projectile Points." *MAS* 35, No. 3–4 (April 1974): 1–8.

—*Ten Thousand Years in America.* New York: Vantage Press, 1957.

—"The Whaletail Atlatl Weight." *MAS* 35, No. 1-2 (October 1973): 14–16.

Gallinger, Osma, Ted Benson, and Oscar H. Benson. *Hand Weaving with Reeds and Fibers.* New York: Pitman Publishing Corp., 1948.

Getoff, Mary M. "Preparing and Cooking Hulled Corn, Hominy, and Samp. The Forgotten Arts." *Yankee* (November 1977): 254–65.

Gibson, Susan G., ed. *Burr's Hill, A 17th Century Wampanoag Burial Ground in Warren, Rhode Island.* Vol. 2. Haffenreffer Museum of Anthropology, Brown University, R.I., 1980.

Gillelan, G. Howard. *Complete Book of the Bow and Arrow.* New York: Galahad Books, published by arrangement with Stackpole Books, 1971.

Gleason, Henry A. *Illustrated Flora of the Northeastern United States and Adjacent Canada.* Vols. 1–3. New York Botanical Garden. Lancaster, Penn.: Lancaster Press, 1952.

Gookin, Daniel. *Historical Collection of the Indians of North America.* 1792. Reprint. Boston: Towtaid, 1970.

Gorham, Anne, and Anne Pierter. "Snowshoe Making." In *The Salt Book,* edited by Pamela Wood. New York: Anchor Books/Doubleday, 1977.

Gringhuis, Dirk. *Indian Costume at Mackinac: Seventeenth and Eighteenth Century.* Mackinac History Vol. 2, Leaflet No. 1. Mackinac Island, Mich.: Mackinac Island State Park Commission, 1972.

Griswold, Lester. "Bead and Quill Handicraft." *Handicrafts* (1931): 267–83.

Hadlock, Wendell S. "Three Contact Burials from Eastern Massachusetts." *MAS* 10, No. 3 (April 1949): 67–69.

Hallett, L. F. "Indian Games." *MAS* 16, No. 2 (January 1955): 25–28.

Halls, Zillah. *Men's Costume 1580–1750.* London Museum. London: Her Majesty's Stationary Office, 1970.

Hammett, Catherine T., and Carol M. Horrocks. *Creative Crafts for Campers.* New York: Association Press, 1957.

Hammett, Kenneth. "Building Powder Horns." *Muzzle Blasts* (National Muzzle Loading Rifle Association) (June 1960): 13–21, 60.

Harlow, William M. *Trees of the Eastern and Central United States and Canada.* New York: Dover, 1957.

Harris, John. *A Relation of the Plantation at Plymouth,* Voyages and Travels I. London, 1705.

Howe, Henry F. *Prologue to New England.* New York: Farrar & Rinehart, 1943.

Hungry Wolf, Adolf. *Good Medicine: Traditional Dress Issue.* Good Medicine Books. Heraldsburg, Calif.: Naturegraph Press, 1971.

Hunt, W. Ben. *The Complete How-To Book of Indian Craft.* New York: Macmillan, 1977.

Jaeger, Ellsworth. *Nature Crafts.* New York: Macmillan, 1950.

Jeppson, Britta D. "A Study of Cord and Rolled Copper Beads, Burial #6, Titicut Site." *MAS* 25, No. 2 (October 1963): 37–38.

Johnson, Lawrence A. "The Indian Broom." *The Chronicle of the Early American Industries Association, Inc.* 10 (June 1957): 13–24.

Johnston, Randolph W. *The Book of Country Crafts.* New York: A. S. Barnes & Co., 1964.

Josselyn, John. *Account of Two Voyages to New England.* London: G. Widdoes, 1675. Reprint. William Veazie, 1865.

—*New England's Rarities*. London: G. Widoes, 1672. Reprint. Boston: William Veazie, 1865.

Kavasch, E. Barrie. *Native Harvests*. Washington, Conn.: American Indian Archaeological Institute, Shiver Mountain Press, 1977.

—"The Typhaceae (Cattails)." *Artifacts* (American Indian Archaeological Institute) 11 (Summer 1981): 28–29.

Kimball, Yeffe, and Jean Anderson. *The Art of American Indian Cooking*. Garden City, N.Y.: Doubleday, 1965.

Knobel, Edward. *Field Guide to the Grasses, Sedges, and Rushes of the United States*. Rev. ed. New York: Dover, 1977.

LaBerge, Armand J. *Woodworking for Fun*. Peoria, Ill.: The Manual Arts Press, 1941.

Lahontan, Baron. *New Voyages to North America*. London, 1703.

Langseth-Christensen, Lillian. *The Mystic Seaport Cookbook*. New York: Funk & Wagnalls, 1970.

Leechman, John Douglas. *Vegetable Dyes from North American Plants*. New York: Hill & Wang (Webb), 1945.

Leighton, Ann. *Early American Gardens*. Boston: Houghton Mifflin, 1970.

Lorant, Stefan. *The New World: The First Pictures of America*. 1st rev. ed. New York: Duell, Sloan & Pearce, 1965.

Loud, Llewellyn L., and M. R. Harrington. *Excavations of the Lovelock Cave 1911–1924*. University of California Press, 1929.

Macfarlan, Allan A. *Living like Indians*. New York: Bonanza Books, 1961.

Mason, Bernard S. *Woodcraft & Camping*. New York: Dover, 1974.

Mason, Otis T. "Man's Knife Among the North American Indians." Annual Reports, United States National Museum. Washington, D.C.: Government Printing Office, 1897.

—"Traps of the American Indians, a Study in Psychology and Invention." Washington, D.C.: Smithsonian Institution, 1901.

Mathews, F. Schuyler. *Field Book of American Wild Flowers*. New York: G. P. Putnam's Sons, 1927.

Maxwell, James A., ed. *America's Fascinating Indian Heritage*. Pleasantville, N.Y.: Reader's Digest Association, 1978.

McGuire, Joseph D. "American Aboriginal Pipes and Smoking Customs." Annual Reports, United States National Museum. Part I. Washington, D.C.: Government Printing Office, 1897.

Montgomery, Florence M. *Printed Textiles — English and American Cottons and Linens 1700–1850*. A Winterthur Book. New York: Viking Press, 1970.

Morison, Samuel Eliot. *Samuel de Champlain*. An Atlantic Monthly Press Book. Boston: Little, Brown, 1972.

Morton, Thomas. *New English Canaan of Thomas Morton*. Introductory matter and notes by Charles Francis Adams, Jr. Boston: Prince Society, 1883.

Murphy, Henry C. *The Voyage of Verrazzano*. New York, 1875.

Naylor, Maria, ed. *Authentic Indian Designs*. New York: Dover, 1975.

"Nessmuk." *Woodcraft and Camping*. New York: Dover, 1963.

Orchard, William C. "Mohawk Burden-Straps." *Indian Notes* (Museum of the American Indian, Heye Foundation, New York) 6 (July 1929): 351–59.

Palmer, Rose A. *The North American Indians*. Vol. 4. Smithsonian Institution Series. New York, 1943.

Parslow, V. D. *Weaving and Dyeing Processes in Early New York*. Cooperstown, N.Y.: Farmers' Museum, 1949.

Pashko, Stanley. *American Boy's Omnibus*. Greenberg, 1945.

Peckham, Stewart. *Prehistoric Weapons in the Southwest*. Popular Science. Pamphlet No. 3. Santa Fe: Museum of New Mexico Press, 1977.

Peterson, Harold L. *American Knives*. New York: Scribner's, 1958.

—*Arms and Armor in Colonial America 1526–1783*. Harrisburg, Penn.: Stackpole Co., 1956.

Petrullo, Vincent M. "Decorative Art on Birch-Bark Containers from the Algonquin River DuLievre Band." *Indian Notes* (Museum of the American Indian, Heye Foundation, New York) 6 (July 1929): 225–39.

Phelps, Mason M. "The South Swansea Burials." *MAS* 8, No. 3 (March 1947): 36–38.

Pope, Saxton T. *Bows and Arrows*. Berkeley: University of California Press, 1962.

"Recently Acquired Mohegan Articles." *Indian Notes* (Museum of the American Indian, Heye Foundation, New York) 2 (January 1925): 38–43.

Richardson, Joan. *Wild Edible Plants of New England: A Field Guide*. Yarmouth, Maine: DeLorme Publishing Co., 1981.

Robbins, Maurice. "A Unique Artifact from Cape Cod." *MAS* 37, No. 3–4 (April 1976): 45-47.

Robertson, Seonaid M. *Dyes from Plants*. New York: Van Nostrand Reinhold Co., 1973.

Rodimon, Walter S. *Collection of Indian Objects*. Westfield, Mass.: Pioneer Valley Press, 1963.

Salomon, Julian H. *The Book of Indian Crafts & Indian Lore*. New York: Harper & Brothers, 1928.

Saunders, Charles I. *Edible and Useful Wild Plants*. New York: Dover, 1976.

Schneider, Richard C. *Crafts of the North American Indians*. New York: Van Nostrand Reinhold Co., 1972.

Scully, Virginia. *A Treasury of American Indian Foods*. New York: Crown, 1970.

Seton, Ernest Thompson. *The Forester's Manual*. Garden City, N.Y.: Doubleday, Page & Co., 1912.

Simmons, Dr. William S. "The Ancient Graves of Conanicut Island." *Newport History* (Newport Historical Society), Vol. 40. Newport, R.I.: Wilkinson Press, Inc., 1967.

Skaggs, R. E. "Building and Scrimshawing Powder Horns." *Muzzle Blasts* (National Muzzle Loading Rifle Association) (November 1975): 8–11, 40, 54.

Sloan, Roger P., and Joseph A. Szymjuko. "Backyard Syrup from Maple Trees." Publication No. 9. Durham, N.H.: University of New Hampshire, 1978.

Stauffer, Florence S. "Maize: America's Miracle Plant." *Early American Life* (June 1976): 18–24.

Stribling, Mary Lou. *Crafts from North American Indian Arts*. New York: Crown, 1975.

Tantaquidgeon, Gladys. *Folk Medicine of the Delaware and Related Algonkian Indians*. Harrisburg, Penn.: Pennsylvania Historical and Museum Commission, 1977.

—"Notes on the Gay Head Indians of Massachusetts." *Indian Notes* (Museum of the American Indian, Heye Foundation, New York) 7 (January 1930), 4–5, 11–12, 14–15, 17.

Thoreau, Henry David. *Journal*. 1856.

Tyzzer, Ernest E. "An Experimental Study of the Manufacture of Articles of Bone and Antler." *MAS* 19, No. 3 (April 1958): 37–39.

Underhill, John. "News from America." London, 1638. Reprint in Orr, C. ed. *History of the Pequot War*. Cleveland: Helman-Taylor Co., 1897.

Vaughan, Alden T. *New England Frontier Puritans and Indians*. Boston: Little, Brown, 1965.

Walker, William B. "Our Neglected Food Source." *Country Journal* (February 1976): 48–51.

Warwick, Edward, Henry C. Pitz, and Alexander Wyckoff. *Early American Dress*. New York: Benjamin Blom, 1965.

Waugh, Norah. *The Cut of Men's Clothes 1600–1900*. London: Faber & Faber Ltd., 1964.

Wilbur, C. Keith. *The New England Indians*. Chester, Conn.: Globe Pequot Press, 1978.

—*Picture Book of the Continental Soldier*. Harrisburg, Penn.: Stackpole Co., 1969.

Williams, Roger. *A Key into the Language of the Indian of New England*. London: Gregory Dexter, 1643. 5th ed. Providence, R.I.: Roger Williams Press, 1936.

Willoughby, Charles C. *Antiquities of the New England Indians*. Cambridge, Mass.: Harvard University, 1935.

—"Antler-Pointed Arrows of the Southeastern Indians." Reprint. *American Anthropologist* 3 (July 1901): 431–37.

— "Dress and Ornaments of the New England Indians." Reprint. *American Anthropologist* 7 (July 1905): 499–08.

— "Houses and Gardens of the New England Indians." Reprint. *American Anthropologist* 8 (January 1906): 115–32.

— "Prehistoric Workshops at Mt. Kineo, Maine." Reprint. *The American Naturalist* 35: 213–19.

— "Textile Fabrics of the New England Indian." Reprint. *American Anthropologist* 7 (January 1905): 88–94.

Winthrop, John. *The History of New England from 1630 to 1649*. New Edition with Additions and Corrections. Boston: Little, Brown, 1853.

Wissler, Clark. *Indian Costumes in the United States*. American Museum of Natural History Guide Leaflet Series, No. 63. New York, 1926.

Witthoft, John. "The American Indian as a Hunter." Reprints in *Anthropology No. 6*. Pennsylvania Historical and Museum Commission. Reprinted from *Pennsylvania Game News*, Vol. 24 (February 1953): 8–13.

Wood, William. *New England's Prospect*. London, 1634. Reprint edited by Alden T. Vaughan. Amherst, Mass.: University of Massachusetts Press, 1977.

INDEX